Family History of Fear

Family History of Fear

A MEMOIR

Agata Tuszyńska

TRANSLATED BY CHARLES RUAS
FROM THE FRENCH OF JEAN-YVES ERHEL

Alfred A. Knopf

NEW YORK

2016

THIS IS A BORZOI BOOK PUBLISHED BY ALFRED A. KNOPF

Translation copyright © 2016 by Alfred A. Knopf, a division of Penguin Random House, LLC

Originally published in Poland as *Rodzinna Historia Lęku* by Wydawnictwo Literackie, Kraków,
in 2005. Copyright © 2005 by Agata Tuszyńska and Wydawnictwo Literackie. This translation is
based on the French edition originally published in France as *Une histoire familiale de la peur*
by Éditions Grasset & Fasquelle, Paris, in 2006. Copyright © 2005 by Agata Tuszyńska,
copyright © 2006 by Éditions Grasset & Fasquelle.

www.aaknopf.com

Library of Congress Cataloging-in-Publication Data
Tuszynska, Agata, author.
[Rodzinna historia leku. English]
Family history of fear : a memoir / Agata Tuszynska ;
translated by Charles Ruas from the French of Jean-Yves Erhel.
pages   cm
ISBN 978-0-375-41370-4 (hardcover : alk. paper)—ISBN 978-1-101-87587-2 (ebook)
1. Tuszynska, Agata.   2. Tuszynski family.   3. Jews—Poland—Biography.
4. Warsaw (Poland)—Intellectual life.   I. Ruas, Charles, translator.   II. Title.
DS134.72.T87A313 2016
929.2089'9240438—dc23   2015020551

Jacket photograph courtesy of the author
Jacket design by Kelly Blair

Manufactured in the United States of America

First American Edition

TO MY PARENTS

Contents

I

The Secret

THE PARENTS

she certainly did not begin with the persecutions and the walls, the marks, the distinguishing insignia of the yellow star. She began by telling me stories. About the curtain, at first. Then, about the chinchilla coat and the muff. Then about the coach in front of the ghetto wall. Nothing more direct. Little by little. To make it easier.

She wanted her child to be without a stigma. She was happy to have brought a little blue-eyed blonde into the world. This little girl had a proper Polish father. She taught me how to live in this country.

She didn't want to weigh me down with a burden heavier than I could bear. She didn't want her child to have to grow up with a feeling of injustice and fear. In her estimation, one could always broach the subject when a child was capable of handling it and taking care of herself.

She is sure she told me when I was nineteen. I have no reason not to believe her.

Every family has a story. Many Polish families have tragic ones. In those days, people did not always tell children about their hardships during the war—the Resistance, the Home Army, participation in the uprisings in Warsaw and fighting in the forests. It took them years to start talking about what they had been through, about the pain as much as the heroism. These stories, when they finally came out, drew the generations together and gave them strength. But my mother's experience was not like that. It was more, much more. Not only in the depth of the suffering and tragedy but also in their consequences. There was nothing in it to brag about or cling to, nothing to wear out by retelling. There were no heroic deaths, no patriotic examples, no sacred traditions, no hope for the future. It had to be concealed. This thing.

Years passed before I found the strength to admit it. Before my spirit abandoned its defenses and took it in. I needed time. Without accepting it, to be sure, but still inwardly weighing the possibility. It took about ten years.

Has it happened? Can I say "I am Jewish"?

*T*his book has been in me for years. Along wit
secret. From the instant I found out I was not
thought I was. From the moment my mother to
she was Jewish.

I was born in Poland, in Warsaw, several years after th
I had blue eyes and blond hair, a source of great pride
mother, whose own eyes and hair were dark.

Today, I realize she wanted a Polish child, for fear of th
her daughter might inherit otherwise, a fate like her own
even though the war was officially part of the past in
socialist Poland, where everyone was equal by definitio
resolved to obscure her origins.

We are our memory. We are what we remember. And
others remember about us.

Even more than that, I often find myself thinking, w
our lapses of memory. We are what we forget, what in
defense we blot out of our memory, chase from our consc
ness, avoid in our thinking. We conceal memories to mak
easier or lighter, so it will not hurt.

I do not remember when my mother told me she was
ish. I remember nothing about it—not the day, nor the se
nor the place; not whether we were sitting at the table or b
window; not the tone of her voice, nor the color of her wo
have no memory of any such conversation. Maybe she tol
that she hid in a cellar during the war. That was not unusu
many Poles were forced to hide in cellars or attics. Mayb
said she had to run away from the Germans, escape, like n
others—Poles who were hunted down by the Nazis, rou
up at work, machine-gunned in the streets and forests, se
the camps.

She does not remember exactly how she went about it,

No.

Did my mother tell me her war stories? Did she actually tell me, or did she only want to tell them without quite having the strength to go through with it? No, it's not enmity that you absorb with your mother's milk. It's fear.

On the subject of the fur coat. It had to be taken out and aired. Especially a coat as respectable as one of chinchilla. Especially one that has been kept in a wardrobe on the Aryan side for years. When Mama and her mother slipped out of the ghetto and reached the safety of their first hideout, they often went for walks after dark. They were afraid of being caught, but they were also hungry for some fresh air and the chance to get their blood moving. My grandmother also wanted her coat to get a good airing. A coat that was already beginning to fall apart, by the way. Fur wears out faster than a human being does. In the end, with a heavy heart, my grandmother had it cut up into small pieces. In a snapshot taken in Zakopane after the war, Mother was carrying a chinchilla muff; the coat didn't make it much farther than that.

Concerning the curtain. In fact, this story is all about salt. My mother and grandmother were hiding in a small apartment at 18 Krasiński Street in the Fourth Colony, where they used to live before the war. The place belonged to two sisters who worked in the neighborhood as domestics. In the kitchen's pantry, a curtain with dark blue flowers on it. One night, the boyfriend of one of the sisters, Helenka, came over. She'd made barley soup for him, but she didn't salt it enough. He complained. She went to borrow some salt from a neighbor. Left alone, he decided to find some himself. In the pantry, behind the curtain. Mama was twelve years old and held her breath. Her mother held the curtain closed. He understood. They had to move out.

If only the soup had been salty enough, they might have been able to stay together a little while longer behind that curtain. Until the moment when a knife or a dish was needed, because that's where they were kept too.

If the boyfriend had wanted to, he could have turned them in to the Gestapo then and there.

If . . .

When my mother came out of the ghetto, it was summer. A chilly August day. The young girl, small in size, with shiny black braids, was wearing several pairs of striped stockings and two dresses, one on top of the other, and a dark blue coat with a collar, and a scarf tied under her chin. She walked beside her mother, who kept a tight grip on her little hand. They had to go right through the courthouses on Leszno Street. She knew she had to walk with a sure step, with no hesitation. Constantly surrounded; it was better in a crowd, where others, many others—Jews and non-Jews, ordinary people—went about their business. The two of them climbed stairs, went down hallways, and then took more stairs, this time going down. So simple. And yet so hard to do. The girl didn't see her mother take off her armband. Nobody was paying attention to them anyway.

She does not recall the faces of the people who suddenly appeared in front of them like another wall. Several men and a woman wearing a scarf, with strands of hair sticking out. Mama and her mother were afraid of Germans. But these were not Germans. "All right, you little kike, hand it over, all of it, c'mon," they heard. "Or we'll turn you in to the Gestapo."

They huddled together as if they were thieves. My mother's mother tried to defend herself, protesting, explaining, and finally begging. To no avail. That was when the coach pulled up.

The driver, one of those Poles with a great thick mustache, took their side. "Leave the woman alone!" he cried. "What's the matter with you? Can't you see the little girl is scared to death?" And to them, he said, "Get in!"

They piled into the coach. Her mother gave him an address in a voice filled with relief, and they drove away. The little girl held on to her mother's coat, watching the buildings go by. They did not recognize that part of town. They had never been there before. It was starting to get dark. Shop windows sparkled all around them. They passed streetcars and black German limousines. A group came out of a corner restaurant, laughing. The hats that the women were wearing looked brand new. A little farther, in a large square by a church, some boys were playing ball. The city was keeping itself busy. The world did not end at Umschlagplatz after all, they thought. The coach turned into Szucha Avenue and pulled up in front of Gestapo headquarters.

The driver turned around. "What did you think, Żydówo, dirty, fucking Jew?? That I wouldn't take you back where you belong?" Laughing, he pushed them toward the entrance.

Polish policemen were prepared for fugitives from the ghetto. They locked them up in a room and demanded money. On the other side of the door, they could hear the sound of German boots and voices. In the ghetto, that meant death. The little girl watched her mother take off her ring and her wedding band, and then her watch. After a moment, without a word, she started to unbutton her coat. Then she reached down toward her garter belt and extricated, one by one, twenty-dollar gold coins that had been stitched into the cloth. She placed them on the wooden table. Six in all. "It's not enough," a man said. "Not enough." It was all they had.

She asked if she could make a phone call. They deliberated for a while, mentioning sums that made the little girl's head spin. Her mother, in an expressionless voice, repeated each amount into the receiver. Who was she talking to? Who was willing to pay that kind of money for us? Her aunt's husband was the only name she could come up with, the one who had arranged their escape from the ghetto. They settled on a time and place. The money would be delivered to that address.

They were on the Aryan side.

That story stuck to me, against my will. It keeps coming back, in various versions, in my dreams. I can't get rid of it.

In this dream, I am the little girl with the striped stockings and the scarf tied under her chin. It is definitely my scarf; it's the color of the ocean, and so is the little bucket filled with sand that I'm holding. I am not kicking pebbles as I go, like the other dark-eyed Jewish children, and in this dream I ask myself why not. I have the same eyes as they do, dark and full of fear. Better look down. I am walking beside my mother. I am not sure whether it's my own mother or the grandmother I never knew. She holds herself very straight, unnaturally stiff, and squeezes my hand. A cold sun shines.

We walk along at a steady pace even though I want to run. Run and yell, as if, after wandering for hours in a gloomy forest, I had suddenly discovered a sunlit clearing. The air feels different on the other side. Feels alive.

I do not recall the faces of the other people who suddenly appear in front of them like another wall. My mind is on the little girl, because nobody else is looking after her, she is only twelve and the Germans frighten her. But these are not Germans. "All right, you little kike, hand it over, all of it, c'mon." They get it; we get it. And then the metallic sound of the word "Gestapo" . . . *sta, PO.* I would not have known the word "Gestapo" at that age. There were no books about the war yet. I learned it much later, even though I was still carrying sand in my bucket.

Mother, or maybe Grandmother, hid her face in her hands, like a child, repeating, "Leave us alone, leave us alone." I cannot move. I just stand there, staring at them, and little by little I recognize the face of this one and that one: neighbors, acquaintances, friends. I look them straight in the eye.

Then the coach arrives. The driver has a mustache, a huge Polish mustache like the one worn by my Jewish great-grandfather, Henryk, from Przedrynek adjacent to Łęczyca's main marketplace. He could even wiggle the ends when he held his granddaughter, my mother, on his lap and sang her the song about the cobbler's wife and her paper slippers.

"Leave the woman alone!" he cries. "What's the matter with you? Can't you see the little girl is scared to death?"

With a shrug, he invites us to climb into his coach. The horse smiles.

But this is not Grandfather Przedborski; this is his Polish brother. Not for nothing have so many generations lived together under the same roof. In the name of this house, shared for centuries on Polish soil, he cannot allow anybody to insult us. He takes us under his protective wing, and the enchanted carriage rolls along, clattering on the cobblestones and carrying us, carrying us, carrying. Grandmother is on the verge of saying, in a strangled voice, clumsy words of gratitude, full of shame and thankfulness, and more. She is about to speak when we turn abruptly. The sand is spilling out of my bucket. "What is a bucket doing here?" I wonder. An hourglass with sand in it, perhaps, time passing. The last moments.

We are approaching Szucha Avenue.

"What did you think, Żydówo, dirty, fucking Jew?? That I wouldn't take you back where you belong?"

What do I do with this dream? I thought. With this story? Life has a cost; you have to do what's right, pay the price. The wedding band and the engagement ring were not enough. The Omega watch, the gold coins sewn into the garter belt, not enough. So they gave the mother and daughter one last chance. A rich relative. You don't come across that every day. Welcome to the Aryan side.

I am still holding the little girl's hand when I wake up. I am protecting her from her Polish brothers. But then I ask myself how I would treat her. I ask myself if I wouldn't be afraid to play with her in the backyard, if I would have shared my slice of sugared bread with her. If I would have had the strength, like others did, to hide her in my closet or in my attic. Even when the money ran out and there was no more hope.

It was easiest not to know anything about all that.

Is that what mattered to you, Mama?

My parents started out with nothing. They were married in 1955, a memorable year because of the Festival for World Youth, which brought students from other countries to Warsaw for the first time since the war. They sublet their first place, one room in an apartment they shared with two other families. That was also my first home, though I don't remember it. A few years later, they were assigned an apartment of their own, a rare achievement for a couple that young. It was located in a new working-class neighborhood called Wola, far from the center of town. Concrete cubes, all identical, uniformly planted in a field that looked like people had just stopped digging up potatoes there. Our street was named Marcin Kasprzak after a hero of the revolution. A black-and-white photo from those days shows a baby carriage, with tiny wheels and removable sides, beside a carpet hanger which soon became the heart of the courtyard. Inside the pram, a chubby little girl puckered her lips as much as she could, for fun.

We had two rooms plus a kitchen and a balcony on the second floor. It was clean and light. My little bed, like a playpen, with netting on all sides, was where I learned to walk. Just before that, my only living grandmother, on my father's side, took me to church and had me baptized, without asking anyone's permission. My godfather, Uncle Włodek, was supposed to attend the ceremony, but he was playing cards at the time and forgot all about it.

My father came from a family of railroad workers in Łódź. Mama's family was from Warsaw. My parents were young and eager for life when they met. Determined to enjoy themselves, to laugh and forget all about their blighted wartime childhoods. They were both active in the ZMP, the Union of Polish Youth, while they were studying journalism at the university. They wore the red ties, they went to gatherings, applauded at meetings of their party, and held long, fervent discussions on the principles of Marxism and Leninism. They wanted to build their lives without looking back. Old paintings in golden frames seemed like meaningless relics to them. In their home, on their walls, they hung reproductions of the French avantgarde. Picasso's and Miró's grimacing faces and multiple eyes and noses scared me to death long before I was able to spell their names. They ordered their furniture from a fashionable designer who regarded our living room as the perfect showcase for his ideas. The combination of black metal, glass, and shiny plastic was a sensation, if barely functional. The brightly colored three-legged stools in the shape of a cone with its point cut off were exquisite torture. As for the chairs, those little red, yellow, and green hollow seats clung to the buttocks. Not easy to sit down on, even harder to get out of. This vista of fanciful modernity was saved by the books, a multitude of them, spreading gradually over more and more shelves, of which there were never enough.

Our house was full of light. Sunday mornings, lazier than all the others, I watched the yellow patches of sunlight rippling across the honey-colored floors of the big room. I closed first one eye, then the other, and watched how the perspective shifted, without moving my head.

I vaguely remember my father being there. Never both of them in the bed together, not that I can recall, never together at the table or out for a walk. In my favorite photograph, my mother is sitting on my father's lap in a cabana at the seashore. They are laughing, with their arms around each other, as if everything still could and would work out.

. . .

As early as high school, in 1947, my father set up a local radio station. He wanted to be a sportscaster. He auditioned for national radio, but they turned him down, claiming that he had absolutely no future in broadcasting because his voice was too "shrill," in their words. He didn't give up.

"From the helicopter, following the race, this is Bogdan Tuszyński"—that's how he always began, every step of the way from Warsaw to Berlin to Prague in the annual bicycle Race for Peace. All of Poland knew my father's voice.

At that time, sports were a matter of national pride, perhaps for lack of other events of a patriotic nature. Whatever the reason, the whole country, young and old, went crazy over that bicycle race. All through the sixties, during those two weeks in May, you might say nothing else of any importance happened in Poland. In towns, in the streets, men gathered around loudspeakers broadcasting from various spots along the route or at the finish line. The sound of radios, turned all the way up, in practically every apartment echoed in courtyards. In mine as well. My father's voice came at me from all sides. The tension reached its highest pitch just at the finish. Thousands of Poles held their breath. When he was in a good mood, he ended the broadcast by saying hello to me.

My father's reporting on the course of the race and the struggles of the Polish team was something more than the simple account of a sporting event. He became the voice of the nation; he created a national legend. The fact that he expressed people's feelings won him a place in the heart of every listener. Everybody considered him a member of the family, one of their own. My father, who at that time had just turned thirty, had become a popular personality throughout the country. Wherever he went—the store, the post office, a café—they recognized his voice. I was so proud.

I remember some times when he got home late after a long journey. He used to wake me up in the middle of the night. I sat on the floor, half asleep, while he unpacked suitcases that gave off the scent of faraway places. They were filled with endless colors, spilling out of clothes that rustled, scarves for Mama, silk and wools finer than anything you could find in the shops, and lace, and perfume by Chanel, and the unforgettable taste of milk chocolates by Suchard. He seemed different himself, as if all those places had rubbed off on him. We had to get used to him all over again, to his smell and the touch of his hands. And then he'd go away again. My father was always on the road.

Foreign travel in those days, when a brand-new passport was required for every journey, was considered to be a great luxury. It was a doorway onto a world that was inaccessible to most of us, full of booty that for me had the taste of Coca-Cola and chocolates in bright little wrappers. My father's homecomings punctuated the calendar of our daily life. Both of us learned how to wait. Me, patiently; Mama, less so. He sent colorful postcards from far away. Innsbruck, Tokyo, Mexico City, Paris,

Berlin . . . the names alone triggered a feeling of restlessness and endless dreams. Even before I started school, I was given a globe as a present. Later, I started to collect maps and learn different countries' capitals and flags by heart.

I started reading early, and I read a great deal. And with a sort of greed. I escaped into imaginary worlds, as if the ones I took part in weren't real enough. I liked stories with wizards and wish-fulfilling beads. My mother used to read poetry to me. Soon, I was choosing books for myself—along with *Mary Poppins* and *Anne of Green Gables,* memoirs of the war, of the Occupation and the camps, Auschwitz and Birkenau. I didn't know why; I just felt I had to read them.

I liked playing hide-and-seek a great deal more than other children my age. I also liked to play dress-up, constantly trying on new costumes and putting powder and eye shadow on my face. I spent hours in the armoire. It had a huge mirrored door. I shut myself up in it sometimes as if it were a palace or a fortress. I was happy to stay in the corner, but I also liked being onstage. When I was six, I was the king's daughter in a play at school. I was attracted to worlds different from my own.

First of all, there was the road. I had the only moments of security in my childhood when we were on our way to Łódź, to visit my grandma on my father's side. Everything made sense because my parents were together, my father at the steering wheel of the black Škoda Octavia, my mother beside him, me in the backseat. They didn't have to bother with me—I was so happy. I listened to their voices; I felt their presence. Nothing bad could happen. Stretched out on the backseat, I watched patches of sky disappearing under my feet or maybe under the wheels, outside my field of vision.

Trains ran right by my grandma's house on the edge of town. Glasses large and small clinked in the cupboard, water gurgled in vases, tomato soup spilled out of the bowl onto the dish beneath. Invariably, Grandma would cry, "The Gdynia Express!" or "The local to Opole!" Trains went right through the round table with its best Sunday tablecloth in the big room.

They woke up the cats dozing in warm patches of sun, shaking the well and rustling the fruit trees. At number 4 Perłowa Street, not far from the tracks, everybody knew them. Even my dolls from Warsaw, after a couple of days, flawlessly recited the arrivals and departures from the station of Łódź Kaliska. "The travelers are going back to their kingdoms," I explained to them, as well as to myself. And then I ran in front of the house to wave to the lucky people in the train windows, who were being carried toward a destination unknown to me but chosen by them. The road was a dream, a promise of adventure.

My great-grandfather Jan, father of Grandma Mania and all her numerous brothers and sisters, worked on the railroad. He came and went in uniform, which he wore as if he had been born in it, although in reality he was born into a household of domestic servants in a miserable little village on the outskirts of Koluszki. As a child, he took the cows to pasture and knew hunger. As a young employee on the Imperial Railroad (called Zheleznodorozhnaia in Russian), he traveled the thousands of kilometers through the heart of Russia to the Far East. He went there several times and often delayed his return for reasons other than work. His wife, Rózia, always welcomed him home. She gave him eleven children. Five survived. The eldest was Grandma Mania.

Sometime in the thirties, my grandfather had built with his own hands the house we would later visit, one story, made of wood, near the station. Even though he earned a good living, he must have put money aside for years. He chose all the wood personally, measured, ordered, and seasoned the timber himself. His first grandson, my father, sat on his lap, playing with ticket punchers and an old-fashioned pocket watch with a fob and a long chain, big enough to count the minutes remaining before the arrival or departure of all the trains. Years later, my great-grandfather used to sit for hours on a little bench in front of the house, in his polished boots and official cap with its visor and its gold braid, as if he were still a conductor. He wrote long columns of numbers in a little notebook, with a fountain pen, grumbling all the while. I was his first great-granddaughter. He used to let me pull on his gray mustache and wrinkle his freshly ironed uniform.

His wife, Rózia, survived him, a woman with a thin gray braid and a dry face, wrinkled and darkened by the sun and by hours and hours in the forest. She showed me where to find mushrooms. For her, mushroom season was a holiday that never lost its appeal, and I'm sure that the pleasure of watching and waiting for the perfect rainy autumn appreciably prolonged her life. She lived past ninety.

Her daughter, Grandma Mania, lived for others. Her enormous family, with its dozens of cousins and distant relations, relied on her. She knew their troubles, their diets, their problems with their children, and their financial situations. She dried their tears, pampered them, and catered to them in every way. Grandma was always on my side, even if that meant contradicting my father, her favorite son. But he was the one who could do no wrong.

She made miles of noodles, thousands of steamed meatballs and plum dumplings, and mushrooms of every variety, fresh, marinated, and dried. When nobody came to see her, she wept. She embroidered wonderfully, with colored silk threads, little animals and birds and our initials on schoolbags. She wove carpets with a pattern of autumn leaves. She had blue eyes and would take me away into the fields beyond the roads. Sometimes, on Sundays, I went to Mass with her. And after church, to street fairs, where she bought me cotton candy and rings the color of rubies or sapphires. She refused me nothing.

On Perłowa Street, they lived in a world that was as plain and simple as a kitchen floor scrubbed once a week by hand, as a front hall lined with buckets of water and rubber boots, mousetraps and milk cans. The milk came straight from the cows, the vegetables out of the garden. We picked apples off the trees or listened to the rain. We looked for meaning in nature, not in books. Nothing was concealed in the lining of daily life there.

My father was away on business more and more. And everything was noticeably different when he was gone.

My mother took me to Kazimierz, on the banks of the Vistula, a quaint little village in a valley where time had stopped. The marketplace, an open square surrounded by Renaissance buildings, with an ancient wooden well in the center, looked like a painting. Visible nearby were a parish church and a convent, the mysterious ruins of the old castle, and the Mount of Three Crosses. When we were there, I used to play with other children who were on vacation like me, in the woods on a hill far from the roads. There, among the ferns, in beds of pine needles, or moss, on the paths and in the bushes, we sometimes came across broken bits of stone. We used to piece them together, trying to reassemble a bas-relief of hands, birds, books. With handfuls of leaves, we wiped off remnants of writing in a strange, incomprehensible language. Someone said there used to be a Jewish cemetery here.

I didn't know any Jews.

It seems that the movie house with the vaulted wooden ceiling in the same town on the Vistula, where I went to children's matinees, had been their church. They spoke of it as "the synagogue." I had trouble remembering the word. Paintings and watercolors that artists sold in the marketplace were full of silhouettes of men dressed in black. They all had beards and hats, and their faces were framed by little round curls. I saw nostalgic longing in their eyes.

At home I rarely heard the word "Jew." Only from my father, and then, always in a mocking tone of voice. To him, Jews were the reason, vague but ubiquitous, for everything that didn't go as it was supposed to. He thought they ran everything and deprived others of the goods and privileges that were their due. He held them responsible for every unpopular law, for whatever problems he currently had at work, for the scarcity of new tires for his automobile. Sometimes he pointed with his index finger at certain people on TV, as if he knew how to pick them out from the others. Them. The others. It was unthinkable that any of them might be found frequenting not only our house but our friends.

I did not understand what any of that meant. I had never met a Jew.

My parents separated when I was seven. I didn't know why my father left us. For a long time, I put his slippers out for him, by the front door, certain he would come back.

In front of my friends, I was too ashamed to admit he did not live with us anymore and pretended he had just gone away for a little while. The fact that he was so well known and everyone admired him so much made the situation more delicate. The principal of my school always referred to me as "the broadcaster Tuszyński's daughter." This only served to heighten the mystery and shame of his absence. Every word out of his mouth was like a message from an oracle.

I was jealous of the dresses that other little girls got to wear for their First Communion, with their long white skirts and lace, their pristine white gloves and their wreaths. I was jealous of the procession they walked in, lined by garlands of May flowers, and of the words they got to pronounce as they bowed: "Holy, holy, holy"—genuflect—"Lord God Almighty . . ." I did not understand why I was being excluded. But I never looked very hard for a reason. As if somehow, deep down, I knew it was no concern of mine. I was very friendly at the time with another little girl who did not go to church either, or to catechism class. One of the games we used to play consisted of burying bits of colored glass in the ground. We also founded a correspondence club by which we communicated daily through secret letters sealed with colored wax and the imprimatur of a genuine seal. We answered the questions ourselves, the first ones and the important ones.

We loved the parades on May Day. There were several industries in our immediate neighborhood: the factory that made Marcin Kasprzak radios, the one that made Rosa Luxemburg lamps, and Polfa, which manufactured medicine. On the first of May, bands from those factories started playing marches early in the morning, and all the employees, in their Sunday best, lined the streets with flags and banners flying. The mood was solemn yet full of enthusiasm. We assembled in front of the school in our Young Pioneer uniforms with white kneesocks that were always brand-new. They chose the oldest for the color guard, plus four volunteers to carry the huge portrait of Maxim Gorky, for whom our school was named. "Mankind—It Resounds Proudly." Later in the day, we marched with all the others in front of the official platform facing the Joseph Stalin Palace of Culture and Science, an architectural showpiece shaped like a wedding cake, which the Soviet Union gave to our capital as a gift. We sang the song "Celebrating May"; we shouted "Hooray for the first of May!"; joyfully, we waved our pennants and our big red crepe-paper flowers. Then, with the satisfaction of our duty done, we all ate ice cream, vanilla bambinos.

I considered myself to be at the same time better and worse than others. I adapted easily to circumstances, and I could handle all sorts of situations with no problem, but I rarely took the initiative. I liked to be part of the group, wholly integrated. Somewhere deep inside, though, I felt different from others and, in a vague way, more important. I performed all my tasks without complaint. I tried hard to please, responding to everyone's wishes, real or imagined. I was an echo.

The feeling of being worse than the others remained superficial, but I never managed to figure out where it came from. It seemed to me that, for who knows what reason, I had to work hard to be better than others. It was really important, and a lot of things depended on it. Better, because I was in truth worse than others. But nobody must ever find out.

I was a good student. They made me read my essays aloud to the whole class, like the one on the paper bird or about *Heart: A Schoolboy's Journal* by De Amicis. I recited poems in assemblies on special occasions. I brought home report cards with perfect grades and the stamp of an honor student. And for me, as for my mother, that was taken for granted. My photograph for being first in the class was displayed in a store window on

Wolska Street nearby, right next to one of the few department stores in the city. My father did not have time to go see it. Summers, he worried whether I was playing ball or if I was riding a bike. Winters, he made sure I knew how to ice skate well. I went to overnight camp with the Young Pioneers, where I earned every badge possible for field exercises.

I wanted to be grown up. Especially so I could begin to live. I wanted to be grown up because adults knew things and were not afraid. My childish world had broken into two pieces that no one could glue back together. With every passing year, I found it harder and harder to believe that these two had ever formed a whole. Power in every sense of the word was on my father's side. Resolute, sure of himself, prominent, supported by a big family, he was firmly planted on the ground and on his own two feet. Even with another man beside her, Mama seemed defenseless to me.

At Christmas, Mama and I decorated a tree. It gave off the same scent of the forest as before, but it wasn't the same. It reminded me of a poor relation in ill-fitting finery. My grandma's Christmas tree in Łódź was more real somehow, much more joyful. We hung little angels, toys and nuts, a ballerina with golden slippers, a little mouse with a red bonnet, and tiny bells. The Star of Bethlehem twinkled on top of the tree. "Hark! The herald angels sing, 'Glory to the newborn King.'" All over the plump little tree, we sprinkled stars strung on paper ribbons that my grandma and her sisters had spent their evenings making. The smell of fresh sweet bread filled the room. We waited together for the holiday to begin. "O come, all ye faithful, joyful and triumphant." We sang Christmas carols. We prepared to welcome the Savior.

On our holiday table, the wafer was prominently displayed, but it seemed out of place. It took me a long time to understand the symbolism. It looked stale to me, left over from the year before, always the same. It tasted like dust, and when the moment came for me to take my share, I felt vaguely embarrassed. I could feel the presence of a lie, but I could not locate it. Something unexplained, something mysterious, secreted under the crust of that childhood.

The same holidays that other children looked forward to embarrassed me. I couldn't wait for them to be over. Mama and I were always alone together. It was painful. An undefined threat hung in the air, and all our daily routines seemed designed for somebody else, as if they'd been cut from the wrong pattern. We were living outside this special parenthesis. Our sense of being shunted aside became more acute. The neighbors on our floor formed closed circles; tightly united in the joy of a common prayer, they were inaccessible. More than ever, I was far from them.

The surprise of presents on Christmas Eve didn't especially cheer me up, either. My dreams revolved generally around new books and were quickly realized. My mother did not approve of impulsive expenditures on principle: you had to have money because you never know what's coming. She got that from the war.

Grandfather, my mother's father, lived on Puławska Street. Armed with a prewar diploma in engineering, he directed an enterprise charged with reconstructing the capital. He loved his office with its huge desk and two black telephones. He often raised his voice. He was constantly photographed in the company of high government officials at ceremonies to inaugurate new buildings and new housing complexes, which were more and more numerous, and to dedicate monuments and the cemeteries for Soviet soldiers that were also constructed under his supervision. His work took him to China and the Soviet Union, from which he returned with collections of things like compasses, and flashlights, and cameras manufactured by Smiena. He accounted scrupulously for every bit of money spent, limiting his expenditures to the bare minimum. He considered many things to be extravagances—not only cigarettes and alcohol, but also the resoling of his shoes if that had not been foreseen in the budget.

He helped me write letters in Russian to Valerka in Leningrad, a pen pal who had been assigned to me at school. "So, what's going on, eh?" he said whenever he saw me, tugging on my ear. That must have been a rare expression of tenderness from such a powerful and austere man who ignored affection or, perhaps, had forgotten about it. He never mentioned my grandmother.

In 1949, he married for the second time, a marriage of convenience to a dry, haughty neighbor who lived on same floor. The mayor of Warsaw himself performed the ceremony. Once a week, without fail, they attended a concert by the Warsaw Philharmonic. It seems he had perfect pitch. He played the violin in his youth. On the occasional family gathering, on Friday nights, he and his sisters would play something from their repertoire of chamber music, by Brahms or Ravel.

I had no idea where he came from or who his parents were. I never saw an old photograph. I could not boast about cousins on my mother's side. Or about their graves. Or the graves of their ancestors. We never told family stories. Or commemorated anything, either.

The most important smell of my childhood was the one in Aunt Bronka's kitchen. They lived in a development of small wooden houses near Ujazdów, in the heart of the city, not far from the Sejm and several old parks. It was a little like being in the country. The minute I walked through the door, I could smell something that I recognized later as garlic. I was in the fifth grade when Aunt Bronka suddenly left Poland with her entire family. Some of her kitchen utensils appeared in our house. Ceramic bowls for turning milk into buttermilk and a great selection of utensils for pastry. The plastic graters to clean the pastry boards still tasted of cake, and apple charlotte, and little croissants with raisins. As my mother listened to Western radio stations at night, she grew worried and angry. And then she began writing long letters to foreign countries. In the place for a return address, she kept up a steady stream of invented names. She signed the letters with the name of our dachshund, Nutka. She was scared.

My grandfather never mentioned his cherished sister's name again, and shortly after that, he stretched out on the sofa and refused to get up. In a conversation I overheard, I learned that they smeared his front door with excrement. He was expelled from the Party and retired from his position.

Years later, I learned what March 1968 represented in the history of my country. Anti-Semitic riots triggered the last great wave of emigration of Polish Jews, those who had stayed after the war and after the pogrom in Kielce and who had not jumped at the chance to flee the country in 1956. Those who had felt the most Polish.

In the little garden in Ujazdów someone else picked the strawberries and cherries. Even in Łódź, on Perłowa Street, it wasn't the same as before. Grandma had gotten sick. We went to visit her in the hospital. As long as she had the strength, she wrote us letters. She died during vacation. I was twelve years old, but it wasn't me crying at the funeral. It was my father. In front of the white marble gravestone adorned with a sepia photograph that didn't resemble her at all, they set up a small bench.

I had to confront everything by myself. I shared my father not only with his new wife but also with their two daughters. No more Grandma to console me. I couldn't get over a sense of humiliation, but I did not know what I'd done. I came home from Sunday lunches at my father's house (tomato soup, pork chop, stewed pears) sated and sad. Our house felt empty, and all my efforts to win my father's forgiveness were in vain.

Early on Sunday afternoons, I would find myself at a street-car stop on Niepodległości Avenue. I was alone. By then, they had decided to let me go out on the streets by myself. I squeezed in my hand a brand-new one-thousand-złoty bill. Alimony—the amount my father had been paying every month for the last few years for my upkeep, according to the agreement my parents made after they separated. The bill was usually new, as if it had come right off the press. I knew I must not lose it. When I was little, it seemed like a very large sum to me. Later, when I learned the value of money, I wondered why I meant so little to him.

We would all wait for him. Usually, in the house, or in successive apartments that changed according to his fortunes and the increasing size of his family. He rang the doorbell several times impatiently and then opened the front door, loaded down with suitcases and bags. He greeted his wife and their two daughters, and then it was my turn.

I always felt like I was intruding on them. Intruding when they hadn't seen each other for weeks. How many times did I vow never to put myself through that again? How many times did I repeat that vow, so that I would never forget it? But I went back. And I kept going back, drawn by some irresistible force. As if humiliated on the scene of my defeat. Afterward, I slipped away to a bathroom or downstairs to my father's office, where he had an armoire big enough to hide in. In there, I couldn't hear anything, neither their joy nor my despair.

I was nine when my first half sister was born. They presented her to Grandma and the rest of the family in Łódź like a big bundle, which they welcomed and unpacked enthusiastically. Nestled inside was a thin little girl with very pale skin. She was crying. Toys had arrived at the same time she did. Little rubber elephants and tiny rabbits that squealed, rattles shaped like little hearts and multicolored paper wreaths that festooned her bed and her baby carriage. The richness and profusion of all this equipment was impressive.

I was nine and twelve years older than my sisters. When they were born, I had a feeling that, for me, things were going to deteriorate. I needed my father. I didn't know how or when to tell him that. I understood much later that for him I was not just a daughter, but a pawn in the game he was playing with my mother. He couldn't forgive her for abandoning him, for not loving him. I knew nothing about that. In my eyes, in my head, he was the one who had packed up and left. I often felt he did not love me at all and that perhaps I was the reason for his going.

I went there every Sunday. I sat on his lap. He teased me about my big feet and about my nose and my hair, but I didn't know how to take a joke. His ridicule hurt. Even the fact that I read a lot provoked mockery. My flawless report cards made no impression on him that I could see. I do not remember any compliments from him or any recognition that I was trying to fulfill all his expectations. I did not know what to do to please him. And that was all I wanted.

It seems he was proud of me. I never felt that when I was a child.

I remember the postcards I would get as a child. Shiny, colorful, sometimes round or elongated. He signed them "Tata" (Papa). Even today, when I get a letter from him signed like that, even today, all the feelings from that period in my life come flooding back.

He always wrote with a Parker ballpoint pen, in black or blue ink. The *T* slightly apart from the other letters, standing firmly on its little leg; the straight line on top—like a roof—attached almost invisibly to the base, and it too is firm and energetic. The *a* resembles an *o* endowed with a little tail written so delicately, and it is attached to the *t* that follows it like a cross hung with another tiny *a*. *Tata*. Papa. My papa. When I see that, it brings tears to my eyes.

On the way to school, I went right by the old orphanage of Dr. Janusz Korczak. I knew his books, but I had no idea that he was Jewish and had gone to his death with the Jewish children in his charge.

I was in my second year in high school when one of my classmates, a redhead named Arturek, delivered a glowing report in our civics class, praising Hitler for having resolved the Jewish problem. He said that Hitler had purified Poland of its Jewish scurvy, something many had tried to pull off before the war without success. The teacher made no objection. I did not understand what he was talking about.

I did not understand why Mama broke down and sobbed during a film about the Warsaw Ghetto. There was no calming her. I knew practically nothing about the Jewish quarter in prewar Warsaw, and when streets like Pawia and Miła came up in the poems she read to me, it never occurred to me to connect them. The tailor Izaak Gutkind might well have been named

Jan Kowalski for all it meant to me. "Izaak" sounded no different than "Mieczysław" or "Piotr." For me, the Jews were as long ago as the Egyptians and as exotic as Indians. I certainly had never met any. I lived with that conviction for a long time.

I graduated from high school with honors.

The world of books took the place of daily life. I felt better at the ball with Anna Karenina than at a party for my friend next door. When I went out for a walk, I much preferred the company of the lady with the dog from Chekhov. Fiction seemed to have only privileges, participation without consequences. There, I was safe. Certainly, Emma Bovary poisoned herself, but you could simply start reading from the beginning again, and there she was. I found nothing ridiculous in Don Quixote's duel with the windmills. Instead of admiring my aunts or my schoolteachers, I was smitten by Phaedra and Antigone, and Cousin Bette and Uncle Vanya were the closest relatives I had. I went for a long time without realizing I was living in the skin of others. Not once did it enter my mind that Mama, my mama, was Jewish. I simply could not conceive of it. Being Jewish was something ignoble. Was a fault. That is what I got from my father.

My mother maintains that she had decided to tell me the truth about her Jewish origins and the fate of the Jews during the war when I turned nineteen. I don't remember that at all. I took my cue from her, but I not only hid it from the world, I hid it from myself. I considered her secret as a humiliation and a disfiguring feature, something it is appropriate to be ashamed of. Otherwise, she would never have hidden it from me. These Jews, who were so rarely mentioned and who were the target of inexplicable outbursts by my father, were suddenly revealed as my family.

She kept silent in order to construct a wall, she said, between me and all the pain I might have encountered in this country because of her. I made an effort to think of this as the greatest possible expression of a mother's love for her child.

After the war, many of the Jews who remained in Poland

chose to keep their origins quiet. They had survived and decided to make a break with all that. They decided not to be Jews any longer. Better not to admit it; you never knew when they would come after you again.

My mother's family had lived in Poland for two centuries. At the beginning of the twentieth century, her grandparents on her father's side—the Przedborskis and the Hermans— were considered Jewish elite, leading very assimilated lives in the little town of Łęczyca, sixty miles from Warsaw. They owned buildings, a printing company, a warehouse of wine and liquor. They held honorary positions as town councilors. On her mother's side, the Goldsteins were much poorer, Orthodox Jews.

When war broke out, my mother was about to enter second grade in elementary school. She remembers a part of the family from Łęczyca arriving in Warsaw and all of them going together into the ghetto. They lived there almost two years in conditions that grew more and more deplorable. And then, one after the other, they were taken to the Umschlag-platz and shipped to Treblinka. Her great-grandmother went and also her grandmother along with her brothers and sisters; also a daughter with her family along with a handful of cousins. More than twenty people in all. Those who had chosen to stay in the ghetto at Łęczyca perished in the camp at Chełmno nad Nerem, located nearby.

Only those who managed to cross over to the Aryan side and go into hiding with false papers were saved. Besides my mother and her mother, who was killed in the streets right before the end of the war, my mother's aunt and her son were also saved. And her aunt's sister, who was married to a Pole. Their brother—my grandfather—spent the five years of the Occupation in an Oflag, a POW camp for officers, in Woldenberg.

I did not learn all that right away. The past was revealed to me little by little, and always in whispers. As if it were still better not to know.

II

Our Home

MY FAMILY, PICKING MUSHROOMS NEAR ŁÓDŹ:
MY PARENTS, GRANDMOTHER MANIA, HER SISTER STEFA,
MY FATHER'S BROTHER, WŁODEK, AND ME

BOGDAN I

BOGDAN

*M*y parents, that is to say, our home. A home should have walls enclosed by their arms, and a roof.

I did not have parents. I do not remember them. I had a mother. I had a father. Each distinctly separate. Why can't I see my parents with the eyes of a child? Are they too close or too distant? What keeps me from holding them close, after so many years, and inhaling our common scent? We were once a family, after all.

Will the fact that we stopped being a family keep me from ever remembering what they were like?

They did not like to be held by the hand, either one; nothing like that was allowed—Mama and Papa out as a family for a Sunday walk in the park. Together. Mama and Papa with a little girl in her best blue dress. She has already eaten her cotton candy and now walks quietly beside them, stealing glances first at one and then at the other to make sure they are still there, and keeps going. She is not tired. Several times she has asked them to take her hands and swing her over the puddles. It rained yesterday but that passed, and there isn't a cloud in the sky today.

Did we ever go on a walk like that? I cannot remember the rhythm of shared family rituals. Sundays usually frightened me a little.

It's easier for me to evoke my grandmother Dela, though I never met her. Or my great-grandfather Henryk. People who no longer exist allow themselves to be described, in spite of nostalgia, and that is a comfort. The living, the nearest and dearest, can cause pain, but their life inside us is not complete. It goes on, in struggle or not, with love or without it. And always with a great need for contact.

How do I look at my parents? I look up at them, from bottom to top, like a little girl—and later, what about today?

My father. Am I unfair to him? After all these years, am I still incapable of forgiving him? I never resigned myself to his absence.

What am I unable to forget? That he was not by my side? He did not want to go. It wasn't his decision, or his desire, for that matter. He was presented with a verdict. He tried to explain to his wife that they had a child. He tried to be understanding and accept that she was in love with someone else; he believed it would pass. He called on her sense of duty. He implored her.

I knew nothing about that. And even now that I do know, it is hard to imagine. I have never seen him lose at anything. It never occurred to me that he was capable of suffering for love.

I saw him weep just once. At the funeral of his mother, my grandma. It frightened me.

I rarely think of him tenderly. With one exception—when I look at snapshots taken in the days when he was young and radiant, with his precious microphone in hand.

The fact that I know now that it wasn't his fault, that he also suffered, doesn't make me feel better, doesn't help. He did not know how to love his child. He didn't know how because he didn't know and that's all—or else, because the mother of that little girl had betrayed him. Maybe I didn't know how to let myself be loved.

Maybe he did love me. Others said he actually bragged about me to them, but instead of filling me with joy, that only increased my bitterness. I already felt that when I was little. My accomplishments, which he made light of to me, were proudly displayed for others. Which of us first shut the door on the other? A door that for years was impossible to open?

My mother, alone, leaning on me and on my life. My father, surrounded by a second family, and with two granddaughters, one from each of his new daughters, and endless projects for books about the history of sport. He never abandoned his efforts at creativity. As always, he railed against the government, against the right, against the left, against the Church, against the Jews. He railed about the lack of respect, respect that he deserved. Well deserved, because actually he had accomplished quite a lot.

Sometimes, I can see it in him still—a brash kid from Łódź, son of a laborer, grandson of a railroad man, who pulled himself up by the force of ambition alone. He made the decision to study journalism on his own, passed his exams alone, without anybody's help, this street kid from Bałuty, Widzew, and Mania, after the war, after a clandestine education, after being forced to pack up and move three times, after his father walked out. Brave. Without complaining. He lived on bread with lard that his mother and his aunt brought over in earthenware jars. He was like quicksilver, bursting with energy and joy, indefatigable. Maybe that is what she loved about him, the young woman who had spent her childhood in fear.

. . .

My father, Bogdan, was baptized on August 27, 1932, in the parish of St. Joseph of Łódź. This grandson of the Karliński family was seven weeks old at the time.

His country was working-class Łódź: Mania, Koziny, Bałuty.

There are photos of little Boguś (as he was called). With a teddy bear and a ball. In the snow, smaller than a snowman. In a field, beside a cow, even smaller then. With a balloon and dressed in the traditional costume of Kraków. And the crowning event: the First Communion.

Of his childhood, my father remembers the priests' visits, the smell of ham cooking for Easter, from which white borscht would be made later. The priest actually came to visit after Christmas, but Bogdan swears by his memory, eliminating in one fell swoop the half year between the birth and the resurrection of Christ. Ham, white borscht, and the priest—praise the Lord.

He remembers his father pushing him off his lap for fear of wrinkling his trousers.

He remembers eating the sugary raisin buns. And that, later, he played goalkeeper in soccer games.

His grandfather Jan Karliński, a railroadman with a mustache, worked or drank. At work he was punctual; dressed in a spotless uniform, he blew his whistle at the precise moment a train was to depart, just as he was supposed to. But when he got home, almost before he took off his cap, he sent his grandson out for a bottle. "Boguś," he said, "run, fetch a *halbka*." At first none of the storekeepers wanted to serve him anything— the kid was little—but then, for his grandfather's sake, they agreed. Occasionally he brought him all sorts of things from the butcher shop: head cheese, liverwurst, smoked sausage. Grandmother Rózia drank with her husband now and then. She made herself a citron vodka, or she heated sugar in a pan and mixed it with pure alcohol. Bogdan also remembers the smell of burned sugar.

Sometimes his grandfather played cards, but never for money. And when his colleagues came over, or the family dropped in, Rózia served sprats at fifteen pennies per can, sausage from Lithuania, pickled cucumbers, and homemade marinated mushrooms. And vodka.

Bogdan's mother was working at the rubber-boot factory, his father in the engine house, hired by the railroad because of his grandfather Karliński. Boguś always stayed home with his grandmother Rózia.

Boguś remembers kindergarten. He wore a smock, the nicest in the class since his mother embroidered so prettily. And he performed in school plays. He learned poems by heart and recited them at home. He often sat at the table turning the pages of a book, pretending to read. "A handsome young page went over mountains and valleys . . ." And then, when he had learned to read, he read to his grandmother from his schoolbooks. She was amazed by what he could do. He loved his grandmother and treated her with respect, always kissing her hand. She not only raised him, she gave him security. She was the one who was always there for him. His grandfather traveled, his father often disappeared, and as for his mother, from the beginning he felt like he had to protect her.

He used to play soccer for ŁKS, the sports club of Łódź. He took part in most of the matches and some competitions. He also tried the accordion with his father's help. At the end of August, he got ready for school.

Shortly after that his father, Corporal Roman Tuszyński, left for the war. He was placed at the head of a squad of heavy artillery in the Kaniów regiment and was soon taken prisoner. He sent many tender letters to his wife and his son from the stalag in the forest of Kampinos. He escaped, came home, and sought work at the engine house. He worked as a switchman through the rest of the Occupation. Sometimes he threw coal on the embankment for them to collect later. Sometimes he drank, and then he became argumentative.

Roman's mother, Maria Paulina, née Hausman, my great-grandmother, of Austrian origin, declared herself German without a moment's hesitation. She registered herself as such on the *Reichsliste*. She left Łódź for Sompolno, where she became part of the local German elite. Her grandson spent his vacations there. Boguś, the son of her only beloved son, was her great favorite. She pleased him in every way she could; she cooked following recipes in books. To this day, my father remembers the pigeon broth she made for him during the Occupation, with little dumplings, as an utmost delicacy. Grandfather Andaszek, Maria Paulina's second husband, used to take him fishing on the banks of the river nearby. As if there were no war.

Roman Tuszyński knew German, which he'd learned at home, but he did not sign up for the *Reichsliste*. In any case, as an employee of the railroad, he was entirely dependent on the German administration. He had been a September soldier, fighting on the front lines during the German invasion of September 1939, and felt Polish. When the Resistance blew up railroad lines and electrical towers, Roman was there.

Bogdan remembers the German woman who owned the boardinghouse in Sompolno, and a Gestapo officer who lived there too. He liked to listen to the conversations of the officer's two sons: they had both fought on the front. They talked endlessly about the power of the Reich. When they went to the local baths to ogle the girls, Bogdan tagged along. The sons did not survive Stalingrad. Bogdan's Jewish friends from Sompolno had disappeared earlier.

In Łódź, life at his grandparents' house was nothing like it used to be. Bogdan began to be afraid. He was frightened because his grandfather had been taken prisoner, and then they took Aunt Stefa away to work in Germany. He was frightened because they buried the radio in the garden. He was frightened because the Gestapo kept hunting men down.

And then, his father got involved in the black market. He made deliveries, tossing merchandise from the train at drop points like water reservoirs. He made a business out of selling goods like lard and moonshine while he traveled. He began to handle huge sums of money. Sometimes Bogdan helped him sell certain goods. Or else, the boy went with his mother to fetch bolts of cloth that she bought from a friend at cost. She would sit at the kitchen table, cutting the fabric into sections and then wrapping as much of it around Roman's torso as he could conceal. He wore baggy coats and carried canvas bags with false bottoms. In these ways, they managed more or less to survive.

· · ·

Bogdan, my father, was about ten years old when he began to take courses clandestinely from Professor Kowalski of the middle school run by the Bernardine order. The professor worked days in the accounting department of a factory; at the end of each day he taught just a few students. They got together at different houses in turn. There was always a lookout stationed in the street in case the police showed up.

Bogdan studied his own language in secret. He played sports in secret. He waited for the war to end. As soon as it did, in 1945, he entered the Bernardines' high school, at 73 Sporna Street, as a freshman.

He remembers his mother at that time, her face pale, her body skinny, her hair gray despite the fact that she was only thirty-six years old. She had just given birth to another son, Włodek, a little brother. She was still nursing him. But she was so frail; she looked like she was going to shatter at any moment. Scrawny and dispirited. She went to visit Bogdan at Boy Scout camp during his first vacation after the war, and she burst out crying when they went for a walk together. She sobbed openly in front of him, even though he was only thirteen. She cried while she told him that she and his father weren't getting along.

He knew it. He suddenly had the image right before his eyes of all those nights she had spent waiting for his father. Yards of thread crisscrossed on her lap like a multicolored spider's web, and she spent long minutes interweaving them with a mechanical gesture, half hours, hours. She said nothing; her right hand moved more and more quickly, weaving knot after knot. Roman would go out for cigarettes or bread and would come back days later. Sometimes he justified it; sometimes he offered no explanation at all. She let herself be deceived.

. . .

Right after the Liberation, Roman Tuszyński presented himself at the national railroad's security services in the "recovered territories." He was promoted to lieutenant. He had always loved the uniform, the boots polished to a high sheen, the reflection of himself in the mirror with the pistol on his belt. He left the house without looking back, but his wife could not resign herself to the fact of having lost him. She took her sons and got on a train for Szczecin. Somewhere near Piła, some drunken Soviet soldiers burst into the compartment. They saw the mother. Bogdan had never screamed like that before. He was a teenager and felt responsible for her. He always had.

Nobody was waiting for them at the station. They went to the right address, but his father wouldn't open the door. They spent a long time in the stairway. Perfect strangers walked right by them. Finally a woman came out of their father's apartment. My grandmother did everything possible to keep the family from breaking up, but things never worked out, then and there or later. Even though Roman earned a good living, she needed to work. She sewed badges on uniforms for the army. She ran a shop. In the street, she always had a dog with her, a German shepherd. In Jelenia Góra, where she followed her husband yet again, another empty bedroom was waiting for her. That, plus Roman returning at dawn, smelling of liquor and perfume, and humiliation. One fine day, coming home from school, Bogdan found his mother lying prone on the floor of the enormous bathroom dating from the days of the Germans. All that blood. Where did it all come from? So black. Two razor blades. Ambulance and hospital. They saved her.

After the war, they were all on the make. That is what defined my father in any case. Starving for everything, especially education and sports. He was already playing soccer before the war. Afterward, he joined the team at school in Łódź, where he showed considerable talent as a goalkeeper. He had excellent reflexes and was good at blocking shots. He boxed a little, too. He was thin. He weighed 122 pounds, was classed as a feather-weight. He had a total of nine fights and won eight of them. His right jab knocked more than one of them to the ground. Or so he says now.

In the succession of schools he attended, he started a series of small newspapers that he edited himself. He reported the events of school life. He pored over *Przegląd Sportowy* (Sports Review)—the only magazine devoted entirely to sports—and went to all the games. At the boxing championship of 1946, someone pointed out an elegant gentleman with a hat and walking stick. It was the journalist Kazimierz Gryżewski. Several days later, Bogdan sent him a letter: "Dear Sir. I saw you at the boxing championship match. I'm passionately interested in sports and would like very much to make writing about them my profession. How does one go about that?"

The reply came in one of Gryżewski's columns in the paper. "Bogdan Tuszyński, Łódź, 4 Perłowa Street. Kindly take up this subject in person with the editor, Wiesław Kaczmarek, *Kurier Popularny*, on the corner of Piotrkowska Street and Moniuszko Street."

He was so overwhelmed by this response that when he went to the meeting, he took his mother along. He was fourteen. He was given his first assignment right then and there: to write a report on boxing matches for young people. Of the six pages he turned in, only one remained after editing. This was his initiation into journalism and the beginning of his association with the *Kurier*, under the watchful eye of editor Kaczmarek, his first mentor.

He felt tied to Łódź, his parents' town, the same Red working-class city where barricades went up in 1905. He thought of Łódź proudly as a city throbbing with socialist life where everyone—the son of a worker, like the son of a peasant—had his place.

He had faith in a bright tomorrow because now the state officially recognized the rights of those who had never had any before. His grandmother and his aunt, who both had to go to work when they were young, could get an education now. Enthusiastically he supported the campaign against illiteracy and for the propagation of knowledge.

In 1949, they needed a new sports reporter for the radio and set up a public audition. His colleagues pushed him to try out for the job. He had a way of describing a match that always made it sound interesting, they said. The jury acknowledged his obvious intelligence and experience in the field. But they rejected his application because of his voice, which was pitched too high, according to them, completely wrong for the radio. One year later, he graduated from high school.

On his final report card, he had practically nothing but high grades, "good" and "very good." He got "fair" only twice—in Polish and biology.

His father did not congratulate him. Not then and not later. The man never said a kind word to him about anything.

His mother wanted him to become a doctor, an obstetrician most of all, because, now that the war was over, a lot of children were going to be born. He had just about decided to apply for a degree in maritime commerce at the college in Sopot. But on the train going home one evening, he read about the opening of a journalism department at the University of Warsaw. He simply had to try.

He traveled to Warsaw. Someone gave him directions from the station to the university. He walked there. Between examinations, he slept under the piano in the big gym of the students' residence, on Narutowicz Square. He did not know a single person in town. He was eighteen years old, in a hand-me-down suit designed for a railwayman, much too hot for August. He had a small wooden cross and a jar of lard that his mother had given him for the trip. He also had a will of iron and many dreams.

In his application for the admissions office, he chose jour-

nalism as his major. He filled in the part of the form reserved
for his background as follows: "I am Polish by birth, a Polish
citizen. My mother tongue is Polish." He signed the form with
a flourish, underlining his signature with a stroke of the pen.
Beneath the signature appears a single word: "Accepted."

It seemed to him—or so he says, it is how he remembers it
and is a feeling he is still proud of—it seemed to him that he
had the world by the tail. The war was over. He stood on the
threshold of a Poland that he could construct with his own
hands.

He took a formal academic oath that day, the thirteenth of
October, 1950. "I put myself and my future in the hands of the
dean of this august academic institution with a solemn pledge
that I will aspire with perseverance to acquire knowledge and
will never sully the name and reputation of this university, that
I will strive to be respectful of its rules and regulations."

They gave him a student ID and a discount card for the
streetcar, and he was given a scholarship and a room in the
dormitories across the Vistula River, on Grenadiers Street. He
also received financial aid the following year. All he ever got
from home were fifty złotys, the equivalent of four pounds of
sausage.

HALINA I

HALINA

*T*here are no photos. Not one from Łęczyca. Not one with her mother. Not one of her childhood. In the first known photograph of her, postwar, Halina is solemn.

Behind the doors of the Batory Secondary School there was no war. No rubble in sight. Green grass, just like before, with a new generation of violets. This last detail is not absolutely definite. Instead of springtime, 1945, it might well have been autumn, in which case glistening chestnuts would lie scattered underfoot. In that area, the old trees had survived air raids and fire. In her freshman year, on the second floor, or maybe when she was a sophomore, on the same floor, a history teacher raved about the victorious Soviet army and how grateful they should all be for having been freed from the tyrant Hitler. He didn't have to be very convincing; most of the students already agreed with him.

She was seated in the last row. She was dark, with curly hair, curly right up to the roots, divided neatly into two braids. With shiny navy-blue bows. Halina was the only one in their class still wearing them. She had round glasses with wire frames that hooked tightly behind her ears. Big brown eyes. Freckles and a clear complexion.

She stood out among the other girls, in their skirts made from blankets, their cotton cardigans and patched hand-me-down blouses. She was neat and well groomed. Her cardigan, dark red in color, was particularly eye-catching. Nobody else had anything that pretty. Nobody had a schoolbag like hers, either, soft black leather with a gold clasp, in which she arranged her books after every lesson. She put them all away carefully and slowly, as if she were afraid they would break, slipping into each nook with a gray paper jacket and her name beautifully inscribed in green ink on a special label: Halina Przedborska. She also had a wooden pencil box with a little sliding cover for her pens and pencils.

Perhaps it would be best to hang on to the version about the spring before the fall of Berlin. Halina was positive she had completed only one year at the primary school sponsored by the Workers' Friends of Children Society (RTPD) at Żoliborz before the Occupation and had entered secondary school after the war. She had forgotten the subjects she had studied informally in groups, with her mother. She went to the blackboard reluctantly. She spoke rarely and only when asked a direct question. With her eyes cast down, she responded in an orderly fashion, leaving nothing out. She was able to remember different constellations and the properties of the elements, to recite Newton's Laws or Pythagorean theorems. She did this without difficulty, but without curiosity as well. She invested all her energy in her schoolwork, as if she were doing her duty. As if she wanted to justify her own existence. She didn't like sports, and she did not know how to ride a bicycle. Books were the only things that really interested her, no matter how the story turned out. A habit left over from the war. At school, nobody ever mentioned the war.

She rarely looked straight ahead. And she blinked constantly. One day, her classmate Romka asked her why. She didn't answer right away. They had only known each other for a few weeks. Halina finally replied that she had read a lot during the war, in very bad light. Nothing more.

A little later, when they knew each other better, Romka got another response: "Behind the armoire where I was hiding, there was hardly any light. But I had to do something all day long. I ruined my eyes." Maybe she also mentioned the basement. She revealed this once, and one time only, and never again. You must not feel sorry for yourself and especially must not arouse pity in others.

Romka lived in Warsaw during the Occupation. She knew exactly what was going on. Her father had taken her right up to the opening in the ghetto wall on Sienna Street once, so that she could see for herself what mankind was capable of. But when she met Halina, she did not make the connection. She did not associate her pretty dark-haired classmate with the people kept starving and in rags behind those walls. She did not realize, haunted as she was by the memory of being chased out of her house during the Warsaw Uprising, that this little girl had suffered a fate even worse than her own. She thought about that later, about the fact that as a Pole, she was better off. She could go to the park. There had always been food on the table. She remembered a child who came to their house around nightfall every day for several months in 1942, and how her mother always gave him a glass of milk and a slice of bread. Then, all of a sudden, he disappeared. Why hadn't her parents been able to save a single Jewish child?

The girls never discussed it at the time. I don't know how Halina would have reacted to it. I do not know if she was even aware of what the people of Warsaw had to bear during the Occupation, the Uprising, the sewers, the couriers, the Szare Szeregi,* the refugee camp at Pruszków where they were sent, and the return afterward to houses without floors or windows. Romka had been all alone with her mother, without a cent, with nothing but an iron stove they found in the rubble. They had managed to bring a few utensils with them. They built a fire in the courtyard for cooking and ate from a single plate with a rusty spoon. They did not speak much about all that, in the same way that it never entered their minds to bring up the old Jewish tailor who made an overcoat for Romka just before the war and who spoke to her like no one ever had. "Young lady, if you would be so good as to turn a little to the left . . ." It did not matter to Romka or her parents that he was Jewish. She would have been offended if someone suggested otherwise. And that is exactly why she never mentioned him. Before the war, they would never have met. The assimilated Jewish intelligentsia rarely had any contact with working-class Poles. The daughters of fathers such as theirs did not play together in the park. They could only become friends in a liberated Poland.

At Halina's house, on Koszykowa Street, in an apartment on the top floor of an old building that they shared with another family, the parquet floor was always waxed to a high shine. There were curtains on the windows, not a windowpane missing, and hot water in the bathrooms. When she went there, Romka thought she was in paradise. She had no idea of the suffering that magnificent kitchen held for a little girl preparing all her father's meals. Halina had absolutely no experience in cooking, and no matter how precisely she followed the recipes in cookbooks, the dumplings stuck together like glue, chops and cutlets came out like shoe leather, and the crêpes for des-

---

* The Gray Ranks was a Polish resistance movement—agents sent by the AK, the military arm of the government-in-exile in London. (A.T.)

sert burned in the pan. Her father was furious. She never complained but she was often in tears. Or else she crouched on a little stool and begged her mother for help. "Mama, you see everything," she said time and time again. "Tell me what I'm doing wrong. I really do want to get it right and keep Papa from yelling so much." Her mother must have been in another part of heaven, because Halina never learned how to cook.

She loved stopping by Aunt Bronka's house for a snack on her way home from school. Her aunt made the most delicious cake. Sometimes she took Romka with her, but she felt uncomfortable on Górnośląska Street with her friend there. She drank tea the color of hay as fast as she could and left with great relief. She liked it better when she and Romka crossed Ujazdowski Park together, bursting with laughter, talking about anything and everything, the new geography teacher and her pretty dress. Something about that open space made her giddy. I know she had to be brave. Not long before then, overhearing a conversation between her father and her aunt, she had learned of her mother's death. The mother with whom she lived during the worst years of the war, who had been the whole world to her, whose love made up for her lost childhood. From then on she had to fend for herself, with that loss and that pain, had to take her own measure in the chaos of freedom recovered, in all the joy, relief, and contradictions of her new destiny. She was learning another duplicity than the one that had been hers until then.

Her relatives patched their wounds. Her father and her aunts lived every day, rejoicing at the end of hell and joining in the reconstruction of Warsaw and of Poland, a new Poland in which everyone would be well and justly treated. These were not slogans to them. They sincerely believed in the promises of socialism. They sincerely wanted to believe that it was the truest of all possible truths. They didn't ask themselves, as others did, whether or not they ought to emigrate. They wanted to be like everyone around them, not merely equal but alike. They erased all traces of the past so that they would never again have to wear an armband with a star on it. They rarely spoke of what had happened, and then said no more than was absolutely necessary.

They chose silence as a sanctuary, and they were not alone.

Like other survivors, they registered with the Jewish committees that came into being in Poland just after Liberation. The first year, the commission of registration and statistics of the Central Jewish Committee recorded more than 240,000 individuals. All of them were given material assistance and help in their search for the missing. They went there, at first, as they went toward houses that no longer existed, hoping that the emptiness was not everlasting and that there were still more, still others like them. They shared their distress, their decision to leave Poland or never again to be Jewish.

On the faded pink registration form, Mama is listed next to her father. They registered together in the summer of 1946. Were they still searching for lost relatives? Did they really think that someone else might have been saved and would miraculously appear before them? Or were they applying for financial assistance? "Przedborska Halina, a student, born July 3, 1931. Parents: Szymon Przedborski and Adela Goldstein"—their real names—"of Łęczyca and Koło." There it was, engraved in the past, the plain truth. "Address as of September 1, 1939: 18 Krasiński Street." Further down, in the space left for wartime changes of address: "58 Leszno Street, ghetto." As if she were informing them that she was fed up with the old neighborhood and wanted a change. The significance of the words was obvious, however, because "ghetto" was associated with Jews, like "camp," "captivity," "Aryan quarter." Number 14 Koszykowa Street meant life outside the walls, meant Liberation. And that, one must not forget, came from Soviet soldiers greeted with cheers on the road from Garwolin.

This file is the only official trace of their identity. The only evidence that her mother was Jewish. As if she were still hanging on to her mother's hand and with her, entire generations. Later, she handled things differently. A defenseless Jewish girl had to transform herself into a Pole. Halina's life would have been completely different if Dela had survived—if.

But she had no mother. She was the only one left, though they were both supposed to die.

I do not know what Halina thought about all that. Or what she had to forget in order to go on. She had to stay alive, had to be saved, as her mother swore she would. She did not know the rules of this new game. She was content to watch from the sidelines. She imitated the people closest to her. They kept quiet. So did she. Hunting down Jews, it appeared, was at an end, but could you trust it? She has no memory of it now. Even so, at the time she had to know, must have heard about the Kielce pogrom. And all the other instances of the murder of Jews, in forests, on trains, when they showed up at their houses. They went back home, but their places were taken. Their pantries, beds, wardrobes, belonged to their neighbors now. The Jews were not welcome. In the years immediately following the war, approximately two thousand citizens of Jewish origin were murdered in Poland, according to estimates.

They had no place to call home. Within two years, more than half of the survivors left Poland forever. Those who remained, like Halina's father, truly wanted to believe they had a right to live in their own country.

She had no wish to look behind her, or inside, either, where there was only fear and shame. Her new fate—Polish, Aryan, orderly, clear—could not be tainted by dread: that is, by the past; that is, by the memory of the ghetto; that is, by being Jewish. That had to stay a secret.

On the first of June 1947, young Halina Przedborska was baptized in the church of St. Vincent de Paul in the parish of Otwock.

Who led her to the church in Otwock, right beside the Catholic cemetery in which her mother was buried? Because it was not faith, not fascination with religious rituals, and not organ music.

She had learned how to pray during the Occupation, in her

first hiding place in Żoliborz. "Thy will be done on earth as it is in heaven." She recited it so often, she could say it perfectly, which pleased the ladies who were keeping her safe in the basement of their house and who shortly thereafter sent her farther away. They told her about Jesus Christ and the Cross, things she had never heard before. "Forgive us our trespasses," she apologized. Later on, that prayer came in handy—"and deliver us from evil"—when the Germans came close, as they did in several of the places she stayed under the name of Alicja Szwejlis, Aryan. This girl also learned how to kneel to pray and how to bring her hands together. "Our Father, who art . . ." She always had to be careful with the Sign of the Cross, though: ". . . and the Holy Ghost," from the left to the right shoulder. "Amen." She had good papers now, Polish, solid. With the seal of the Cross. She knew she needed the same ones after the war.

Who could have put an idea like that in her head? Someone in charge of dealing with the outside world? Could it possibly have been her father—the Communist, the master builder, who went to great lengths to avoid even passing a church? No, it never would have occurred to him to take refuge in the Almighty. He did not pray to any God. He believed in the Party. Could it have been his brother-in-law, then? Oleś, Aunt Frania's husband, the one who had saved them, who trusted no one? Who saw that his three sons, born of Jewish mothers, were all baptized? In the church where Halina received the sacrament, Oleś—Aleksander Majewski—appears on the registry as her godfather.

My mother does not remember the ceremony. She does not remember the priest looming over her and pronouncing, "Halina, I baptize you in the name of the Father, the Son, and the Holy Ghost," or if the holy water had any taste.

Nobody forced her to do anything. What counted most, no doubt, was the will to live, an urge so strong it consented to practically anything. It is difficult to draw the line precisely between my mother as a sixteen-year-old and the young woman she wanted to be. The parents of that young woman—

the father, Szymon, forty-four years old, engineer, and the mother, Adela Zmiałowska, whom he married in 1930—were both Roman Catholics.

Father Jan Raczkowski never suspected a thing. The official stamp of approval, purchased for ten złotys, was authentic.

Some of Halina's classmates claim she was always withdrawn, as if she were hiding something that she couldn't shake off. Though the two of them were close friends for years, it took her almost half a century to tell Romka how her mother died. Was she haunted by the past? Did she dream about the war? She could control herself during the daytime, but what about the nights? Was she frightened of them? Sometimes, on Górnośląska Street, after devouring chicken broth with lima beans or chopped liver, which they never called by its Jewish name, Aunt Bronka spoke of Łęczyca. Whatever the subject was—delicious dishes that only Grandmother cooked on Poznańska Street, the wine and liquors in the cellar, the right way to chop and marinate meat, or about a good Tokay or the special set of dishes used for Seder, or the view of the meadow— neither she nor her cousin Maryś wanted to hear a word of it. Absolutely everything else was more important—school, friends, games, their wonderful new life without the slightest hint of fear. They could go to school, meet people, walk in the streets with their heads held high, normally, just like other people. They did not want to hear even the merest echo of the past. What was beginning was so much more important. They had a brand-new world to build, houses and lives, with modern foundations made out of concrete and no looking back. As in the myth, one glance back might wipe it all out.

She does not remember hearing about the founding of the state of Israel. The year 1948 was not particularly memorable. She did not go to the unveiling of the monument honoring the heroes of the Warsaw Ghetto on April 19th of that year. The ceremony took place on a plot of land in the old Jewish quarter on the fifth anniversary of the Uprising. It was cut out of the same black granite from Sweden that Hitler had reserved for all the monuments to his own victories. She avoided that part of the city.

Reconstruction. She was engrossed by it as the daughter of a man who had dedicated a large part of his life to figuring out how to raise Warsaw from its ruins. She took no direct part in the effort, unlike her friend Baśka, who frankly remembers more of their childhood than she does. The two girls spent a lot of time together studying for final examinations at Kochanowski Secondary School, which Halina attended after Batory Secondary School, and they have remained good friends ever since.

Baśka was a child of the Warsaw Uprising. Her apartment building was burned to the ground. Her family lost everything. They came back to an ocean of rubble. She remembers the Old Town as a gigantic wreck of a place, with piles of rubble one story high. They loaded children into army trucks after school and drove them to Krasiński Square, where they handed out hammers and pickaxes to separate the bricks. All the necessities were missing. They did not have proper material for construction, or tools, or adequate means of transportation. But people were bursting with energy, drunk with a thirst for life, for the opportunity to negate the destruction of their city.

Baśka stressed that. People were coming home, all sorts of people, and as soon as they had told their stories, they wanted to act, to do something for Poland. "You can't imagine what it was like then. How could you? Today, people sit around talking about politics. It wasn't like that in those days. We had to pitch in and do something for the country."

My mother felt that way, and so did her father. And her friends, the daughter of the cleaning woman at the Central Committee and the shoemaker's daughter from Mokotowska Street.

Everybody knew Halina was Jewish. This is how they remember it today and how they tell the story. How she and her mother, who was a schoolteacher, were stuck in the ghetto during the Occupation and then, after that, went into hiding.

But for them, it was exactly the same as knowing that Baśka's family remained loyal to the AK, the Home Army, or that they fought in the streets during the Warsaw Uprising. Or that so-and-so escaped from Auschwitz. Or had never returned from some other concentration camp. Each of them had a wound to bear. Only the degree of pain varied. They were not interested in adding prejudice to the mix. No scar was considered more important than another. The only real difference between them was the destiny assigned to each by the war. Otherwise, they had different parents and lived in different houses. That's all. And when they shared it in secret, as little girls do—friends tell each other all sorts of things—when they were told about that, it simply wasn't mentioned again. Considering the pace at which events were moving, they had more than enough material to discuss. Like joining the ZMP, the Union of Polish Youth, for example.

One fine day, the principal of the school came into their classroom and said, in a tone that brooked no objections: "Young ladies, you are to join the ZMP." And so they did, eight out of nine. Almost every one of them sincerely believed in the ideals of socialism. It was hardest for Baśka. She had to hide her relationship with the Marian Society/Sodality of Our Lady. Still, none of them regarded enrolling in that organization as a political gesture. They had agreed to give their wholehearted support to the system that was in place at that time. Now, they felt even more connected by the shared discipline of the organization and by its rituals—for instance, marches and social activities. Besides, they all knew membership in the ZMP was their ticket to the university.

December 21, 1949, was Joseph Stalin's seventieth birthday. Stalin, master builder of the first socialist country in the world—according to the wall posters—leader and educator of the workers of the world, of progressive youth the world over, and Poland's greatest friend. She believed it; she wanted to; just as, when the war was ending and all the children were waiting for their parents to appear, she had believed her teacher's prom-

ise that the Russians would come and that no one, from that
day on, would ever hurt them again. The Russians did come,
and actually, nothing that bad had happened, for which they
all had Comrade Stalin to thank.

They had been celebrating his birthday since the beginning of the month. The ZMP held one program after another.
There were discussions of Stalin's life and work, and all sorts of
contests organized around the common theme of his achievements. The best participants were rewarded with books by
Soviet authors glorifying the heroic struggle against the fascist
invader and celebrating the establishment of socialism. I am
sure my mother got one. I remember seeing a book by Fadeyev
on the shelves at home.

She was one of the first to put together a complete library
of her own. She knew how to speak with conviction about the
superiority of the current system over the old one, using as an
example the availability of cheaply priced books. Created in
March of that year, the Committee for the Propagation of the
Book brought out volumes of Polish classics for one hundred
złotys, the equivalent of three kilos of bread, seven eggs, or a
pint of vodka.

She kept these accounts meticulously and reported them to
scholarly journals, full of enthusiasm and pride. Several dozen
titles out of the two hundred projected had already been published, each with a print run of at least fifty thousand copies.
Before the war, even the most popular works sold a few thousand copies at best. That was a big difference. Soon she realized
that she wanted to know more about everything to do with
books. The Week of Public Education, Books and Publishers,
which was held for the first time that year, 1949, was as signifi-
cant an event in her eyes as the campaign against illiteracy.

Sunday mornings, most of Halina's friends went to church,
but she never did. That was as it should be, she thought. It
did not surprise her that Catholics and Party members prayed
together every week. Regina, who was president of the ZMP in
their class and came from the working-class district of Wola,

never missed a May Day parade or a Sunday Mass. Political commitment, diligence, and piety did not necessarily have to conflict. For her father they did, but not everyone was as much of a stickler about the basics. And even he made exceptions.

Sometimes, after breakfast, they went for a Sunday walk together. Or else her father and stepmother would go and Halina would stay home alone. She had never taken Catholicism to heart. She did not feel she was missing anything. She never read or thought about the Bible. She never felt the need. She did not know how to behave at a Mass.

Before graduation, all the girls in Halina's class went to confession, two by two, at the Convent of the Sisters of Nazareth. The whole class also took Communion. One after another, they knelt at the altar and received the body of Jesus. All of them, without exception.

My mother denies it categorically to this day. She swears that she never, ever went to confession. That she never took Communion. It is how she remembers things.

"Religion" is clearly indicated on her diploma, written in dark ink with a firm hand. Very good. Her classmates remember. We can assume that she took part in all the compulsory religious ceremonies at school. And then she blotted it out. In the graduation photograph, she looks demure, in a navy-blue uniform with a little round white collar, her hands folded on the bench in front of her. An excellent student, satisfactory in Latin and physical education, determined, with a serious expression, next to Miss Ronthaler, the Polish professor and hall monitor. Of the nine graduates, three were admitted to the school of journalism at the University of Warsaw. In the autumn of 1950, high school diplomas in hand, they embarked on a new chapter of their lives. Perhaps the most important one of all.

BOGDAN II

MY FATHER, BOGDAN TUSZYŃSKI,
A POLISH RADIO SPORT REPORTER AT WORK

B ogdan still looks back on those first few years in Poland right after the war as a time of tremendous enthusiasm. He remembers how grateful they were to the Soviet army, which had delivered them from the Nazis. No one spoke then, as we do today, of the yoke of communism, but of building a socialist country "on the model of the sister state of workers and peasants." They took seriously the slogan "Workers of the world, unite."

He did not know what that really meant. In other words, he was not aware of anything beneath the surface. In those days, like many others, he was oblivious. None of them felt they were under lock and key, captives of the "Red menace." They did not use terms like "regime" or "under the yoke." There was nothing shameful in their political involvement. Only Poland and the future mattered. On every official form, he emphasized his working-class background and his left-wing pedigree. He included his parents' membership in the PPS, the Polish Socialist Party, although his mother was never an active member, and his father's ties, after the war, with the PZPR, the Polish United Workers' Party, although he no longer maintained contact with his father. Bogdan's political activism started as soon as he entered secondary school, when he joined the ranks of the "Red Scouts," which gathered working-class youths under the socialist banner. He adopted their ideology as his own. At this time he also joined the ZMP, the Union of Polish Youth, but—as he stated on the official form—it was only at the university that he came into contact for the first time with "the real work of the youth organization" and "the scientific view of the world." They elected him secretary of the local group.

He was involved in sports, he attended the dances, and he wrote his first articles. He started contributing to the popular daily *Przegląd Sportowy,* a sports paper. He was nineteen years old in 1951 and knew exactly what he wanted. He was skillful, he wrote a great deal, and very quickly. He was so successful that one day a professor pleaded with him to moderate his pace, because the other students could not keep up. "You have all sorts here, people from the countryside, collective farms; it's a question of fairness."

It was his success in sports, no doubt, that brought young Tuszyński to the attention of the director Leonard Buczkowski. He was filming *Pierwszy Start* (First Start), the edifying story of a country lad who wants to become a glider pilot. A team of intrepid fellows from the association called In the Service of Poland bravely helped him. Bogdan had a part as a telegraph operator. The young actor Stanisław Mikulski appeared in several scenes, and the high-school student Roman Polanski was in one frame. Bogdan's characteristic gesture of brushing back his hair from his forehead was caught on film.

He soon fell in love.

He knew everything about Halina. She herself had told him. It was an important element of their relationship. He immediately felt responsible for her and wanted to be her protector.

To me they seem very young, slender and radiant, at that time. Always together, in a group. Wearing red ties. If they marched, it was jauntily. If they sang, they gave their all. If they took action, it was with conviction. They were permanently at the height of euphoria—in the trenches, in their social life, in their propaganda work in the countryside, in the gathering of *stonka* (potato bugs). And in the parades on May 1.

"Feel sorry you couldn't be here," wrote a student to her friend—it could have been my mother to her girlfriend or any one of them. "Something phenomenal. I was in the front row wearing a red tie. There was a red banner raised high in the sky, and my eyes were riveted with admiration on Comrade President Bierut. People streamed past for hours on end, for a whole day. Then the military parade. What power!"

They would remember the first parades of their student years as idyllic.

At the universities, everyone was debating the issues of Communist education. Among them were subjects such as "Why we adopt as our own the tenets of communism and morality." Or else: "On patriotism and internationalism." "The moral and ideological profile of a member of the ZMP—a young patriot and future leader of the country" was particularly popular.

Right after the war, the department of journalism at the University of Warsaw provided a diverse environment. On the one hand were young members of the ZMP just out of secondary school, and on the other, noticeably older students in their twenties and even in their thirties, as well as "comrades" of both sexes selected by branches of the Party to continue their studies.

The young were brimming over with energy; they wanted

to construct socialism from the ground up, as they had a profound faith in the new order. They also believed in the profession of journalism and its mission. The newspaper, in the words of Lenin, was "an organizer, a propagator, an agitator." The newspaper was the "cultural bread." They were conscious of its power. The press had to mobilize the broadest public opinion for the tasks facing the country in the struggle to achieve peace. "From a banal scribbler serving the bourgeois class," wrote Bogdan, "the journalist in our system has raised himself to the function of social militant before whom stand glorious goals." That's what was drilled into them: they had to be politically vigilant; they had to pay attention to public opinion, stigmatize evil, and react by composing letters, complaints, demands. The militant students were placed under the supervision of the dean of the faculty, first Jerzy Kowalewski, then Aleksander Litwin.

The transcript of the department listed all the subjects that had to be mastered by the students in the journalism section during their three-year course of studies. My parents studied from 1950 to 1953. It was the political economy of capitalism, with Professor Lipinski, that took up the most time, four hours a week. They devoted two hours to dialectical and historical materialism with Adam Schaff. The students were required to participate in work-study organizations—at a daily paper, at a weekly, on the radio—as well as learning the techniques of printing. In total, more than twenty subjects, among them military training. In the second year was added the history of the All-Union Party (the Bolsheviks), logic, style, and literature.

The lectures were attended by large numbers of students, and the tutorials were broken down into smaller groups. Teams of readers reported on the short stories by Prus, Sienkiewicz, and Konopnicka, *Volkolamsk Highway* by Bek, and *How the Steel Was Tempered* by Ostrovsky. The printed word had to reach the masses and strengthen them in the spirit of socialist realism. The students voiced their contempt for films "made in Hollywood"; they were enthusiastic about art based on the simple life; they debated the moral dilemmas of the welders and foremen.

When they started their studies in autumn 1950, you could be thrown out of the university for telling a joke. It was necessary only that someone rush to inform the right people: "He told me a joke about the USSR." Meetings were organized at the faculty level to debate the horrors of wearing narrow trousers or of making the moves of a "cool cat" while dancing. As a general rule, denunciations concerning participation in the Warsaw Uprising or belonging to the AK, the Home Army, were really dangerous. Someone in their group recalled an accusation made against a colleague who was threatened with expulsion from the organization because she took notes during lectures with an American fountain pen. This must have had a deeper meaning.

The propaganda brochures for internal use warned: "The disruptive aspects of the enemy's work are hostile manifestations, especially those linked to the question of Katyn* and the defacing of newspapers posted on walls. The enemy also depraves the young through drunkenness and debauchery, into which they even lure members of the ZMP. In some cases the depravity is masked specifically as communist morality: It's to enjoy life that we have communist morality. Residents of the university dormitories are particularly vulnerable."

During his student years my father had no other residence in Warsaw, like the five other members of his group from Rypin: Daniel, Czarek, Edek, Włodek, and Witek. Among them were four couples, Halina and Bogdan included, who formed a circle of friends. My father enjoyed laughter and telling jokes. You could hardly avoid noticing him socially; he had to stand out, no matter at what price. No doubt he was careless in what he said, because he had confidence in people, in the times.

* Katyn: the site and burial grounds of a mass execution of Polish officers during the Soviet Occupation, which the Soviets tried to blame on the Germans. (A.T.)

I have trouble imagining my parents this way: always together, in classes, during recesses, during the evening meetings. Always near one another, at no more than arm's length, side by side, knees touching, shoulder to shoulder. He was generally in action, always "between"—between a match and meeting someone, a conference, returning home. She was calm and serious. But she also enjoyed laughing, especially in his presence. To the others, they both seemed without a care. For that she was also grateful to him.

They seem to me so dissimilar, coming from such different homes, heredity, and environments, each carrying baggage of distinct experiences. Following different gods. And yet many things united them, above and beyond their initial feelings. Above all they wanted to live, at last live, walk, and breathe, attain their happiness. Holding their heads high, she and he, with the same privileges, the same promise of a favorable destiny. In Poland, in their country. The daughter of an engineer and the son of a railroad worker, the granddaughter of merchants and the grandson of peasants, coming from different planets, on this same piece of Polish soil.

How did it happen? How could they brand as an enemy of the people this lad from working-class Łódź, so that he was stripped of his rights as a member of an organization to which he was completely devoted? No one can remember. The whole faculty gathered for the meeting. No one can reconstitute the sequence of events of this organized entrapment, or the succession of accusations.

From that moment something started to change in the life of my father.

May 1952. Certainly it was May: he remembered the chestnut trees in bloom. One morning he was leaving the student dormitory on Grenadiers Street, his soccer shoes slung over his shoulders. He was on the team representing the university in a game that afternoon, vying for the championship of the top-ranked schools. He was in a hurry. He was coming from the other side of the Vistula by bus and wanted to go over his notes before classes. And see Halina.

He had hardly entered the university hall when he was called to the office of the ZMP. On the right of the entrance hall, up to the second floor. There were several men in the room. Without any warning, one of them put a revolver to his back. Even though it now seems unbelievable, that is what he remembers: "You son of a bitch, come with us." Downstairs, near the Geography Institute, a car was waiting. They drove him to Mostowski Palace, headquarters of the Internal Security Services, the political police.

His friends at the residence had seen him leave for the university, but he did not show up there before noon, nor afterward. Halina became worried. By evening they went searching for him.

Someone had seen him as he was being intercepted in the entrance hall of the university. Someone else told Halina. She was in a panic. She who had never asked her father for anything now ran to see him. I am not absolutely certain, and she does not remember, but somebody must have intervened. Or else all of this would have taken another turn. It was the only arrest made in a class that numbered more than a hundred students.

"In the course of the first fortnight of this month of May, Tuszyński was arrested by the authorities of the Internal Security Services for having commented on a broadcast of the BBC in a public place in a manner prejudicial to our current relations." That was the statement in a note bearing a "Confidential" seal.

My mother cannot remember those days. But she recounted her visit to the Mostowski Palace to a girlfriend, thanks to whom I can imagine her there. Had she been summoned, or did she go there on her own initiative? No one can tell today. It was a blond young man from the countryside, "with a broad face, semi-literate, you see," who questioned her.

They reproached Bogdan for telling anti-Soviet jokes and listening to Radio Free Europe in the apartment on Puławska Street. She denied it, as she also denied he had made disastrous comments, for trumped-up political reasons, about a certain match against the Russians. She didn't remember what match; sports did not interest her, she had an indulgent attitude toward what was called "physical culture." She was in love and ready to do anything to protect her man.

"Is it true?" The blond young man wouldn't let go. "Is it true, because there is an accusation against Tuszyński, that he is an anti-Semite?"

They all remembered that he had made Jewish jokes. But no one took it seriously; neither did she. She stood up and, facing the officer, who was seated, she said, "Look at me closely. He is my fiancé."

I like her making this small theatrical gesture, full of confidence. Did she risk anything at all by doing it? It seems not. She admitted that she was Jewish, as if that rendered the accusation absurd.

She fought for his release, she defended the man she loved. It's extraordinary to me, but perhaps I am mistaken. I never knew her thus. I don't know if in other circumstances she had ever admitted her origins so openly and defiantly.

Aside from the accusations of anti-Semitism, having told anti-Soviet jokes and listened to Western radio, Bogdan was accused of hanging a cross above his bed in the student dormitory and of "spreading false information about the massacre in Katyn"; he had declared that it was the work of the Russians. This sort of offense meant two to three years in prison.

The accusation concerning Katyn was the most serious. That concerning anti-Semitism had some weight but was also shameful. There were rarely any consequences. His friends all affirmed this. As for listening to hostile radio, it was not necessarily proof of ideological depravity. People who were implicated were often absolved if they reacted appropriately to the hostile propaganda. Knowing what the enemy thought could be valuable. But Katyn, that was dangerous.

One night they released Bogdan, after seven days of detention. They asked him to appear in the office of the ZMP so they could review the case and so he could provide additional explanations. "They will take care of you." The chairman of the board was one of Bogdan's close friends.

The meeting was set for mid-June 1952 in a large hall on the second floor of the Casimir Palace. No one can remember whether they had gathered only the journalism department or other faculties as well. With the distance of time, some recalled the podium in the middle of the room; others, friends speaking from the lectern. Tables and chairs were arranged in three rows, or perhaps two with an aisle in the middle. Several dozen people were present, or perhaps several hundred. In the back unknown people sat on tables, workers from the UB, the Internal Security.

His comrades got up one after the other, the same ones with whom he had played ball, gone drinking, those with whom he roomed. They made accusatory statements. They repeated what he had said in the course of a dinner, or while shaving, or in a café, or playing cards. About Katyn he had said that the crime had not been committed by the Germans and that while the Soviet Union was promulgating a policy of peace, at the right moment they could start a war. As for the economic problems, he was dissatisfied and blamed it on the environment rather than looking for the root of the problem.

"Although he is the boyfriend of a certain Przedborska, who is of Jewish origin, he is an anti-Semite, which is evident in the statements he made."

Those who tried to raise objections were rebuked with a categorical "Sit down!" One or two announced that they were going to monitor him on the ideological level. For a moment he tried to defend himself by invoking the proletariat from Łódź and insisting that this was a misunderstanding. However, by a unanimous decision of the collective he was expelled from the ranks of the ZMP as a hostile element with alien ideology.

The signature on the note with the label "Confidential" and dated June 17, 1952, is illegible.

They crossed the enormous courtyard of the university holding hands; no one came toward them. Bogdan still remembers today that she was by his side.

Expulsion from the ZMP almost invariably meant being

expelled from the university. Yet Tuszyński was allowed to remain there.

The matter had run its course when he had to take his examination in dialectical materialism with Professor Adam Schaff. He remembers the exam because he took it at the same time as four Jewish, he says, girls, each of whom received five out of five. As for him, Schaff had written, in his own hand, "Unsatisfactory," which he rarely did, people said. Someone heard him say that individuals like Tuszyński, unworthy of the trust of the organization, did not deserve any other grade in Marxism-Leninism.

Professor Schaff's teaching assistants claim that it was unbelievable that a major Marxist philosopher had anything to do with such an incident. He had more important matters to take care of. Besides, he rarely supervised his own exams. It was they, his teaching assistants, who were in charge of Schaff's signature, who gave the exams.

My father failed. This grade, "Unsatisfactory" (two out of five), appeared in his transcript with the signature of the professor. Adam Schaff was Jewish, that was not a secret.

In the fall, Bogdan passed his makeup exam in dialectical materialism with a four out of five.

As an enemy of the people, his life was made difficult in the department. That's what he says today, that's what he really believes, and he knows who should be held responsible for it. Were the Jewish professors effectively all prejudiced against him, or was his persecution only the result of his imagination and his biased outlook? In those days no one wondered if brilliant students were Jewish, no one had singled them out; it never occurred to anyone to link intellectual capacity with genealogy. No one talked about it, any more than they discussed the number of Jewish scientists. No one can recall any conflict of this nature. No one ever wondered who were the grandparents of Professor Schaff, the author of *Introduction to Marxism,* the most frequently reprinted textbook.

Bogdan never spoke ill of his Jewish friends at the university.

He continued to affirm that when Halina and he first became acquainted, their backgrounds had no meaning, did not count, and certainly were not a problem. His friends have the same recollection. Did his aversion only concern those in the upper echelon?

It was said that his final thesis, *Sports in the Service of American Imperialism,* was a pioneering work, judged favorably as a propaganda pamphlet. He passed his exam on June 23, 1953, with the grade of "Excellent." He obtained his diploma from the department of journalism, graduating in philosophical and social sciences.

In July 1953, Halina wrote him in a letter that she had had a frank conversation with the vice-chancellor, who made it possible for her to continue her studies in literature, a necessary condition for obtaining her bachelor's degree, and helped Bogdan find work with the radio station. "The staff member Tuszyński started working at Radio Station of Warsaw on the 1st of September," she wrote him proudly. "Are you happy?"

"I am very pleased with the work assigned me," he wrote in his report. "I am fully capable of devoting all my faculties to my professional tasks, in order to add, in the small measure of my work, my own contribution to the edification of socialism in our country."

In an evaluation dated May 1954, he was deemed politically honest, "a man who is devoted to us."

HALINA II

*W*ho first noticed the other?
Did she notice him: blond, athletic, with blue eyes? Or did he notice her: delicate, brunette, with a serious expression? Where did it happen? In the courtyard of the university, or at a meeting of the ZMP; at the dean's office, or in class? It happened quickly, as if each had been waiting for the other. Or perhaps it was in the class on dialectical materialism, or history. Let's say history. Neither knows how or when, but they remember that they quickly became a couple.

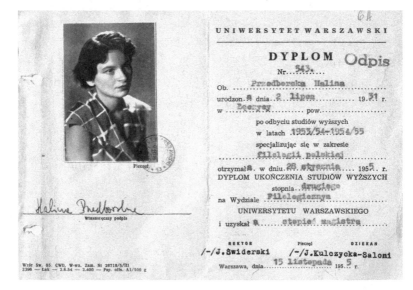

MY MOTHER, HALINA PRZEDBORSKA, AND HER WARSAW UNIVERSITY DIPLOMA. SHE OBTAINED A MASTER'S DEGREE FROM THE FACULTY OF PHILOLOGY IN 1955.

When they met at the beginning of autumn in 1950, my mother was nineteen years old; he was younger by one year. Both were born in the first week of July. Halina weighed about 108 pounds dressed and wanted to gain some weight. He had been boxing until recently in the featherweight division.

He was her first boyfriend, and she was his first girlfriend. Almost in one outburst, she had told him everything about herself. They visited the grave of Halina's mother in Otwock.

My mother was eight years old when war broke out. Two years later she walked along the streets of the ghetto looking for green trees. A high wall separated the Jewish quarter from the Poles. She had to look up, and even then a narrow frame of barbed wire and glass shards hemmed in the sky. She knew a few places from which you could see the Krasiński gardens on the other side. She liked to think about this garden; she knew that her aunt Frania strolled there, pushing her newborn in a carriage. People said Frania was on the other side of the wall because she looked as if she belonged there.

In the course of the summer of 1942, my mother left the ghetto, although it was forbidden for her to walk in the streets of the city. She spent her twelfth birthday in the Żoliborz neighborhood, in the basement of the same house in which she had lived with her father before the war. She was always afraid. She read for hours on end by candlelight. People said that her looks betrayed her. They changed her first and last names and taught her how to pass from one hiding place to another and never ask questions. They also taught her Catholic prayers and how to make the Sign of the Cross.

In July 1944, friends of her father sent her to a summer camp for orphans in Wilga. There she was known as Alicja Szwejlis. Her mother visited her there once. She came on foot from Otwock, where she worked in Mrs. Czaplicka's boardinghouse. She couldn't take Halina with her then, but she promised to come back as soon as she could. She never returned, neither after the flight of the Germans nor later, when the guardians came to fetch their wards.

After the war, my mother decided to look at herself in the mirror for the first time in five years. She liked the little girl she saw. "Pretty little Halina," she said. "Pretty little Halina," she repeated.

The war had left her with nothing, except her life and fear.

. . .

My father was seven years old at the outbreak of war. He lived with his family in his grandfather's house in Łódź. He had light-colored hair and piercing blue eyes. In a photo taken the day of his First Communion, dated May 1940, he looks in good health. He stood amid trees in bloom holding a bouquet, wearing a fine suit with short pants and a shirt with a spread collar. Next to him was his mother, Marianna, in a suit trimmed in white and wearing a hat. He came out of the war convinced that with a little luck he would get along fine in life.

It could have been the other way around, with my father the one reading in a basement, afraid of the dark, and my mother wearing a white First Communion dress, standing in a park by the church. It would have been more difficult for a boy to be saved. Mother could have been on the sunny side and Father in the dark.

Halina wrote love letters to Bogdan in green ink on sheets of white notebook paper now yellowed. In neat handwriting, slightly angular, she counted the days and the hours, the days and the hours she waited. She waited to throw herself into his arms, she waited to snuggle up against him, to forget all her troubles and worries.

It was he who saved her letters. Twelve letters, all twelve beginning with "Darling," "My love," "My little cat." Today I can't think of any way to describe these terms of endearment other than futile.

He had a sunny disposition and was unaware of everything that frightened her within herself, the flashbacks that returned and surged in her head and wouldn't let her sleep. When she was alone on Sunday afternoons in the apartment on the third floor, the others having gone for a stroll, she sat at the oak table, listening. "In the small café where you whispered 'I love you' to me for the first time . . ."—the old tango interpreted by the Trida Sisters. A sad and languorous melody, similar to the rain on the window and the monotonous ticking of the clock.

"The book is lying shut on the sofa, my knitting has fallen on the floor and I don't even want to pick it up . . ." She went out only as far as the mailbox, to send her latest letter, or else she waited for the mailman.

One evening she had gone to the train station because she thought Bogdan was coming back. He had gone to Tczew on family business. Her waiting led to disappointment. She took a long time returning home from the station. Then she had written, "You can't do that. Show a plate of warm food to someone famished, and take it back without her even having a taste. Mean!" She thought about going a second time to wait for the train, but she dreaded another solitary return home.

Besides, it was getting late and her father did not want her to be out at night. Once he had left her on the doormat for half the night as punishment for being five minutes late.

• • •

Her father was so distant, separated not only by his own silence by also by his wife, to whom he was completely subjected. She had a strange first name, Żena. Halina held it against her father for wanting to change his life so quickly and radically. Certainly he had not seen her mother for ten years, but she had been dead only for five years. How could he have forgotten her? Perhaps you have to forget; how else to continue living? But couldn't he have found another woman, a woman like his friend Marysia, whom she liked so much? What really transpired between those two? Halina sometimes visited her secretly; she received presents from her, dresses in packages from London or secondhand clothing. After alterations she wore them to dances and they matched her *trumniaki,* old tennis shoes she had dyed black herself. If Żena had only known . . . She could confide in Marysia, but Żena had never even hugged her. Neither had her father. Żena would shut herself up in her room or would ask herself rhetorical questions: Why did her father marry this woman? He needed someone to do the cooking? But she never cooked. We have Miss Józia, who comes to clean the house; Żena has to attend meetings. He wanted to have ideological discussions over breakfast?

She remembered what she overheard Aunt Bronka say late one night in Ujazdów. Everyone thought she was asleep. They spoke in muffled tones, almost whispering. Bronka always spoke to her brother cautiously, as if to a child.

Halina had known for a long time that she would hear these words one day. She couldn't ignore it. "If she were alive, she would never have left her daughter in such a state." The absence of her mother caused a permanent pain she felt at every step. Mother wasn't here and would never be here.

It was on rainy days that she missed her mother the most. She still had the stockings of Scottish wool that her mother had brought to her at the summer camp in Wilga in 1944. They had become too small for her but she kept them in a drawer. She would bury her face in them to recapture the smell of that moment.

Of those years, Żena remembered that Halina was uncommunicative. "Distant" was perhaps too strong a word to characterize her relationship with her father, but it certainly never went beyond the bounds of correcting her behavior. Żena says, to the astonishment of my mother, that she was very disturbed by this. They did not relate to each other as a family. She heard Halina complain to Bronka that after the Liberation her father had not been in a hurry to fetch her. Żena said that it was unfair to blame Szymon. He had to come to terms with many absences at that point.

They never had the time to learn to know and grow to love one another, little Halina and her father, the father and daughter. And in the end they had not known how. Before the war, he was rarely at home in Łęczyca, which he left to work in Warsaw. They saw each other on Saturdays and during holidays. She was closer to her grandparents than to him. She had not seen him during the whole Occupation, five years: the ghetto, the hiding places were always with her mother. He was not with them in the most difficult times. He appeared when nothing could be saved any longer. There were so many things that he did not understand.

She would find echoes of the warmth of Łęczyca again in Aunt Bronka's house in Ujazdów. There everything was in motion, alive—the kitchen, the laundry, the neighbors, the friends, the conversations, the card games. Not only did Aunt Bronka serve broth with beans and the same gefilte fish as at Przedrynek Place, but she gave Halina the feeling that she belonged to someone. She gave the feeling of being confident that the future would come out fine one way or another. The war widow, who in addition to her husband had lost her whole family, brought comfort to others.

In her father's house on Puławska Street a chill atmosphere reigned. Halina escaped by joining her friends and Bogdan at the university. Disciplined and concentrated in her studies, she took notes, which the others in the group benefited from subsequently. From the beginning she was interested in literature.

She enjoyed learning carefully, while he had to force himself, with more or less success. She assiduously took notes in history classes, in English vocabulary, and in printing techniques. She paid special attention to a book titled *The History of the All-Union Communist Party (Bolshevik),* which was considered very important. Her friends copied from her notebooks all her notes from the materialism class.

When Bogdan returned home to Łódź, where he was often needed, she tried even harder to take charge of everything concerning him. She attended the administrative meetings of the ZMP, placed calls about his internships. She missed him and wrote letters even during classes, reminding herself not to sit too close to the front of the room, which she generally did. Her eyesight wasn't the best, and besides, she wanted to know what was going on.

"Everything follows its habitual, worn path," she wrote to him in the autumn of 1951.

> The wheels of university life continue working as always, ignoring the enormous changes that have transpired in one of its microscopic circles.
>
> Who is even aware that I feel so awful, and everything is so painful to me without you? How this little noisy and crowded world is now empty for me, that nothing interests me or has any meaning? My thoughts are constantly about you. I count the hours until I receive your letter.

It was during the vacations that they were separated for the longest time. For her, time dragged then, and the days were drawn out to frightening length.

She expressed longing in all its forms. She reread his letters, looked at photos of him, thought about him. She couldn't bear the fact that they had to wait for the end of the vacations to be together again, permanently. "Always together—isn't that so?"

She felt alone. Bogdan's presence gave her strength; his absence devastated her. She became scatterbrained; she lost books that she had borrowed. Once she even left her handbag in a bazaar, with all its contents; by sheer luck an honest customer found it and brought it back to her. It was fortunate: how could she ever have explained it to her father? "Come back quickly, otherwise I will leave my head somewhere," she implored Bogdan. When he did come back, everything fell into place again.

He had become her refuge. She counted on him, she dreamed of a little place that would be their own, nothing more than a room in the student dormitory on Malczewski Street, so long as they could be by themselves.

Quickly it became natural that he should be there, that he should leave his suit at her apartment, the only suit he owned, and his dress shoes; that he would come when no one was there and she would iron his linen shirts. He had so little and she received so much from him. He was always broke. She offered him money, but he always refused; he assured her that he would soon earn his living, that they would become independent.

He kept his promises. Today when she thinks back, she can't tell what was most important in their love. She has forgotten the flame. She remembers what she thought: he had blue eyes, he was Polish, he had loved and accepted her as one of his kind.

They wanted to get married immediately, but Halina's father did not agree. First your studies, he repeated, the most important thing is to have an education. No one knows whether he wanted to test his daughter's feelings or hoped that perhaps she would change her mind. It was clear that he had wanted a different son-in-law than this one. It was hard to say if it was Bogdan's social standing or his background that was the problem—both would clearly be in conflict with the ideals of the engineer Przedborski—or if their different temperaments were the cause. He treated Bogdan with indulgent condescension. He hardly ever addressed him. They shared this feeling of reciprocal aversion.

At Bogdan's home in Łódź, they received Halina the best way they knew. The first time was on a Sunday. There was the smell of laundry, of cooking, and of church. His mother had spread a special tablecloth, she had prepared a *czernina,* a soup made of the blood of a goose, and in the heat of her emotions she never noticed how difficult it was for young Halina to swallow it. Everyone did all they could: they with their Polish hospitality, unique in the world, filled with concern and tenderness. A young lady, so very thin, you must eat to avoid misfortune! She forced herself to hide how ill at ease she felt. They were so very different from the families that she knew. At the same time she wanted so much to be a part of them, to laugh along with them, loudly, to eat the soup and the marinated mushrooms, drink the vodka with caramelized sugar, wipe her mouth with the back of her hand, to answer nature's call in the pail behind the curtain, to eat the red currants right from the bushes. To answer questions directly.

To not appear superior and to accept the value of simplicity. What right did she have to feel more important than they, privileged perhaps? Because she had read more books and knew how to behave at the Philharmonic? Because she understood words they didn't know? Yet she was the one who had hidden in a closet, not they; they were never hunted down, but she had been. So was she worse, or better?

How was her grandfather Goldstein of the coal depot different from Bogdan's grandfather Karliński, who made the trains run? Only their prayers were different. But they, the younger generation, were not obstinate about faith.

She would have preferred that they had been different, Bogdan's parents, his family, but that wasn't the case. They didn't have oak bookcases with generations of books, they didn't recite *Ballads and Romances,* and they didn't share the cult of Beethoven or Brahms. Yet they were interested in her, they opened themselves up to her, which never happened to Bogdan with her father and his wife. They had enabled her to feel at home here, as in her own house. On her first visit to Perłowa Street, she had told Bogdan's mother, the good mother Mania, that she wanted a big family and many children. Many, at least six. My grandmother, who wasn't yet Grandma at the time—Bogdan's mother, I don't know if Halina ever called her "Mother"—smiled and asked, "My child, do you know what you are saying?" Or something like: "Do you know what it means bringing up six children?" Perhaps she didn't know, but then in Perłowa Street, next to her blue-eyed man, that was what she aspired to the most: to make a family, a big Polish family. She wanted to surround herself with a protective wall of love that was Polish. Not to be afraid. I don't know if at that table half a century ago, anyone had wondered why this young couple clung so closely to one another.

Bogdan's mother appeared to her wise and so caring.

Halina was as taken by Bogdan himself as by his Polishness. The simplicity of Perłowa Street and its inhabitants, railroad workers, contributed to it equally. "Workers of the world, unite"—the headlines of *Trybuna Ludu* (Tribune of the People), immutable over the years. Why would she have anything against them? She had to admire social progress, the aspiration to rise higher, overcoming difficulties, ambition. The dreamed-of, promised new world left no one behind; the Red proletariat, working together toward a better, socialist future.

To what extent did Bogdan himself believe in this future? Sometimes he would be funny and tell terrible jokes, mostly when he was drinking wine in the students' dormitory or when they had too much beer with their dinner at the Bristol. For the meal they had coupons, but they paid for the beer out of their own pockets. It would happen that she heard him make statements about Katyn, or the economic difficulties; he would even say that the Jews were guilty of something, but it never bothered her. She knew who he was and she trusted him.

Years later she learned that her own cousin Maryś, active in the ZMP at the Batory Secondary School, had tried to interfere in their relationship. He did not consider Bogdan a suitable match for Halina and had telephoned him on several occasions to prevent him from meeting her, but without any result.

She was very shaken by Bogdan's arrest, the subsequent tribunals accusing him, and everything that happened later. Bogdan was crushed; he felt violated and deceived by his friends as well, who suddenly testified against him. He constantly wondered who could have turned him in: someone close, someone from the student dormitory, someone who had seen the cross above his bed and heard what he said before going to sleep? That's when he stopped being a boy; he matured, forcing himself not to say everything that he was thinking. He saw through different eyes those whom he had once called friends. He complained that they were destroying him, persecuting, spying on him, wanting to make him fail his exams, those guys from the UB and the others. The vague "them."

She spent the month of August 1953 with her father in the mountains at Krynica. She was twenty-two years old, and it was the first time they were together for such a long period.

They had gone on vacation but always in the company of the family. This time they were both to benefit from the care of a state-owned resort, Szymon to lose weight, Halina for her nerves and to become stronger. She wrote Bogdan detailed letters about their stay and her disappointment at the absence of any closeness to her father.

They went on excursions together, striding along the trail to Góra Parkowa. In the afternoon they played cards. Newspapers in the reading room, water in the thermal baths, Soviet films at the cinema. They talked a lot. She was under the impression that it was all "very warm"; however, they spoke about everything but never anything personal. They made fun of people they knew as well as strangers, but not a word about Żena or the new course of studies planned for Halina. Also they avoided speaking about Bogdan and their relationship. They never touched upon anything really important.

She missed that, even though she did not believe that anything could change suddenly. Obviously, she thought, there was a wall that separated them. She had a word to describe it; although not the most precise, it was telling: "impenetrable." Their time together every day did not break down the wall. She wrote to Bogdan about it with an open heart, as to no one else.

Perhaps she and her father had become too distant. Perhaps there was never a meeting point. For some reason they had never learned to express their warmth to each other. Perhaps they couldn't, perhaps closeness frightened them. And that's how they remained.

Bogdan became all the more important because he was cheerful, with his shock of blond hair and a thousand ideas. It wasn't enough for him just to write about sports, he had to talk about it. There wasn't any television as yet, so he presented himself at the radio station on Myśliwiecka Street. His examination before the selection committee was a failure. But Bogdan did not like to give in; he had already heard this evaluation and had started working on it. He developed by himself a set of exercises to lower the pitch of his voice. As a professional aware of the need for regular practice, he sat down in front of a mirror several hours a day. She admired him.

"First your diploma, then marriage," her father had declared. Halina Przedborska passed her final exams in the department of literature at the University of Warsaw on January 28, 1955. She received the highest mark for her work on the Second World War writer Ksawery Pruszyński. Two days later, on January 30, she and Bogdan presented themselves for a license before a clerk at the town hall of the Mokotów district in Warsaw. To her maiden name, Przedborska, she added that of her husband, Tuszyńska.

She wore a brown woolen suit that was nice but not too festive; her stepmother had not given her enough money to buy a better one. What she did have needed to stretch to cover the hairdresser and the reception. The young groom in a navy-blue suit a little too tight, dating really from his secondary-school graduation, greeted the guests. She stood by his side, not near her father. She embraced his mother and brother, who had come from Łódź by train in the morning. They shook hands with Szymon and Żena, who both barely uttered a word; they had to be satisfied with their dryly spoken "Congratulations." Many of Bogdan's friends from the university had come, dressed in their best outfits. The officiating clerk stuttered, which lightened the atmosphere. They laughed as they made their vows.

They proceeded on foot to Szymon's home on Puławska Street. It is difficult to say whether a family dinner was served. If yes, it was the first time that Mr. and Mrs. Przedborski had received the family from Łódź. Bogdan's eleven-year-old brother, Włodek, remembered a handsome hostess, and a cake that he had devoured with abandon and then had to pay for it on the way back home to Łódź. Others said that the reception consisted of a cold buffet of hors d'oeuvres—without herring, as Żena was allergic—but this was made up for by preserves and pickles from Perłowa Street, with black pudding and an array of sausages. The elders quickly left the young people to themselves. Perhaps after the first toasts made to their success, with a demi-sec from the Party's shop with yellow curtains? They danced until midnight to music on the phonograph.

That year, as they recalled, was a year of fun and joy. During the summer they took part in the International Festival of Youth and Students, organized in Warsaw under the banner "Friendship and Peace." Thousands of participants from abroad gathered; for the first time they saw something different and exotic. Again they danced to Polish and Soviet standard tunes in parks and on the stage in front of the Palace of Culture, and in the apartments of their friends. In a very short new dress of gray silk, with straps and a little bolero with three-quarter sleeves, she looked very pretty. She had to constantly resole her one pair of black high heels, but she didn't have to listen to advice from anyone anymore. Her husband gave her a necklace of artificial pearls. She worshipped him.

She said that he was the only man who was really close to her, who loved and understood her and was good to her. She wanted to be his Little Mouse.

She had brought nothing from Puławska Street. She did not forget to return the wooden hangers. Without a dowry, she had gone to live her life. They had arranged a place in a sublet on Washington Circle, which they shared with friends from the journalism department.

Two years later, three aluminum pots filled with diapers were boiling on the stove in the modest kitchen.

OUR HOME

HALINA AND BOGDAN, MY PARENTS,
AFTER THEIR WEDDING, 1956

Number 9 Kasprzak Street was our first address, the first one I remembered. The first that I wrote on envelopes as my return address. But I don't remember fields around the factories, or the suburban landscape and flat horizon. All these things are in the photographs of a little girl who has just learned to walk.

It was only later, in school, that I learned that Marcin Kasprzak was a revolutionary hero who had been executed on the embankment of the Citadel, the tsarist prison. In this working-class neighborhood, the streets were named after militant heroes of the workers' movement. My happy young parents had moved to a new residential complex in the industrial section of Wola at the end of 1957. Without the help of Szymon, who played such a large role in the reconstruction of Warsaw, they could only have dreamed of having their own apartment. He facilitated their being assigned to an apartment without needing to be on a waiting list, sparing them the necessity of letters of application, registration forms, and other procedures. It was a gift of inestimable value at the time, even though the security deposit recorded in the payment booklet they received from him along with the keys amounted to only a symbolic seventy-five złotys. They had to pay the subsequent installments themselves. They had two rooms with a kitchen and a loggia overlooking a courtyard that would one day be filled with greenery.

It seems that they had the possibility of moving to Żoliborz, to the old intelligentsia quarter so prized by Warsaw natives, but it would have required patience and they gave up. They were in a hurry to be together. The neighboring lamp factory and pharmaceutical laboratory did not bother them. They could see, at the end of the street, the Palace of Culture and Science, a gift from the USSR to Warsaw. For them there was no better or worse address, it only mattered that they had a common one. Often I wish that I had known them then.

Perhaps my mother preferred to be far removed from her courtyard in Żoliborz from before the war, in the Fourth Colony of the Warsaw Housing Cooperative. Perhaps a new life required a new start and being cut off from her memories. Perhaps somewhere, unconsciously, she was pleased with this new environment, and with her neighbors, locksmiths and bus drivers. No one knew her, and she knew no one. All the same, it was to be her Polish address.

It's a shame they didn't wait. Every neighborhood seems to me better than that one. But over the years as I was growing up, my world was framed by the playground and by school, so that I never realized it was any better elsewhere. Only now, returning from the places that were my ancestors' homes before the war, do I know that Mother wanted to erase the past. To be as far as possible from the basements where she had to hide. I was never to know this. On Kasprzak Street she was the wife of her Polish husband, and the mother of a daughter with blue eyes. Always.

During the next four years, Bogdan and Halina scrupulously made the home payments when they came due, which came to ninety-five złotys a month, the price of a liter and a half of vodka. As the sports correspondent for the radio station he earned nine hundred złotys plus benefits.

In 1954, Bogdan found himself on the team covering the most important international sports event to take place in Poland, the annual bicycle Race for Peace.

Two years later, when they introduced live coverage from a helicopter, a novelty at the time, he was promoted to announcer. It so happened that his colleagues who had been selected before him suffered from vertigo. However, Bogdan had done some gliding. Without hesitating for a second, he accepted the assignment. He enjoyed challenges. At each stage of the race, he would broadcast live several times a day: "This is Bogdan Tuszyński, from the helicopter."

I still hadn't learned to speak, but at the question "Where is Papa?" I answered by pointing to the radio.

My first word was "Papa"; then "Mama." The third word I chose, for a long time the most important, was "give." I stretched out my arms to whoever wanted to carry me. I stayed with whoever read to me. There was nothing sadder in my life than the end of a fairy tale.

Grandma knew how to turn the button on her heavy radio

set in its dark brown case in such a way that she found Papa's voice. I thought that it only required coming close and searching on the dial to have him very near. It was only when he brought me for the first time to a broadcasting session that I saw the microphone and the studio, and I understood everything that was required.

At the kitchen table in Łódź, Grandma was very proud of her son. And I was also.

As a sports reporter for Polish Radio, my father began to travel abroad. He was one of the few selected. His job opened the world to him at a level undreamed of. The neon lights, the streets alive with cafés and tempting shop windows. He was passing through areas not accessible to others. For a while on his return he would trade the local Carmen cigarettes for Winstons.

I recall my excitement at the first mint-flavored Wrigley's chewing gum he brought back for me. I saved it by chewing it over several days, and keeping it in silver foil. The bottle that once contained Coca-Cola was a precious trophy for many years. It served as a vase. I kept lengthening my first pair of real Levi Strauss jeans for as long as possible.

My father had always worked a lot, and he worked still harder when he had a family. He went to the Olympic Games and to world championships. In addition to bicycling, he specialized in hockey and track and field. Journalists and athletes were outfitted for their trips: suits with shirts and ties with the emblems of the events, shoes, suitcases, and briefcases. I know that Mother looked at him with admiration. He smelled of a far-off world, a combination of tobacco and eau de cologne, and something indefinable. He was a successful man. He started then, or perhaps a little later, a collection of miniature liquor bottles. Like everything that came from "there," they were brilliant with all the colors of their labels and had exotic shapes. One of them resembled a full inkwell. In time he needed several shelves for his collection.

He was rarely at home, because he was at the radio station or else covering a race or attending some competition somewhere in the country or abroad. He forced himself to feather his nest by bringing home presents and by putting money aside. Eventually he bought his first car. I don't remember if it was a Wartburg or a Škoda Octavia—he has owned both models. The owners of the domestically manufactured Syrenas marveled at the elegance of their lines, their brilliant finish, and all their fixtures made of synthetic materials.

Immediately after completing her studies, Mother was employed by *Życie Warszawy* (Warsaw Life), which was reputedly the best daily published in those days. She took her work as the local editor seriously, although she started by reporting the problems of faulty drainpipes, the opening of a leather-goods shop, or the stocking of lemons in grocery stores. She was quickly transferred to the cultural department. She ran from bookstores to book fairs and watched for anything new being published, and kept herself informed about what writers were working on. In the editorial staff of *Życie Warszawy*, a paper livelier than the Party's daily filled with propaganda, there were still professionals from before the war. However, I am not certain that professional ambitions were the driving force of her life. Probably not. New earrings, a new scarf, an evening out at the theater, in the cafés, a stroll: she knew how to enjoy her life.

Above all she was my mother. "The baby deserves the whole world," that's what Halina always used to say. Her girlfriends remember it.

My baptism was a birthday present. I was one year old. Grandma Mania arranged everything. My mother probably agreed to it, to keep peace within the family, and to get Polish documentation. Grandma Mania brought her first granddaughter into the fold of Christians. They celebrated the event with a festive reception. I must have received a little cross, but I don't know what happened to it. There aren't any photos, either. My father was becoming the protector. Growing up in a home with an absent father, he felt responsible for his mother and his little brother as well as his grandmother. In Kasprzak Street he had a wife and a daughter. He needed someone close, a proven friend with whom he could share his problems. At the beginning of his marriage, he had tried getting close to his father-in-law. He tried to break through Szymon's coldness. But Szymon never bothered to hide that this sort of son-in-law was not to his taste.

He respected neither him nor his work. Szymon held himself aloof and seemed self-important. They seldom met.

I was still very small when for my birthday Mother invited our close relations. Szymon came with Żena, his two sisters, and their families. Even though I wasn't aware of it, they must have brought presents. I know these stories because they were told to me, and they form a coherent whole. Żena had no children of her own. When I started screaming at the sight of her, she looked at me with an aversion close to disgust. But my aunts were all delighted with the only girl in the family.

Mother placed a cheesecake and liqueur on the table. Courteously they moistened their lips to toast the occasion. They didn't feel at ease in this situation despite the bonds of marriage and family: my grandfather Szymon held an important position and was an official of the Party. One brother-in-law, Danek, had been a fellow prisoner of war at Woldenberg and was a colleague at work; the other, Oleś, Polish, fundamentally anticommunist, never spoke of those who governed as anything other than "savage beasts." They argued with each other, repeating the same things year after year.

Bogdan, a generation younger, came from a world without political passion, but he joined in as best he could. He repeated the same jokes that made him popular among his colleagues, Jewish jokes among others. He told them with verve, like the old stand-up comedians, the old Jewish jokes from before the war, mimicking the accents.

I don't know if my father was aware of what he was saying. Perhaps he wanted to persuade them that he was one of them. A little intimidated, a bit of a show-off, he faced a strange family, different from his own, more difficult to decipher.

Maryś, Aunt Bronka's son, was furious, but his mother

looked kindly upon Bogdan. She took his tactless jokes as a sign of playfulness, not as an insult. He was alone facing the clan. He made it clear that he knew this, but it didn't really bother him.

Bogdan was from a world that was slightly different. He would have appeared strange to native Polish intelligentsia. But the Przedborskis really believed that the new system was without any discrimination. They considered themselves progressive. There was no reason they wouldn't trust someone who had married into the family simply because his behavior was sometimes inappropriate. "The most important thing is that he is good to the child. It would be worse if he drank," Aunt Bronka repeated her favorite expressions. They accepted Bogdan.

In her professional life my mother signed her articles with her maiden name: Przedborska. But in the neighborhood, at my kindergarten, and later at school, she was Tuszyńska, like her husband (later, ex-husband). My parents led different lives from the parents of my friends from the playground. The words "broadcast," "transmission," "editing the copy," "setting up type" were more important to me, and more understandable, than others concerning what was being manufactured in the local enterprises. I went to the printer with my mother, and I knew what a newspaper consisted of well before I could read one. I remember the noise in the great space with the presses continually running. Each released a printed sheet, the newspaper. Several men, all grimy, worked in their respective places. They called one of them the typesetter. When the typesetter had the time, he would set my name in small letters of different type. He was showing me how books were born.

In our house on Kasprzak Street, there was nothing more important. We could consult books, touch them, caress them, breathe them, hug them, and keep them under our pillows. I could always rely on them. Some could be tamed, like the rose in *The Little Prince*.

From the time I was a child I was familiar with the offices

of the radio station on Niepodległości Avenue. My father often brought me along to recording and editing sessions. In the great entrance hall, there was a guard who, with a smile, let my father pass and made pleasant remarks in greeting me. I felt that Dad was important, and I was at his side. We would climb up one or two stories by the great staircase. It formed a deep funnel inside, like an open cage with a hole in the middle. Shortly afterward, they stretched a net across the space, because someone had jumped from the top story and crashed down on the stone floor.

As we walked along the hallway, recorded voices could be heard from each studio. Men's and women's voices, the chirping of birds and the sounds of the forest, conversations and monologues. Some glided along the winding tape or raced in an accelerated rhythm till it came to a stop. Others made the confused sound of a small stream only to suddenly change rhythm and become loud and a moment later fall back into monotony. Usually my father hurried toward the studio, but I paused before every door, trying to decipher the mystery behind it. Then we entered one of the rooms, and the padded door closed behind us. In the studio I had to remain quietly seated during the recording. On the soundstage I watched my father's work with the same amazement that I felt on looking at a magician pulling multicolored scarves and doves out of his top hat.

Father placed his hands on the flat spools of the editing table. He lent an attentive ear to the different sentences that he then carefully rewound once and sometimes played again, looking for the places that he had to correct. When he found a place with a slip of the tongue, or stuttering, a word needlessly repeated, a "huh" or a "say," he edited this fragment from the tape in front of him by finding its place and with the help of a small X-Acto knife removing it. He rejoined the two ends with white adhesive tape. In the same way he cleaned up all the hemming and hawing, every cough and false start. In time, he let me cut the adhesive tape into little pieces that I placed for use on the edge of the editing machine. He gave me the key to the art of polishing and perfecting the form of words.

After several years Mother quit the editorial staff of *Życie Warszawy*. A school friend worked at *Dziennik Ludowy*, the publication of the Peasant Party, aimed at rural readers. The cultural section was much smaller than at *Życie Warszawy*, and there were fewer demands. She had more time for her child. She must have been a little bored; she was indifferent to agricultural problems. She couldn't tell the difference between rye and wheat, uprooting and harvesting. She didn't know, and still doesn't know to this day, what is spring wheat and what is winter wheat.

Yet she got used to the editorial staff of *Dziennik Ludowy*. She took great pleasure in theater opening nights and in reviewing books. She brought home all the latest publications that editors sent to reviewers. Our shelves were lined with the choicest titles. She didn't care about any other benefits.

Mother liked entertaining. She invited school friends and mutual friends with whom they shared so much. Later, people from the editorial staffs made their appearances, from her office and from his. Sometimes they danced, not only on New Year's Eve. Bogdan invited his colleagues from the sports section.

I don't know when my mother began inventing pretexts for not attending these gatherings. Irena, the oldest of my father's colleagues in the sports division of Polish Radio, remembered that one day Halina had asked her to act as hostess of the house in her absence. She had placed the vodka in the freezer, the salads and hors d'oeuvres in the refrigerator, and she showed her where the plates and glasses and the knives and forks and napkins were. She made sure that Irena would take care of the guests. When asked where she was going, she answered, more or less in jest, that she had a date.

I have no idea where she went. Bogdan's colleagues liked to drink, as did he. Halina never touched alcohol and still doesn't.

There came a time when the house on Kasprzak Street was a house without a father. And nothing could be done to make it otherwise, even though I placed his slippers by the door, and I firmly believed that he would return if I were a better daughter.

I don't remember the day, the precise day when he moved out. He left often, he packed his bags, he returned. I don't know how his clothes had progressively gotten fewer in the closet, or where I was when my parents had serious conversations. I didn't notice the time when his shaving brush disappeared for good from the bathroom. My mother also did not seem any different. It was only when by accident she slammed the car door on his right hand that I thought she must have been distracted.

Was I such a poor observer to that degree, or had she made such an effort to hide things? A new love and sorrow, disillusionment and problems, the necessity of a separation, the inconvenience of moving away. They had to protect the child, for the sake of the child.

That was now her second secret.

I never knew that after seven years of marriage my mother had fallen in love with another man. She wouldn't listen to the advice of her more experienced friends: nothing is worth breaking up a family. She couldn't wait. She didn't want her new love tested by time, or to lead a double life.

Neither did I know that Bogdan was ready to forget everything and make a new start. He asked her to do it, at least for the sake of the child. I never knew that he paid the price of the separation with his health, or to what extent he felt wounded. I hadn't the least idea.

He still is not over the pain.

What he finds the most painful today is that she said nothing to their child. The child grew up thinking that her father had rejected her. He finds this unacceptable.

I didn't know that he had met my friend Agnieszka walking with her grandmother on Krakowskie Przedmieście, one of the main thoroughfares in Warsaw, one afternoon. He offered to drive them home. She was in the backseat of the car, a little girl in a red coat with a mushroom-like red hat; she had forced herself not to hear what he was saying and not to see his tears. She remembered it like a scene from a film for adults seen despite being forbidden by the parents.

No one explained to me why Father had disappeared. The simplest thing was to search for the fault in myself. He had stopped loving me. I could see no other reason for his departure, nothing else was comprehensible. I never associated his absence with the presence of Maciek. It never occurred to me.

Maciek was Maciek, big, heavy, clumsy, always holding a newspaper and a cigarette, which in time he changed to a pipe. The Dutch tobacco Amphora in its red package seemed to me a luxurious attribute of masculinity. Mother had met him on the editorial staff one afternoon when she went to hand in her day's work. As the technical editor he supervised the composition of the newspaper. He appeared older than she and was passionate about politics. Later he would give me long explanations about the situation in the Middle East, about which I understood very little. He would shut himself in for a long time in the bathroom, where he read. He replaced no one, he never moved in with us, he was neither a replacement nor a successor.

I missed my father.

I felt that my mother and I were alone. One day late in the afternoon, Mother came to fetch me at school and we walked home together, a short distance. We were accosted by a drunk who started following us. I felt then for the first time how easy it would be to hurt us, how thin was the sheet of ice on which both of us were walking. Two feelings: panic and resentment. Forbidden to be afraid, I had to fight for myself and for my mother. We were alone, and alone we had to manage.

My mother was pretty, not tall, but thin, with dark eyes. She wore glasses. In the sixties the feline frames that made eyes look slanted were in fashion. Hers were gray, spotted like the fur of a leopard.

In her photos she wore necklaces of seeds, which I used to make in craft classes. They were dyed red and heavy, but she wore them to please me. During the end-of-the-school-year ceremony in second or third grade, my mother was filled with pride when she held my report card in her hand: nothing but straight A's.

But the principal of my elementary school, who had been a scout before the war and had participated in the Warsaw Uprising, admired my father passionately. She never called me anything but "the daughter of the broadcaster Tuszyński," and on my reports she wrote enthusiastic praise that I did not always deserve.

It would have been easy to appropriate, if only a little bit, his popularity and fame. I could not do it. Somewhere inside me I had a feeling that prevented me, like the feeling that I was lying. Perhaps he was my father, but no one knew that he wasn't really, since he didn't live with us and only came by to visit me.

My mother never spoke of love. Very early she gave me a tale by De Amicis to read, from *Heart.* The cruel son rips out his mother's heart to satisfy one of his whims. On his way to take the heart—to whom and why I don't remember—he trips and falls. The heart slips from his hands. Then he hears the soft, tender voice of his mother: "My son, I hope that you are all right."

I was secretly disgusted by this story, and at the same time I felt guilty. It never left me.

Years later I learned that this story was among the canon of books read in the ghetto. The magic blue bead of my favorite storybook was getting paler as the successive wishes were realized. I constantly had the same wish: to be invisible and see what really happens. To enter houses, go into rooms, and overhear the most secret conversations. To see where Papa was when he was far away and to hear what Mother was thinking when she stopped smiling.

At home I was not taught any religion, and I didn't miss it—except on certain days when the church became a stage and you were guaranteed a long white dress with lace and a floral wreath. In going and returning from church my friends paraded in the courtyard like princesses. Otherwise I would never have known that I was being deprived of anything. I was resigned. I never received my First Communion, and I never took part in any procession.

The month of May offered rewards, village festivals, and Sunday book fairs. Mixing with the crowd in the marble halls of the Palace of Culture, I collected folders and bookmarks given out by Western editors in the foreign booths. I remember my happiness in filling plastic bags with my loot of promotional prizes, which were a novelty in Poland in those days. Surrounded by the multilingual crowd, I felt myself more distinguished than at any time in front of an altar.

In my house we didn't discuss the most important things. It was as if the answers were in the books or suspended in the air.

Was the divorce an act of courage? Was my mother being brave in choosing love, and deciding to bring up her child without her father?

As a journalist, she had a position and earned a fair living. Supporting a child didn't present any problems; the professional unions helped her by organizing vacations and providing various benefits and free tickets to events. In this environment everyone lived modestly but comfortably; there didn't exist any great differences. Even those who earned the least had enough to buy their hams, filets of pork, and early vegetables in the spring. We celebrated the first tomato, the first strawberries, by the ritual of pinching your ear at the first bite. Most important was that she had housing, and the rent didn't take up much of her salary.

Poland seemed to her a land of well-being and relative liberty. She never complained about missing any supplies or when errands became difficult; at the time she still didn't complain about anything. She always managed to procure the necessary supplies: butter, lightbulbs, linen. She still remembered the war, and life after the war among the ruins. Now houses were springing up and roads were being built. Poland was reborn of the effort, as they wrote in the propaganda articles.

I don't know if my mother ever regretted what happened. It

seems to me that she never felt guilty toward anyone. She didn't try to defend herself against a new love. She didn't want to refuse herself the right. She was shapely, not tall, with beautiful breasts. I wasn't able to judge at the time, but I can see that today in the photos. Men were attracted to her; she was very appealing. When she rushed to the hearing for the divorce on April 1, 1964, she wore a black skirt and a fine sweater with a rolled collar the color of ripe bananas; she was very pretty. They dissolved the marriage of nine years without citing any cause. For my mother, the divorce meant a new life; for my father, a tragedy.

Mother claims that seven years is a magic number in her relations with men.

The court awarded custody of the child to the mother, with responsibility for education, well-being, and administering the rights of the child, who was a minor. The father was granted the right to maintain his personal relationship with his daughter and the supervision of her development, with all that it implied. His share of child support was evaluated at one thousand złotys monthly. It was a quarter of his minimum salary, not including benefits.

I never liked Sundays; I was afraid of them, and that has remained with me. Sunday was a time reserved for happy families, a day of established rituals that was beyond our reach. Morning Mass, long strolls, family lunches, and afternoon tea with home-baked apple tart. Everything together, each thing in place. Mother, Father, and me, as in a storybook. My mother's mother, Grandmother, and mother's father, Grandfather. It wasn't that way in any household close to me. Not on Kasprzak Street, without any father. Nor at my father's place, Batory Street, where I was a stranger. Nor with Grandfather on Puławska Street, with his second wife, Żena. Even in Łódź, Grandma Mania didn't have a husband any longer, and subsequently, very soon after, we no longer had her. Thus it was not quite like a storybook. Nor with Frania, of the two aunts. Perhaps with Bronka. Yes, in Bronka's home everything looked perfectly ordinary. I had learned to do without the ordinary.

• • •

From the start when I began going back and forth between my father's place and my mother's, with a thousand-złoty bill, my mother appeared to me wretchedly abandoned. It was as if I had to defend her, within me, against myself. I soon learned not to repeat in one place what happened in the other. Not to say how he was with his new wife, and certainly nothing about her and Maciek. I learned to keep quiet from the beginning, whence came my skill in living a disguise and adapting to different realities, often very removed from each other.

Adapting, adjusting, knowing how to strike the right chord with many people, knowing how to separate from each one. And letting no one really know you.

III

Perłowa Street

GREAT-GRANDMOTHER RÓZIA

MY GREAT-GRANDMOTHER ROZALIA KARLIŃSKA,
MY GRANDMOTHER MARIANNA'S MOTHER,
MY FATHER BOGDAN'S GRANDMOTHER, THE 1980S

*G*randma Mania had a mother, my great-grandmother Rózia, with a mousy gray braid that she wound into a small chignon. She lived in the house on Perłowa Street in Łódź; the entrance was on the left in the hallway. Beneath the window overlooking the small garden was a wooden table with a drawer, and in the corner stood a coal stove. And next to it was a chipped enamel washbasin with a pail and a cup for pouring water. On the wall hung an embroidered motto, with this inscription in navy-blue thread: "To him who rises in the morning, God lends a hand." It was cold in the room. Perhaps the gnarled pear tree cast a deep shade. But for me it was about my great-grandmother Rózia, robust and burned by the sun and the wind. She was old.

I didn't like her hugging me, I didn't like her smell, the odor of mice, starch, and sweat, sweat dried by the wind. She wore flowered dresses over which she slipped an apron, and round glasses, with lenses that grew thicker year by year.

In the photos kept in the drawer among useless items—nails, spools of thread, rubber covers for jars—she was young. Thin, blond, she had lovely-shaped eyes and wore a string of coral beads. She liked large collars that she wore over her dresses. In the course of years she more and more began to resemble her mother, whose face was reminiscent of a sunflower.

I couldn't imagine that she had been a young girl who had walked barefoot six days of the week, with the exception of Sunday, when the whole family went to church. Her mother and father, her brothers and sisters—there were more than ten in the thatched cottage in a hamlet near Rokiciny. She knew how to milk cows, care for pigs, and feed the chickens. She knew what animals ate, and she was sure that they spoke with human voices on Christmas Eve. Her parents, Agnieszka and Józef Krześniak, had never been to a city, but she had gone to Łódź and had married someone from the neighboring area, Jan Karliński. He had worked his way up to ticket collector on the Warsaw–Vienna railroad line.

She started bringing children into the world, the first, the second, the twelfth—only five survived. She brought children into the world and she cooked, cabbage soup, broth with barley, and buckwheat kasha with buttermilk, sprinkled with fried pork fat. Yeast dumplings, potato pancakes, and pierogies with blueberries. Some fruits and vegetables came from her garden; from Polesie she brought back honey, cranberries, and eggs. She prepared jams and carrot marmalade for the winter. She always stocked up extra in reserve. Blood pudding, sausages, and head cheese that they made from their own pigs which they kept in the country. She sprinkled veal with vinegar and covered it with pepper and laurel leaves to "tenderize" it. I didn't like soup made from the blood of a goose, a specialty of my great-grandmother. Nor the huge down comforter that covered me more closely than the familiar salmon-colored quilted blanket saturated with my milk dreams. I didn't let her kiss me good night. In her white starched nightgown with her gray pigtail that fell down to her hips, she got into her large marriage bed by feeling her way, like a ghost. She was completely swallowed up in it and generally alone, because my great-grandfather, a railroad worker, was usually traveling. He didn't write letters; he didn't know how, no doubt because no one ever took the trouble to teach him. His move to the cemetery wasn't in any way different from his usual departures.

During the day I managed to avoid her caresses. I hid in the garden or ran off to the railroad embankment to wave at the passing trains. Trains were always at hand and in our thoughts and memories. I didn't know then that my great-grandmother Rózia had travel in her blood. Perhaps with a husband who was a carpenter or clockmaker, she would never have discovered that in herself, but the tickets of her railroad-worker husband had given her the possibility of adventure. Employees of the railroad company could obtain these gray tickets with a red border, free for themselves and their families up to twelve a year, valid throughout the country up to the border. Grandmother Rózia would set off on these travels often without any fixed destination, just like that, from station to station, going from one view through the window to another landscape. There are photos of her on the platform with bags, suitcases, children; at the window, on the footboard of a departing train.

First she would fry quantities of pork cutlets, then she would bake sheets of cookies and pack bottles of sweetened tea with lemon. At the train station's buffet she purchased only boiling water, so that it would cost them the least possible. Bread, butter, rolls—she arranged everything in a small suitcase, and they took off. If they could stop somewhere for the night without incurring great expense, often in convents, then they would stop. If it wasn't possible, then they returned home from their excursion. First she had always taken her five children without exception; later only the youngest accompanied her. They went with pilgrimages to Częstochowa, to the monastery of St. Barbara. And to Zakopane to see real mountains and breathe mountain air. As proof that they really went there, her daughter Stefa kept a small carved wooden shrine from the mountains. And thanks to his grandmother, little Bogdan still remembers the roar of a mountain stream he had seen before the war. They visited Gdynia when it was still a village, not at all a great port. They went swimming in the sea, and once they hired a motorboat. They went to Poznań for the opening of an international exhibition, in the thirties, and there for the first time Stefa saw a black man. She couldn't take her eyes off him. They ignored Warsaw. There was no one there.

Rózia had learned everything that life demanded of her. Mend, take care of things, fill the pots and the plates. From breakfast to dinner, with blessings and prayers. From the cradle to the grave. Put everything in order, make welcome, and say goodbye. During the Occupation she had smuggled meat. Wrapped in layers of lard, pork and veal that she had cured with her own hands—she covered miles every day. She helped transport people over the border. She had replaced Great-grandfather, who had been taken prisoner.

To me death seemed to be the sister of my great-grandmother. She outlived her husband, she outlived nearly all of her children. From funeral to funeral, it was only at the end of nearly a century of daily service that she consented to leave. In the coffin that was kept open at the request of her neighbors, despite the presence of grandchildren and great-grandchildren from town, she looked as graceful as a young girl. She smelled of the meadows.

My great-grandmother used to sit on a small bench in front of the house. She could remain seated that way for hours. She would look at the garden, the scraggly apple and pear trees, the cherry trees in bloom; she watched or she dozed. Her immobile figure was slightly curled in as if she were cuddling an invisible baby, forever etched in this place between the window and the well. The heaviest were her hands. Joined together on her apron, like intertwined old roots, they seemed to have a separate existence. They didn't belong to her, they belonged to the earth; they had taken its color and had its strength. As long as they had worked, dug, carried, hoed, cut, washed, as long as they had served others, they had lived; in themselves they were only a burden.

My great-grandmother had only her hands. It was her means of communicating with the world. She spoke little.

I realize this now; I grew up to understand that her cooking was the way she expressed tenderness. She believed that feeding her family was her ultimate caress. Because she did this every day, it became banal and commonplace. That was why we hardly noticed. But she didn't know how to care for us otherwise.

. . .

My great-grandmother did not know how to read or write. Neither did her mother. She didn't think it could be useful. She listened to the earth and to the seasons, to spiders and flies, to plums and apples, to birds and the rain. She knew how to come to an understanding with the animals in the stable and the barn, the sun and the moon. That is what she taught her children.

WANIA

RAIL CONDUCTOR'S CARD OF MY PATERNAL
GREAT-GRANDFATHER, JAN KARLIŃSKI, 1915

He didn't last long. My great-grandfather, the father of my grandma Mania. White mustache with a smile beneath. A picture seen from below, and when he bent down, gentle blue eyes.

He wasn't even nine years old when he left home to work as a servant in the manor house. He didn't complain; they treated him well. He helped in the stable and the barn, he carried and he carted—simple tasks that he was used to doing at home. They had stopped counting the children in his family, which never stopped growing. The village of Rokiciny had perhaps twenty cottages straggling along a road. It was near Koluszki, whose train station was a transfer point, an inaccessible dream for a boy who shared a pair of shoes with several siblings. The village church, with its statue of a barefoot Jesus with a grayish body, was located not far from the inn and the only stall where you could buy soap and kasha. People went shopping at the fair in the neighboring village. There next to the Polish merchants were Jews with whom it was easy to bargain, although they never touched vodka, even on concluding a deal.

He had fled the house, left his parents and misery behind. He was hanging about the trains in Koluszki looking for work. At the station they did not need anyone, neither for the cars, nor for the locomotives, nor for the cleaning. As for serving travelers, he had not even dreamed of it. They looked at him suspiciously, because he looked like a child who had just received his First Communion even though he was past sixteen and had already gone to the barn with Rozalia, the daughter of Krześniak, his neighbor.

For Rozalia, life was also painful. They lived in the farmhands' living quarters, and her father took care of the horses for the masters. They had taken on his daughter to help with the children of the manor. Rozalia, small, taciturn, was used to working all her life. He had met her once, and again, when she had gone to the English people to work in the thread factory. However, that was not the reason that among several possible trains he had chosen the one to Łódź. Events simply turned out this way. He was hanging around the deserted platform, another cold night before him, and he didn't have the money to buy a ticket in either one direction or the other. Without thinking he had jumped on the train going to Łódź Kaliska.

He told the ticket collector that he wanted to pay for his ticket by working.

"What's your first name?" asked the Russian official.

"Janek."

"You mean Wania?"

"Wania," he agreed.

He started as the assistant to the mechanic.

. . .

He married Rozalia, then started working on the major railroad lines, first as a ticket collector. On his return children were born. During the First World War he had been held in Russia for several months. His Russian railroad company Zheleznayg Doroga, issued in 1915 in the name of Jan Karliński, son of Szczepan, was valid for five years. Under the heading "Position" he wrote "inspector for brakes," which meant that he was responsible for the brakes. In the photo he looks elegant, in a tie and white shirt. He wears his uniform with evident pride, even though his jacket with gold buttons seems a little big. He has short hair, light like his mustache, and no beard. He holds himself straight. He signed with an illegible zigzag.

In a hardcover notebook he wrote down all the successive train stations: Vladivostok, Odessa, Lvov—this took hours, as he wrote with indelible ink in the Cyrillic alphabet, which he had painfully learned in the tsarist school. In the service compartment, he drank a glass of *kipiatok*—boiling water—he didn't have much to do. He jotted down the hour and minute of arrivals and departures—they were never late—and the words to Russian songs. He wrote nothing else.

. . .

"*Wanka z Pietra prijechal*" (Russian for "Wania is back from Petersburg"), laughed my great-grandmother when he returned from a distant journey. He smelled different. But she never made any comments. The important thing was that he was here again, there were so many things to look after. "Hey, my little vagabond." She patted him on the cheek, careful not to ruffle his mustache.

He traveled, he earned his living, he worked. He was more often far from Łódź than at home, but Rózia, his legitimate wife, patiently prepared his breakfasts, washed, sewed, looked after everything. For seven years he never touched a drop of vodka, he only put away money for a house. One after the other the children were born. He didn't keep track of household expenses. He no longer knew who was who, except for the eldest, little Marianna, because she was the firstborn and the first to call him Papa. And she quickly became so perceptive, she would climb up on his knees and ask him to tell her about his travels. She played with the cardboard tickets and learned to read the names of the stations: Ra-dom, Ka-lisz, Kra-ków. She wanted to be like him. He laughed when, bent under the weight of his leather bag, so small, so thin, she asked him, in a serious voice, to show her his ticket to be validated. She learned the train schedule by heart. She was also the first to sing the songs of the legion to which her father's brother, a veteran from Piłsudski, belonged.

In time they changed their address, moving from Wapienna Street (Lime Street) to Perłowa Street (Pearl Street).

Great-grandfather's house was toward the end near the embankment.

He earned by the sweat of his brow every cord of wood that went into building the walls, the doors, and the roof. He won every square meter of earth where were planted the apple and cherry trees, the currant bushes, and finally the sunflowers. He had converted the hours, in the pounding monotony of the wheels, into the nails, the cement, the glass panes, and the parquet. He built the fence and the well. They celebrated their first Christmas by the light of oil lamps, and the Christmas tree seemed all the more embellished in this half darkness.

They often sat down at the table without him for a solemn supper. In the crowded sideboard, near the crystal glasses used for special occasions, near the carafes and the coffee set, was placed Great-grandfather's itinerary. He had written in his own hand the dates and the hours of his schedule so that Great-grandmother would know what and when. His work was the essential thing. Holy day or not, he had to travel.

This was a house, like many others, in which absent men reigned, often from far away.

Jan Karliński, my great-grandfather, loved being photographed. Especially in uniform standing on the platform by the locomotive holding a carbon lamp. He had raised himself to the rank of train supervisor: salary of 220 złotys, double with overtime, and a cap with gold trim. It was the cap he was most proud of. With overtime he earned ten times more than an ordinary worker, more than 500 złotys before the war—that is more than one hundred dollars. He was considered an aristocrat of the rails.

"Ready!" he shouted on raising high the lantern he held so that the ticket collector would see it. Then, on receiving a confirmation, he called out: "Departure!" and lowered his arm.

He was a formalist. Oh Lord, formalist, that he was! That's what his children said. His pants had to be ironed, his shoes polished. Around him every person was busy with a special task—with a brush, with a cloth, with the hot iron. He also had to have a small white collar properly folded, one for each day. He was always ready for work.

GRANDMA MANIA

MARIANNA TUSZYŃSKA, NÉE KARLIŃSKA,
MY MATERNAL GRANDMOTHER, BEFORE THE WAR

At the hospital, Grandma Mania was lying behind the door at the end of a long hallway. I felt nauseated the moment I entered. The walls the color of vanilla pudding made me think of the skin on milk; the smell of chloroform was suffocating. The world I had just come from had breathed the promise of spring, the windows were open to greenery. Here at the hospital I felt ashamed, because my heart was filled with joy and I wanted to run among the trees. Grandma, fragile and imprisoned by heavy bedclothes on a metal bed with wheels, belonged to another order of things, as if the rights of the living that had prevailed until then had stopped being valid. Once she tried to pat my head, but her arm, pierced with IV needles, had fallen back onto the bed.

"Grandma, where does it hurt? Does it hurt more than when I banged my knee and you put a bandage on it? You gave it a kiss, and the pain went away. Where should I kiss you?"

I visited her only a few times, because she was soon transferred to a hospital wing where children were not admitted. They checked bags and clothing for infectious diseases and took away unclean flowers. It was forbidden to place the pots and colored jars brought from Łódź on the white nightstand by her bed. Grandma had lost her appetite even for the pear compote her sister had prepared. And for the oranges so difficult to find. Because of her suffering, I was no longer her darling little girl. She now preferred my father, her elder son, to her younger son, whom she had always favored before because his birth was a demonstration of love and was supposed to save her marriage. I did not understand then that she was looking for support— she who had always been supportive.

Then they placed her in isolation where she was even more alone. She was taking up less and less room in the world. Her time was being more and more reduced.

She wrote letters that were increasingly brief. Sometimes I heard my father speaking about her in a whisper to his new wife. They spoke about her blood chart, red and white corpuscles, and uneven circulation in her body. I understood that she was suffering from a deficiency of red and that she needed some. For her I started painting flowers in the loud colors of the posters I used for decorations on May Day. For her I saved up all the raspberry and strawberry candies; I asked them to bring tomatoes and beets to her at the hospital. With the money from my piggy bank I bought her a red scarf. I had dreams in which we escaped together in a purple carriage drawn by dogs with rainbow-colored fur.

I didn't understand what was happening, and in those days they didn't speak about such things to children.

I was playing hopscotch in front of my father's house, one two three, a step to the side, another set and one to the side and a turnaround. As he came over he said, "Grandma is dead." It was as if he had struck me. He took me by the hand without a word and brought me upstairs. They lived on the tenth floor of a big building. From the balcony I saw the same town as several hours earlier. However, in the spot where the hospital on Szaserów Street was located before, there floated a milky radiance.

I returned home to my mother by myself in the streetcar. "I don't have any grandma," I said on the threshold.

She had called me "Agunia" or "Agusia." From the pile of toys with which we greeted the birth of my first half sister she had selected one for me. It had never occurred to anyone else. She hugged me very hard against her and when she could, she made me come to her bed at night until I became accustomed to the fact that henceforth everything would be different for me. She had eyes the blue of cornflowers, the same as the flowers in the fields.

In the house on Perłowa Street nothing was lacking, although they lived modestly. Bread and lard, that was a treat. I disliked lard and fried pork bits. I felt an instinctive disdain for the slices of bread with lard and fried pork bits, and yet she had given it to her family, my grandma with her blue eyes, so good and so close. That was the first sign of strangeness.

I wasn't finicky about the potatoes with sour milk, or about the borscht with potatoes, but I felt that I belonged somewhere else. How was it possible that I could perceive this through food? Was it because my mother called this "peasant" food? She had not been able to bear the *czernina* soup made with the blood of a goose or a duck that they served her on her first meal in Łódź just after the announcement of their engagement.

They had done everything to give her a treat, and they had obviously missed all her culinary preferences. The same way that freshly steamed noodles with a greasy sauce had seemed to her unsuitable for such an occasion.

There the rhythm of the seasons dictated daily life. The little garden presented the succession of plantings in the beds, the sequence of flowering bushes and fruit trees.

The most important was the autumn. Mushrooms were gathered in pails or large, round wicker baskets. The mushroom gathering was the most important holiday; whole days were spent in the laborious aftermath: peeling, washing, cooking, marinating. They knew each clearing and every narrow path, the places for boletes and for cèpes, and the hedgerows for chanterelles. Only Christmas could rival the ceremonies of the mushroom harvest, although Christmas was shorter, including all the days of preparations.

The Karliński sisters—Marianna, Stefa, Sabina, and Wiesia, the daughters of my great-grandmother Rózia and of my great-grandfather Wania—started working three weeks before the Christmas celebrations, in secret, so as not to be seen by anyone. With long strips of shiny white paper especially cut out, they wove braided stars. They cut out little ballerinas from cardboard, pasted on wings and fans. They decorated their angels with cotton batting. They were finicky in making little girls from Kraków with scarves and necklaces and ribbons. And on Christmas Eve when the tree was trimmed in the main room, in addition to their decorations, they hung different sweets, apples and gingerbread, chocolates wrapped in colored foil. For the finishing touch, they hung a silver garland from every branch, in preparation for the mystery of the Nativity.

Grandma was simply there, just like the furnace and the fire. Like day and night. She was the affirmation of the simplest truth. The powerful voice of the radio announced noon by playing the "Hejnał" from the steeple of the Church of Our Lady, symbolically recalling the arrow of the Tartar invaders.

The trumpeter suspended his note. The melody hung in the

air, interrupted. Then Grandma started the Sunday dinner. The railroad whistle on a string was hung near the sink, and the ticket puncher lay on the oilcloth spread on the kitchen table. And the tickets, precious promise of adventure.

Trains crisscrossed my childhood, and they continue running. Across the table, in the middle of the meal, sounded the local to Gdynia, between soup and the chicken, sometimes earlier. The Opole Express came with the strawberry compote. Today Grandma keeps house in other firmaments. She watches over another star.

She taught me how God was born, and how the powers tremble. In the winter she put me to sleep with a Christmas carol and in the spring she awakened me with the colored shells of Easter eggs. There I was safe and warm.

She died in the spring of 1969. I wasn't yet twelve years old, too soon for me to understand who she was.

In the photos taken of her First Communion, Marianna is thin and childish even; her curly hair is piled very high. She is standing under a lilac bush. A little later she was photographed in the style of a nymph of the end of the last century, half lying back, wearing a decorative scarf, her hair falling down over her shoulders. At her feet a spray of white roses. Behind her is a painted backdrop of an avenue of big trees. At that time she still had her future before her, like the other little girls at the boarding school of Madame Laszczycka. She was taught how to write beautifully, how to draw and do needlework. She recited poems. She produced the most beautiful embroidery in her class on napkins and tablecloths. She could read the web of the most complicated patterns. She also created her own; she had that gift in her fingers and in her eyes. She was infallible in matching colors. On kilims, embroidery, doilies, tablecloths, her touch was unmistakable.

Life verified her dreams. At first she had worked as an assistant in a pharmacy, then she went to a plywood factory, and finally to a rubber factory. Instead of embroidering bouquets she made galoshes.

It's not known how she met Romuald Tuszyński, or why she was fixated on him. She had other suitors, nice looking, with jobs, but only he mattered.

Romek came to see Marianna twice a week, always elegant and well turned out. After Marianna had served him tea, the younger children, her brother and sisters, sniffed his glass because it smelled of perfume. They made fun of her, but to tell the truth, Romek impressed them: a locksmith of precision work, three years younger than she, tall, stylish, with brown hair. But he was the jealous type, wouldn't let her see anyone. She became pregnant.

They were married in St. Joseph's in the spring of 1932. She had prepared the wedding reception at her parents' home on Wapienna Street, with her mother and her sisters. Her stomach was already bothering her. It was hard on her to be in the kitchen kneading the dough for the dumplings, for the poppyseed cakes; to marinate the herring and make all the salads, with everything that had to be cut up—onions, potatoes, vegetables. And all the cutlery to be washed carefully and the table to be set. And at the last minute to make elegant canapés with little English rolls. She was tired and her legs were swollen, but she danced with her young husband as if her happiness depended on it.

Jan Karliński gave what he could to his eldest daughter for furniture, two hundred złotys, half of his monthly salary. Rozalia made the trousseau: a duvet cover, two pillows, two sets of sheets, some fine white and cream tablecloths and linen, six sets of blouses and underwear. It was a big event, this marriage: Jan Karliński was saving up for the house, and soon his first grandson was going to be born.

My father's father, Romuald Tuszyński, was the grandfather I barely knew. I have no memory of him from my childhood, as he was already no longer living in the house on Perłowa Street. Grandma had never said a word about him, as if she had never had a husband. During my whole childhood, my father never mentioned him. Sundays, in her holiday best and accompanied by her husband and her son, Grandma went to have lunch with her mother-in-law, Romuald's mother. In the middle of the thirties, they had a little money. As they were both working, she could afford to buy a better woolen suit and a decent fur-lined coat. But whatever she wore and despite all her efforts, for Maria Paulina Hausman, a Viennese, Marianna remained a proletarian from the workers' quarters of Łódź. Romuald's mother, stout, with a fox collar and glasses, made it understood without any ambiguity to the whole Karliński family that they should feel honored to be associated with her only son and herself.

She was originally from Vienna, and her father was Austrian. A man of means, he built roads and bridges. He arrived in Łódź at the end of the nineteenth century and settled in the Koziny quarter, Włodzimierska Street, not far from the old cemetery. He never knew how or where his daughter Maria Paulina had met Walery Tuszyński, a Polish hairdresser, the owner of a barber shop. She fell in love at first sight, and this led to the altar despite her father's opposition. I don't know what disturbed old Hausman more: the milieu his future son-in-law had come from or his nationality. They were married in 1912, and soon afterward a son was born, Romuald. The young mother received an armful of white lilacs from her husband.

Walery Tuszyński soon marched off to war. He fought for a long time, up until Poland became Poland again. He returned victorious to Łódź in 1918, but it wasn't the same man who came home. Suddenly he would burst out laughing, start talking out of context, or start weeping, all inappropriate for a soldier. He couldn't sleep; he had hardly fallen asleep than he woke his lawful wedded wife with a loud cry. She would change his shirt and console him like a child, but he couldn't be calmed. "Leave me, leave me, you German woman!" he said one day for the first time. After that he repeated it all too often.

One fine day he went to the barber shop without having eaten and put his razor to the throat of the first customer. Walery died shortly afterward.

Grandmother Tuszyńska, née Hausman, soon remarried, this time to a good man, a railroad worker named Andaszek. He was a good grandfather and taught his grandson, little Bogdan, all about fishing.

They lived through five years of German occupation. In a photograph taken during the war, in May 1940, my grandparents are seated at the table at the Andaszek home. Grandma Mania is wearing her best dress, black trimmed with lace. She had pinned a little corsage of roses on her chest. Romuald, also in his Sunday best, is wearing a polka-dot butterfly tie, with his dark suit and vest. Also dressed up, their son Bogdan stands by their side, but unsmiling. It was probably the day of his First Communion.

In a photograph from after the war taken in a park in autumn, it looks as if their life together has already come to an end. On a bench, wearing a black hat and a coat with a fur collar, Romuald is avoiding looking at her. Grandma is still forcing herself to convince him of something. I can feel the pervading chill that reigned.

She couldn't resign herself to the idea of losing the man she had wanted so much. She lost him the way she lost her strength, year after year, slowly, bit by bit. However, I can't picture her with a razor in her hand trying to end her life. As I knew her, Grandma Mania could take care of everything; she was capable of bringing help to all who despaired.

He would leave and return; she would welcome him again. Łódź, Szczecin, Jelenia Góra, and once more Perłowa Street. Usually he didn't drink, and he wasn't quarrelsome. He could be charming, he brought her flowers, he pounded his chest, promising he loved only her. "And he would lapse again," said Stefa, Marianna's sister.

Grandma excused him, because some take to drink and others chase women. Besides, what do you do with a man like him? Perhaps the war had removed any moral sense, or perhaps it was in his character. Sometimes she would say to Stefa that her life was eternal worry. She wept, but she never stopped waiting. According to her sister, the Lord had taken her mind away.

I have a ring that came from her, a little diamond set in platinum. I received it when I turned eighteen. I wore it until it broke. No one wanted to repair it for me.

STEFA

STEFA KARLIŃSKA, MY GRANDMOTHER MARIANNA'S SISTER.
SHE WORKED AS A LETTER CARRIER DURING THE
GERMAN OCCUPATION, IN ŁÓDŹ, 1940.

*T*his year swirls of snowflakes greeted Easter. But on Perłowa Street, windows were washed, there were freshly starched bright white sheer curtains. The odor of cleanliness, of wax and laundry soap, announced the holiday, in time to be replaced with the aroma of sausages, white borscht, cooked ham, and grated horseradish.

Aunt Stefa has grown stooped; it has been a long time since
I've seen her. Grandma's younger sister has survived her by forty
years, millions of soups, roasts, marinades—an ocean of inconceivable fatigue. She looks like a mean bird with curved claws.
Her neck emerges nearly from the middle of her back, which
is defined by a soft hump. Leaning against the door, without
any preamble, she starts the litany of sufferings. A rosary of
maladies: shortness of breath, anemia, coughing, nightmares,
itches, scabs, more and more. She raises her blouse and makes
me feel her skin, her bones, places where breasts and stomach
used to be. She seems proud that there remains so little of her,
proud of the pitiless way that time has treated her.

"Come, I want to show you the dress I am going to be buried in."

"Show me."

"I'm going to show you, I'm going to show you, you'll see
how pretty it is."

The armoire smells of mice and the remains of desiccated
mothballs. A pale echo of the smell of lavender permeates the
plastic cover of a clothes stand. Set free from its plastic container, it spreads for a moment before melting into an old perfume, the scent of the childhood of this house, the smell of
duvets, of whitewashed walls, of fire and sickness.

"Look how pretty it is!"

A black jacket and skirt of heavy material, carded material,
that's the word that comes to mind, although I have no idea
of what that looks like, but the word is suited to the coarse
weave of this material destined for death. "Look how pretty
it is!" repeats Aunt Stefa, stroking the skirt and jacket laid out
on her bed. "Look how artistically embroidered"—with a bent
finger, with fingernail chewed down to the quick, she points to
the frill under the collar. "Artistically" sounded strange coming
from her mouth, but linked to that sad little decoration hooked
to the collar, it awakened a tenderness in me. It reminded me of
her seamstresses' monologues she had subjected me to all during my childhood. What delight my little celadon-green cape
with little flounces excited in her, or my little cloth pumps with

tiny bows. It was a fervor close to a prayer. She always used diminutives: Like a little garland of small roses. Like my little fingernails that she trimmed to a point ("fox-trot" trim, she said) and painted with real nail polish the color of rubies—my first manicure, for which I was so grateful.

. . .

I looked at her huddled on the bed with her painful hump. I saw her dress was too big at the waist—she must have bought it years before. I saw her deformed legs with the swollen big toes. "You want to see how it is?" She took my hand and slid it once again under her blouse, tracing her chest, resigned. Then she pulled down her heavy tights. The dried stomach sagged, making the pelvic bones jut out; her skin was rough and deadly pale. "It will be cold lying like that," she continued as she took out lingerie of thick white cotton. A blouse with slightly soiled lace, bloomers, and a thick pair of underpants with elastic. "You know what it's like to be laid out like that." She pressed her patent-leather shoes with little heels against her face, squinting her eyes: "How pretty they are. The best! I saved a long time for them."

She will go to her grave wearing lisle-thread bloomers and slightly worn Sunday patent-leather shoes, and without a hat. "You don't have to walk very much, and it will be comfortable to be lying down."

They were already all dead. First, her father, the railroad worker from whom she never took her leave. "Papa had caught cold, but he was stubborn, and he got up with a fever to go to work. He came down with pneumonia, and the cupping glasses were useless. God, how we cried, Marianna and me!" They had curled his mustache with an iron for the coffin, and he wore his full uniform, also his good shoes. And in his hand the railroad whistle, next to the rosary. "And afterward, it was my sister. I went to the hospital in Warsaw once a week. She would ask, 'Bring me cucumbers, but salt them yourself.' Or 'Bring me fresh steamed noodles.' Then after a while she stopped asking. She repeated only, 'Take me home, I want to die at home.' They brought the coffin back by train. My sister Wiesia also died—she had to be nursed like a child because she had remained at the stage of a child; and my brother, Mietek, who wouldn't learn anything, a ne'er-do-well. Now they are all gone. They've worn out so many shoes. There's only me who remains."

In the photos of her taken when she was young, she wore a mail-carrier uniform. Her hair was brushed back and held by a barrette. She was first taken to work in the Reich, and she worked in a margarine factory. She smuggled out margarine in an oversized coat with special openings worked into the lining behind the pockets, or even in her hair—she hid it under a mass of hair worn in a roll. When she returned home, she worked for the Germans as a mail carrier. She quickly discovered that every day there were some denunciations in her bag. A lot of people were in hiding, they had come back from Germany, they had fled, they were lying low. At first she didn't know what to do; she was afraid of betraying herself if the letters didn't arrive. She hesitated for a long time, looked around her to make sure no one was watching, and ended up slipping the folded papers into one of her galoshes. Then she became bolder. She even wanted to keep the denunciations for later, after the war, to have proof of what and when and whom she had saved. But one day the Germans raided a house nearby, a few streets away; they chased people with dogs, shouting all the while. So she grabbed all the papers and threw them in the furnace. "Oh, right here, in this furnace, they all went in . . ."

Nearby is the round oak table covered with a white tablecloth, surrounded by four wooden chairs. Under a pillow, on the right, is a colored magazine, and inside, an article about me with big photos. They bring it out when someone important comes, the doctor or a bill collector.

Stefa always gave me something secretly. For example, a bedsheet, or an inexpensive brooch, a blouse with frills that I never intended to wear, or stockings I have never worn, a jar of pickles or of pear compote. It embarrassed me, but I was incapable of hurting her feelings by refusing.

She remembered my father from the day he was born, and she had taken care of his brother like a mother. She herself could not have children. She had been sent for treatment several times to a clinic, but without any results. Even when I was a little girl I felt that fate had deprived her of something. I let her play with my dolls. Her husband, Manius, a good man, worked in the locomotive hangar on engine maintenance, but he drank. He would pick me up and spin me around toward the ceiling. He wasn't quarrelsome after drinking, he went to sleep. Toward the end, after several cataract operations, he could hardly see. Something had come loose in his eye, and he was forbidden to drink. He remained seated. Or he stayed by the window. She tortured him, because not only did she keep him up all night with her fits of coughing, she also nagged him. She complained and she reproached him every which way: He hadn't chopped wood or repainted the walls, the water pump was stuck, the waste bucket hadn't been emptied. He still hadn't gone to the market, or chopped the onions, "yet again, but I've told you often enough, it's always the same . . ."

She ended up dying before him. He wanted to hang himself. However, he sat in the kitchen dead drunk, after the funeral dinner.

During my last visit there, at Easter, as the snow was falling, she took from a drawer a little rubber doll without arms and started weeping, explaining that the doll had belonged to Marianna, her eldest sister, her beloved sister, my grandmother. Again she wanted to give me something secretly, when no one was looking. I asked for the little doll. She refused: "That's all I have left of her." She said several times that she was going to die. She was preparing for the journey. When I teased her, she became angry and shook her twisted finger at me just like when I was a little girl: "You can't make fun of the good Lord!" With time her fingers were twisted in all directions, like the branches of a stunted tree. They darted out with their tips gnawed, like wounds that had healed. "Agusia, pick some gooseberry for yourself—there's also a good crop of currants this year. Na, there's a bowl here."

I don't like gooseberry, I don't like black currants. I am ashamed of the memory of my childhood shame when I heard this "na." "Na, take, pick." "Na" meant "here you are." No one spoke like that in Warsaw.

I had expected her death. I understood very well that the day would come when the news would catch up with me. It wouldn't strike me, it would catch up with me. And I would think, it doesn't concern me.

Instead of that, I see her in mourning standing in front of the freshly dug grave of my grandmother, with a weeping little girl who is hanging on to her hand with all her strength. It was summer, like now; there is no longer any little girl, I have grown up, and I flew away. I had forgotten her for years, I didn't even send her postcards, not a sign of life. I didn't telephone, I never invited her. As if she didn't exist. It was as if she had never saved me from a flock of geese, hadn't shown me the horse in the pasture, had not placed the potty next to my bed, and hadn't warmed my milk. As if she had absolutely never been concerned about me. She is not there. On the other side of the world, I light a fire according to her way: a piece of newspaper, some small pieces of wood for kindling, a well-stacked pyramid, several logs on the side, some pinecones for the smell, and some birchwood for the aroma. A drop of resin. It bursts into flame like on Perłowa Street.

THE NEIGHBORS

I never heard the word "Jew" on Perłowa Street. All the neighbors were Polish, and it never occurred to me that it could be otherwise. For a long time I didn't know if Jews had ever existed in the consciousness of my family in Łódź. When I wanted to ask them, only Stefa was left, and she is not here any longer.

We spoke about it once. I never told her that it was important to me because of Mother. When I asked her to tell me about it, she spoke willingly. According to Stefa, in Łódź the Jews lived everywhere. They lived as well on 11 Listopada Street as on Jaracz Street, Śródmiejska Street, and Zachodnia Street; on Wschodnia Street also, and in the Bałuty neighborhood. There were fewer in the Mania neighborhood, on our street, but not far away, on Koziny, there were two or three. One of them had a shop on Srebrzyńska Street.

When we had to buy anything, then we used to go to the Jews in town. Great-grandfather Karliński would give money to his wife, Rozalia, who would take Marianna, their eldest daughter, and off they would go to run errands. When snow boots were needed, they went to buy snow boots. You bought sweaters at Weberka's or from someone else who had a workshop. The same for gloves or a coat. Everything was cheaper at the Jews' and also of irreproachable quality. They had a large selection of pretty materials. They would buy a light-colored wool, or wool dyed green, burgundy, or black, or perhaps a patterned cretonne, which they would give to a seamstress to make into dresses. Stefa especially liked frills and gussets. Then they were always bargaining over something. The Jews agreed to a discount on what was bought. From butter to eggs, you could find everything there: flour and socks, stockings, herring and tea.

"At the *żydek*'s [little Jew's]," repeated Stefa. "Mother shopped on Nowomiejska Street. The curtains were purchased from a *żydek,* they were pure cotton, very strong, pretty." And I nodded. How is it that language becomes impregnated with the emotions of the users, and with whose permission has "Jew" been changed to *żydek,* said with familiarity and indulgence, and with a tone of superiority and a shade of disdain. But perhaps I am mistaken, perhaps it's better this way, perhaps "Jew" would sound harsher? A curse word, a word of insult: Jew. They bought from their Jewish neighbors.

My grandma had Jewish schoolmates at her secondary school, her sister Stefa told me. They had become friends and went to dances together. Stefa also had some in school. They studied their lessons together, and saved up their money to buy candies, and played all sorts of games. Wiesia, the youngest, had the most Jewish friends: there was Chajka and Laja and Bronka. They went to each other's homes and ate the chicken with carrots and the gefilte fish. They sang a song: "At the Blawiczes there are guests, because their daughter is engaged, fiddlelaï, -laï, -laï, fiddlelaïlaïlaïlaï, and *tate komt* and *mame komt* and there is even some kugel."

She couldn't remember what came next . . . fiddlelaï, -laï, -laï, fiddelaïlaïlaï.

No one ever sang that song for me. No one mentioned those who sang it. No one ever showed me the shops in the Koziny neighborhood where they bought on credit, and said to me: "She lived there, they took her away, she perished." Ryfka or Sura. The Jew who was part-owner of the halvah factory where their brother, Mietek, worked would give sweets to his employees for the holy days, and they were so grateful to him because these were Catholic holy days and he did not have to. About him they were also silent. But they said of other neighbors,

"He was taken prisoner," or even "He was sent to work for a *Bauer*," a peasant. Or else, "Drunk he fell in front of a train." They never mentioned the dentist Żytnicka, who took care of their teeth. Nor the Jew from Bielsko, even though he made the rounds of all the houses, one after the other, selling textiles for credit, returning to fetch what was still owed him a month or two later. There was also one who went around in a cart and bought rags. For useless bits of cloth he would exchange some pots for the kitchen, buttons or little combs. Even children waited for him.

How is it that they did not leave an empty place, even in their memories?

At that time the Karliński family no longer had any contact with the ghetto, even though it was nearby. During the Occupation they only went to their aunt's in the Widzew neighborhood, because everyone was afraid to go out. The children who studied in the evening would come home by going over the back fence and crossing courtyards. They weren't very big, seven or eight years old. All the same, each person had to watch out.

Once Stefa had seen a little girl—she could have been the same age as little Bogdan, her nephew, my father—so mud encrusted, so grimy, she was drinking water from a puddle not far from her window. Stefa wanted to call out to her, night was already falling, but she did nothing.

It could have been my mother.

My grandma Mania, could she remember this little girl, or little girls like her, children like her? She was so good, she believed in sacrifice and mercy, she could not bear them to be hungry. I know very well that it was during the war, that they didn't have very much themselves, but in memory of her schoolmates she would have certainly given them bread. I don't want to think that she didn't have the strength for the misery of others.

I don't want to know it. I will never know it. Me, the daughter of a little girl like that one.

But, to tell the truth, why should she have fed Jewish children? That's the question I ask, the daughter of that boy behind the window. My grandma, had she ever thought about that? In any case danger lurked everywhere. And Jewish mothers, if the madness of the world had taken a different turn, would they have been concerned about her own son?

My father, who was ten years old then, remembered that not far from his house on Strykowska Street, and Zgierska, was the ghetto. He used to go by there. He no longer knows what he saw or what he was aware of. They had shut in people. Whole houses, all the people. The children also? No doubt also the children, they couldn't play ball like him or learn Polish. On the first of September he had to go to school. He was afraid of the Germans, but he ran with his friends around the empty lots in the Mania neighborhood to kick around a ball made of rags, and they threw stones at the street signs that were in German. The war lasted a long time; he had the time to grow up.

But then, like the others, he forgot those people.

I V

Łęczyca

A DAY AT THE MARKET IN ŁĘCZYCA, THE 1930S

MIREK

*I*came to Łęczyca for the first time during the winter of
1991. In the town square, the graying snow was starting to
melt. I had a sheet of paper with two addresses on Przedrynek and Poznańska Street written in my mother's hand, and
a few names I had confused. Even the stone statue of the Virgin
in front of the municipal building looked perplexed.

A limping man resembling the Boruta Devil—a local
legend—tried to guide me through icy little alleys until we
reached an empty area dominated by a gas station. I was following the invisible trails of the past. I had discovered nothing.
At the tavern I entered to warm up, I overheard a sentence
that made me leave the town where my mother was born with
a sense of relief: "You shouldn't have taken on such a burden;
there are still so many Jews here."

Curiously said. Not offensive, properly spoken, certainly
not vulgar, and strangely aesthetic. But offensive all the same.
I never react directly to such remarks. I fade into the background, I do not defend myself, I don't argue. I don't give any
explanation, I flee. That time also I had fled. For nine years. I
had slammed the door.

I then thought of Mother. She didn't want such statements
ever to touch me. I always think of her when I hear any words
of this sort.

This statement reminded me of another, much more
brutal—that Hitler deserved a monument in Poland for what
he did to the Jews. It brought back the tragic return of the Jewish survivors to their small towns after the Holocaust, going

home to their houses occupied by Polish neighbors who didn't hide their surprise that they had survived, had come back, were still there.

When I went to Łęczyca for the first time, my grandfather's younger sister Frania was still alive. She was the one who spoke of her dreams of escaping her hometown, to flee forever and never come back. She couldn't understand what I was looking for there when she had done everything possible, her whole life, to forget.

I had succeeded in finding someone who remembered Frania from Przedrynek Place. He remembered her, despite the family's absence, even though half a century had elapsed and the house at number 9 was gone. He remembered the young Misses Przedborski as cultivated—they had gotten their baccalaureate diplomas—and very pretty, who had nothing Jewish about them. "No, madam, you would never have thought . . ."

I found the address of Mirek, a local history teacher, at the Jewish Historical Institute in Warsaw, in the folder labeled "Łęczyca." I knocked on the door of his apartment on Żydowska Street in May 1999.

They constructed the main street of the Jewish quarter in the fourteenth century, Żydowska, "Jewish Street." The name hasn't changed for years.

In Łęczyca, Żydowska Street had been paved since the Middle Ages. During excavations, leather shoes were found dating from that period. It was the oldest evidence of Jewish presence in this fortified town. They had arrived wearing shoes. Strangers. Some left barefoot. Some surrendered their clothing. Others had their shoes stripped off them when they could no longer defend themselves.

By the end of the eighteenth century, the Jewish settlement on the shores of the Bzura was one of the most important in central Poland. The Jewish quarter had spread up to the town square. A synagogue had also been built of stone. In the nineteenth century Jews represented half the population of the town, and in the 1920s they numbered four thousand.

Before the war only two Polish families lived on Żydowska Street. All the other inhabitants spoke Yiddish: the tailors, the boot makers, the shopkeepers. In their wooden houses piled one on top of the other, they lived and worked, sewed, hammered, tanned hides, traded in herring, cucumbers, challah bread, and vodka. The street smelled of sweat and poverty. Children and rats ran loose. Every Friday there was a celebration—prayers and the Sabbath meal.

The sad, crumbling building from the 1950s where Mirek lived was built on the remains of structures several hundred years old. After the war, in the ruins of the wooden house next door they discovered nearly a dozen ram's horns hidden in the wall. The shofar is used by Jews to welcome their New Year, Rosh Hashanah.

As a schoolboy, Mirek was ashamed of his address on Żydowska Street. But he soon outgrew this feeling of shame. Now it's prominently displayed on his envelopes as the return address, even with a certain bravura. Since childhood he has been proud of the Collegiate Church of Tum, located nearby, where the history of the town began in the sixth century with the castle and the facetious Boruta Devil. He knew by heart the dates of the kings of Poland, the history of the Order of Teutonic Knights, the location of the ruins from World War II, and the crimes committed by the Bolsheviks. He was curious about the past and the triumphs of the Polish military. But who was to teach him the history of the Jewish Talmudists and the *tzaddikim*, the merchants and the *melameds*, religious leaders? He had been ignorant of their existence.

He wanted to learn about them as soon as he had overcome all those who were prejudiced—the peasants who had fallen into debt to the Jews for centuries, the middle class for whom they were competition in business, and the priests who for centuries had proclaimed from the pulpit that the Jews had killed Christ. Freeing himself from this widespread prejudice that had gone on for years required the courage of an independent thinker.

Perhaps that is why he became a history teacher.

I knew nothing about him when I knocked on his door. I didn't know who he was, and what he was like, this grandson of a baker from Łęczyca, the son of a worker, this teacher from Żydowska Street.

I don't know how it happened, but very quickly, almost all at once, I told him what I was really searching for. This is where my mother's side of the family had come from: the Hermans, the Przedborskis, the Goldsteins—all Jews from Łęczyca.

I had told him this, something I had never mentioned to a stranger, and certainly not in Poland; I had perhaps confided in a few friends, not all, only a few selected ones. We were in a dark room in the ground-floor apartment. It had a small bookcase filled with books, a tile stove, an old typewriter. He had clear, attentive eyes.

He showed no surprise, as if every day someone brought him the same sort of problem. Without hesitation, he promised to help me.

The first envelope from Żydowska Street arrived several days later. It contained a list of the inhabitants of Łęczyca who had sworn allegiance to His Majesty Tsar Alexander II in 1855. Three Hermans were on the list, a landlord, a merchant, and a shopkeeper, as well as the peddler, Hersz Lejb Przedborski.

Other letters soon followed. Not only about my great-grandfather Henryk Przedborski, a municipal councilor for the town of Łęczyca, but also his brother, Bernard, an alderman. In time Marcus, their father, also was found. Their wives and children. They all had Jewish first names, which made the identification difficult. The order of their appearance on the scene was proof of their eagerness to be heard.

Thus, step by step, I began to go through the list of tenants, the municipal archives, and the registry of mortgages. I was impatient to receive the next letters, with more information about my past, the notes of municipal councils, the list of the inhabitants of such and such street, and those who contributed to the salary for the watchman of the synagogue. Mirek gave them to me little by little as he discovered them, the fragments more than one hundred years old telling of the fate of the Jewish inhabitants of Łęczyca linked to my own destiny. I started not being able to do without his letters.

It was like working on a puzzle whose subject I didn't know. It became clearer as I was given the pieces that had been missing. Out of nothing came a picture that grew more detailed with time.

He wrote. I telephoned, and I rushed up as soon as I could to Żydowska Street to sit by the tile stove a few steps away from Poznańska Street and the printing press of my great-great-grandmother Salomea Herman, to be able to speak of her as if she had just stepped outside the room for a moment. Or else of the way her daughter Justyna played the piano, or of her tutor, later her husband, Henryk. Mirek had started referring to him as "Handsome Henio," the nickname given to him by the Przedborskis.

In old notes we found traces of the fragile family legend. They had left traces for me, in a registry of the population of the towns of Kalisz and Łęczyca; in birth registries, in legal declarations, in reports and certificates. They had left traces because they wanted to be found. They wanted to come back from Treblinka and from Chełmno, from the burning barns, houses in ruin, forests, and gas trucks.

It must be radically different if you can remember your own great-grandmother seated in an easy chair, her head held high, her braids wound into a narrow crown. It's enough that she is seated; she doesn't have to say anything, but if she did speak, it would be good to distinguish her voice from the other voices. Or the shape of her hands, the way she held them over the piano keys, the expression on her face when she played. Or when she made her apricot preserves.

For me, my unknown grandmothers are only traces on paper, thin lines of ink in a signature. The echo of a shadow.

They had never sat down at the table with me. They never ate either broth with yellow noodles or prune compote with me. They never took part in the daily life of my childhood, not even as shadows. I had to discover them, sometimes even against the wishes of their living relatives, mute heirs of their memory. Many times I got lost among their genealogies, and in the signs that they slipped me, and sometimes I wandered far afield from the clues I had already found.

The documents testify to the fact that the Hermans had been present on Polish soil for more than two centuries, in Kalisz and Krośniewice, in Łowicz and in Łódź, in Łęczyca and in Płock. After 1815 these territories were incorporated into the Russian Empire, where the position of the Jews was more difficult than in other annexed territories. It was only then that they started being called *starozakonni,* Israelites, referring to the Old Testament, which replaced the qualifier then in use, "infidels." Toward the end of the nineteenth century, half the Jewish population of the world lived in the tsarist state. In the kingdom of Poland, the number had multiplied by eight in the matter of a century to reach a million and a half. Despite this, Poles would still call Jews "transients," or strangers to their land.

According to the stereotypes, all Jews were tenants, innkeepers, or shopkeepers, busy multiplying their fortunes, generally indifferent to the conditions of the country in which they lived.

My most distant ancestor was Szmul Herman, a spice-and-wine merchant. At Łęczyca he ran the family business, which was founded in 1804. He also sold lottery tickets in his capacity of collector for the National Lottery of the kingdom of Poland. In the middle of the nineteenth century he had taken his seat as municipal councilor, which testifies to his particular position in society and the level of his education. Only privileged Jews, wealthy and educated, had the right to vote and hold public office. He owned a house with a wheat granary on Poznańska Street, where he stored his reserves of wines. Sometimes he organized theater performances for children, with the proceeds going to benefit the needy.

He died after the insurrection of 1863, against Russian rule, leaving debts that represented three-quarters of his fortune.

The enterprise survived, passing into the hands of Salo-mea Herman, most likely Szmul's niece. My great-great-grandmother, called by her Jewish name of Sura Ruchla in the census of the town, is registered as a merchant or a bourgeois citizen thereof. Very early on she had married her cousin Sam-uel Herman, with whom she had four children. By the end of the nineteenth century, in addition to their commerce in wine and spirits they owned a printing press. The local corre-spondent of the *Kalisz Gazette* complained that a Polish print-ing house had passed into the hands of a Jew who was a wine merchant and who made people pay high prices for shoddy work and would also create an unbelievable number of spelling errors in all printed matter, whether Polish or Russian.

It's completely possible that the Hermans did distort the Polish language. No doubt they spoke Yiddish all the time. I don't discount the possibility that they committed errors, but I am not convinced whether this complaint about the compe-tence of the Hermans was linked to the reality of the situation or rather was only the result of the antipathy of Polish printers.

The mark of the Herman Printing Press appears in the daily newspapers of Łęczyca in the 1920s and 1930s on the reviews of the activities of the fire department and the choir associated with the Jesuit church, the prospectus praising the wheelbar-rows of a local manufacturer, and the death notices posted on the walls.

I thought of my great-great-grandmother while listening to stories about the Jews of Łęczyca between the two wars that the inhabitants of the town still remembered. I listened to how they came out of the synagogue looking down on other people. How they took over the streets, "our streets, from their syna-gogue to our church," I see them walking and there is among them . . . a shared feeling of superiority. "They were self-sufficient, they didn't arouse any sympathy, they were arrogant. They did everything possible to exclude us from commerce; they went out of their way to destroy Polish businesses."

Jachet Gitel, or Justyna, daughter of Salomea, my great-grandmother, didn't have any distinguishing characteristics.

Not in 1930, when she filled out an application for an identity card. With chestnut-brown hair, blue eyes, and an oval face, of average height, she didn't attach a photograph with her application. It seems that I resemble her. She had long hair, and she liked to have it combed by someone sitting next to her on a stool. Then she arranged it in a chignon or in a crown. Her granddaughter, my mother, remembers that. But the one who remembered her best was Mirka, a friend of the family, who was young at the time; she spoke to me about the combing ritual on the seaside promenade in Tel Aviv. I traveled thousands of miles, from Warsaw to Israel, to hear this. The comb was made of bone. The stool came from the drawing room furniture where the piano was. There was a candy bowl of Meissen porcelain. They were seated by the window looking over the fields at number 9 in Przedrynek at Łęczyca.

Why am I obsessing about this comb and her hair? In the gas chamber did hair burn before the body? And how did it burn? From the roots or starting at the crown? And the pain? She had left the contents of her pockets outside the door; her ring—I don't know if she still had it—went into a heap. They had captured her on a street in the Warsaw Ghetto, where she had gone to rejoin her family. She had not resisted; she was searching for her youngest daughter and her small son, who had been caught in an earlier raid.

Thus: medium height, oval face, brown hair, blue eyes. The handwriting of the clerk is bold. Her signature appears timid. She obtained her identity card on September 20, 1930. She was then forty-five years old.

JAKUB GOLDSTEIN

JAKUB GOLDSTEIN,
MY MATERNAL GREAT-GRANDFATHER

*T*here were many Goldsteins, more than a hundred in Łęczyca alone, but also in Ozorków, Krośniewice, Koło, Brześć, Kutno, Gostynin, Piątek, Stawiszyn, and Łódź. Their genealogical tree made a dense forest, overwhelming even with my obsession with minutiae.

My mother's mother was a Goldstein. The Goldsteins were poor Jews, ordinary, without any distinctive traits, who left their traces by the thousands for hundreds of years in little towns along the rivers of Poland. You could see them everywhere, or not see them, all the same, as they blended into the routine of weekly markets and Sabbath prayers.

Jakub Szlama was born in Łęczyca; his wife, Chana Rauf, in Koło. My mother remembers them as her Jewish grandparents. They had six children, five girls and one boy, David, who was a painter by trade.

The eldest daughter, Udel Sura, called Dela, the mother of my mother, was born in Koło in 1902. They were proud of her because she became a schoolteacher.

Jakub Goldstein sold coal, and his income barely sufficed to meet his family's meager subsistence. He had been threatened more than once by the bailiff. Among the documents of the town of Łęczyca are numerous letters from my mother's grandfather concerning the rescheduling of the payment of his debts. He paid them conscientiously. His letters are handwritten in fine Polish, though I am not certain that he wrote them himself. Nevertheless they employed a servant, they contributed regularly to the salary of the night watchman for the synagogue, paid their share of the school fees, and gave to poor Jews.

Jakub Goldstein was the only one of his whole family who revealed his face. In June 1930 he submitted a form for the renewal of his identity card. Description: medium height, oval face, graying hair, gray eyes. Distinguishing characteristics: untrimmed beard. On the left he had attached a small photograph.

My great-grandfather had a large nose and ears that stuck out. He wore a yarmulke on his bald head and had a sagging mouth as if several teeth were missing, and a salt-and-pepper beard.

His overcoat with the collar twice rolled down was closed by a metal button and looked threadbare. His eyes, slightly narrowed, looked straight ahead.

He was fifty-two years old and was already an old man. He is frightened. He was murdered several years later.

PRZEDRYNEK

THE PRZEDBORSKI FAMILY

O n Przedrynek Place at number 9, in a big L-shaped building, my Przedborski ancestors occupied an apartment on the second floor in the front. The apartment was light, with windows overlooking the square and the meadows. My great-grandfather Henryk's office was dominated by a mahogany bookcase.

In the mortgage registry there is mention of a stone house of several stories with a wing also of several stories, a ground-floor annex, a courtyard, a garden, and a meadow. Before the war, almost one hundred people were registered at this address on Przedrynek Place: the families Fau, Szpigiel, Cynaderka, Engiel, Cwang, Monter, Moszkowicz. After the war, the authorities found, with great difficulty, one surviving heir.

I never saw the house on Przedrynek Place, although it was not destroyed during the war, or even in later attempts to erase the past. No one can say why, in 1981, they pulled down this handsome building that had sheltered the lives of ten families. It is also difficult to find photographs of it.

The only photograph of number 9 on Przedrynek Place that I succeeded in obtaining belonged to the woman who administered these properties after the war. She kept it only because it showed in the foreground the funeral cortege of her favorite neighbor. The house is gray and sad. It had a different way of maintaining its silence than what I had imagined. My mother was born on Przedrynek, and she lived near her two sets of grandparents, the Goldsteins in the wing, and the Przedborskis at the front of the building. In Łęczyca, a town of ten thousand inhabitants, the Jews represented a third of the population.

My great-grandmother Justyna Herman was married early. She became pregnant by her tutor, who was fourteen years older. In time they had four children. The firstborn, Samuel, called Zamutek, came into the world several months after the wedding in 1903, the year of the pogrom in Kishinev. Then in succession, every two years, the daughters, Bronka, Frania, and the youngest, Madzia, in 1913.

Henryk Przedborski, my great-grandfather, this industrious tutor, had been called Handsome Henio in his youth. They had lived on Przedrynek since 1914, when my great-grandfather, already settled at that time, also became a town councilor for Łęczyca. He held this position for the next twenty years on the committee for charity and the budget; he was also a member of the administration of the municipal savings bank. He had been elected from the list of the Union of Orthodox Jews, although he was not excessively religious. Within the municipal administration he was entrusted with tasks that required a thorough knowledge of Polish history and the Polish language, as in preparing an announcement for the townsfolk of the hundredth anniversary of the death of Tadeusz Kościuszko.

In his daily life, Henryk Przedborski kept the books for

his mother-in-law's wine warehouse, against his inclination and not very scrupulously, although the day-to-day life of the whole family depended on it. He considered commerce, the proverbial realm of the Jews, as something inferior, unworthy of his attention. He preferred the sessions of the town council, although even there he was often marked absent. The compensation for an alderman came to six złotys per session, which enabled him to buy a kilo of excellent salami. He liked non-kosher meat, but most of all he liked books. With his future brother-in-law the dentist Mojżesz Kuszner, he founded the Jewish Society of Libraries and Reading Rooms.

He never used his Jewish first name, Enoch, other than on official documents. He knew Yiddish from home and Hebrew from the cheder, and he had obtained his baccalaureate diploma from the Imperial Lycée in the Russian language.

His father, Marcus, was born in Łęczyca. His grandfather Baruch, to all appearances, also. One of his ancestors came from Frankfurt, but they had all been raised on Polish soil for generations. Perhaps they came from the neighborhood of Przedbórz, on the Pilica River, where a Jewish community had existed since the fourteenth century, with a dynasty of *tzaddikim* and a synagogue built of larch wood that had been admired by Napoleon. The name they bore had been also given to Jews from Łódź, the neighboring town. In the 1840s, it was among the popular names.

Łódź had developed in the nineteenth century from an agricultural village into the Polish Manchester, seat of the textile industry and a financial center. The value of its industrial output was estimated in the hundreds of millions of rubles. The Przedborskis of Łódź, essentially descended from Aleksander, the brother of Marcus, formed a fairly important clan there.

They were born and died within a radius of a hundred kilometers between Kalisz, Łęczyca, Przedbórz, and Łódź. It was only during the generation of my grandfathers that they had established themselves definitively in Warsaw.

At the end of the nineteenth century, Handsome Henio was

part of the golden youth of Warsaw; that's where he received his nickname. Dashing from his earliest youth, he sported a bushy mustache, and people said that he had an elegant sense of style. There was nothing Semitic about him, which was repeated as the greatest compliment.

He had been a bachelor for a long time, and for a long time he had been searching for where he belonged. He took care of his father's business and traveled to Warsaw, where he entertained himself by going to the ice-skating rinks and attending balls. He had administered the manor house at Kuchary, which he subsequently divided into lots, and supervised the family shops in Kalisz by organizing the deliveries. Only his marriage constrained him to lead a more settled life, although he never gave up reading.

He believed that you had to assimilate. He appreciated what was Polish, and he believed that he had the right to it. He felt that he was entitled by the presence of several generations of his family in this land.

He was not conflicted within himself. He was born into a Jewish family with its traditions. His forebears sold alcohol, and the Poles called him "brother" because he gave them credit and did not hound them to obtain what he was owed. He already spoke Polish. He opened himself to the world, as did his children and their children. His business was carried on among Poles, and he lived with them and among them. Henryk considered it a lack of decorum to overly stress his particular differences.

He paid his quota for the maintenance of the synagogue and his contribution to the poor Jews, but he spoke about it in Polish. For the educated and upper classes, French was the second language of Eastern Europe and Russia right up until World War II. In the same way, he read Tolstoy and Flaubert in Polish, and he sang opera melodies. And perhaps he also counted in Polish. It seems that one counts best always in one's native language.

Yet my great-grandfather did not take his meals at the mess

hall of the garrison, or play bridge at the Gentlemen's Club. He did not participate in amateur theatrical performances, or go on hunting expeditions by sled in the winter. In Łęczyca all these things were reserved for the Polish. The members of Polish national organizations stood at attention for the musical fanfares at holiday celebrations and prayed during services in churches and in public places. Oftentimes the patriotic celebrations were accompanied by concerts, which Henryk was enthusiastic about: to listen to Chopin, Corelli, and Handel. He sometimes would even go to the Bernardine church.

How can I know when the Poles speak about the Przedborskis with sympathy and approval? They stress the fact that they absolutely did not in any way resemble Jews. This was more about their appearance than about their behavior—their noses were well shaped and small, the opposite of Jewish noses, which were prominent, hooked, and pointed. Their eyes and complexion were light and not dark, somber, diabolical. A high forehead and mustache can still be Polish, but rarely the lips, and never the beard.

How and to what extent and in what way was Poland the homeland of the Jews? Had they not, like the Poles, fought for her, spilled their blood? A small number, not the majority.

Henryk's father, Marcus, and his uncle, Aleksander, refused the call to arms under the flag. Was it out of aversion for battle, according to the stereotype of the Jew running away from violence and not liking to fight—or were they afraid?

Henryk joined the first civic committee put in place at Łęczyca in 1914 after the departure of the Russian authorities from the town. It was composed of Polish and Jewish inhabitants. Henryk supervised the security in one of the four districts. Like the other members of the committee, he wore a sky-blue armband.

Language defined the zones of influence. The knowledge of Polish was a must for knowing your rights, applying for a post in public administration, and daily contact with the majority. Assimilation brought with it upward mobility on the social ladder. Adopting the language, the dress, the customs of the majority created a sense of belonging. Hence, there was often a feeling of condescension and a sense of superiority on the part of assimilated Jews toward the religious masses. It wasn't only in Łęczyca that they constituted a majority.

Sometimes it seems to me that the Przedborskis looked down on the religious Jews. Not only did these masses not belong to the spheres to which they aspired, but they also butchered the Polish language, and in daily life they spoke Yiddish. Educated Jews considered Yiddish a jargon, a corruption of German. Even though there existed a rich literature in the language, it took many years for its value to be appreciated, not until the Nobel Prize was awarded to Isaac Bashevis Singer in 1978.

Among the memories of the Przedborski family, the most important were the Friday evenings at Przedrynek. After having dinner, they played music together, the most deeply rooted of family traditions, the one dearest to them. Even if they burned dozens of candles in the seven-branched candelabrum, and didn't take milk with meat, their world was not circumscribed by religion. It seemed as if the liturgy was observed for the sake of Grandmother Salomea Herman. But the weekly concerts stayed with them for good.

The men, father and son, played the violin. The sisters, alternating with their mother, played the piano. They practiced quartets even though they lacked a viola and a cello for the string quartets and a third stringed instrument for the piano. Zamutek got all worked up and made them repeat the least peccadillo until it was correct. Bronka played off-key gracefully, not bothered by all the numerous imperfections of her interpretation. Frania agreed to everything. They played Mozart, Beethoven, and Brahms.

The three Przedborski sisters and their brother had received a traditional Jewish education, but they spoke Polish exclusively. As they grew older, Przedrynek became more and more secular. At first they had been taught at home, before entering Polish primary schools and then the Lycée of the Polish Motherland Circle in Łęczyca. The first baccalaureate was Zamutek's, in 1922; he was an exemplary student, which counted a great deal in his entrance examinations to the institutions of higher education. There was no quota officially set, but they limited the admissions of Jewish students where the most applied. The Polytechnic Institute of Warsaw, which he chose, was the most in demand, along with the medical and law schools. Zamutek passed his examination and was admitted to the civil engineering faculty.

He was a student with Bolek Kuszner, a fanatic liberal, whom Bronka eventually married and followed to Warsaw. Frania was enrolled in the history department at the University of Warsaw, leaving the family home. Their adult lives naturally took place in a Polish milieu. There was no need to rebel. It required leaving Przedrynek Place.

The Kraszewski brothers, who often visited Aunt Bronka because she was a friend of their mother's, used to say that the Jews had killed Jesus. They mocked the Jewish gabardine coats and threw stones at the decorated huts the Jews erected for Sukkoth. Their father was Polish, which is why they attended a nursery school run by the Ursuline Sisters. They also served as altar boys at the church.

In 1935, when the town clock in Łęczyca no longer kept time, despite numerous complaints to the municipality and notices in the newspapers, there were only the parents and Madzia, the youngest, at home at Przedrynek Place. In 1937, Henryk's mother-in-law, Salomea Herman, sold the printing house. A year later, at the municipal cemetery, the family bade farewell to my great-grandfather Henryk Przedborski, son of Marcus. Undoubtedly they played for him, as leavetaking, the Kol Nidre of the Jews. But perhaps also the Ave Maria? His widow moved to Warsaw with her grown children. For them Przedrynek Place had ceased to exist.

THE WAR

THE SYNAGOGUE, ŁĘCZYCA,
ON A GERMAN POSTCARD, 1942

On September 3, 1939, a Sunday, the inhabitants of Łęczyca committed to God their country, the Polish army, and their families. The first bombs fell upon the town in the afternoon.

Ten days later, the Germans marched into the town. They renamed Łęczyca "Lentschutz" and incorporated it into the Reich. They called the town square Adolf Hitler Platz, and Żydowska Street became Judengasse; Przedrynek Place is on the map as Vormarkt. The *kirkut,* the Jewish cemetery, was still there, and the synagogue remained standing.

Who was what became known only when the Germans made it obligatory to wear the star; the streets were a constellation of them. Converted Jews wore even bigger stars than the others, stars on the back and on the chest. They were ashamed and tried to hide the stars under their coats. When the Germans noticed, they forced them to sew on even bigger ones.

At rifle point the bearded elders were made to march through town singing this song: "Marshal Śmigly-Rydz* didn't teach the Jews a thing, but Hitler came and taught them how to work."

The gibbets were set up in the town square, where the old treasury building had been destroyed. The police rounded up the inhabitants of the town there.

They hanged more than ten Jews and ordered the townspeople to watch. One of them was a tailor, Szpigiel, whom everyone knew because he sewed the school uniforms. No doubt they were left hanging until dark.

For a long time they searched for a volunteer to pull the bench from under the feet of the condemned men; they wanted a Jew to present himself. Finally, the son of one of the condemned men became very upset: "I can't stand my father's suffering any longer." He stepped up and took care of it.

The Kraszewski brothers from the building on Przedrynek Place, whose mother was Jewish, were also in the crowd. They did not wear the star because their father was Polish and Catholic and they had studied with the Ursuline Sisters.

· · ·

All this must have happened in the first two years of the war, before they created the ghetto in February 1941. They

---

* Edward Rydz-Śmigly (1886–1941) commanded the Polish forces at the outbreak of World War II. Fleeing to Romania after the defeat, he secretly returned to Poland, where he died in 1941. (A.T.)

shut in about three thousand Jews, those who remained after the sweeps preceding the closing of the ghetto.

There exists a postcard from the ghetto. Like a postcard from a vacation spot, a postcard with greetings from the seaside or the mountains. Who was this German photographer who decided to send across the world pictures of the extermination?

His name was Geschke, and he had a shop at number 1 Adolf Hitler Platz—that is to say, the town square. He certainly took the pictures himself and afterward retouched them. He printed them up as postcards and distributed them. I found two: the synagogue in flames with the caption "Brennende Synagoge," and Żydowska Street in the ghetto.

The synagogue was set on fire in February 1940. It had stood there, leaning against the city walls, for more than 170 years. The monumental building with thick walls started burning from the top, the high-arched roof called a "Polish roof." The flames shooting from the upper level take up a third of the postcard. The fire is black like the window recesses.

They ordered the Jews to clear the wreckage of the burned synagogue.

On the second postcard was Żydowska Street behind barbed wire: "Judengasse." In the background, the building with the numbers 2 and 4. Barbed wire, wooden barriers, wooden doors, a gateway. Barbed wire in the foreground, the entrance to the ghetto, several children, and a woman pushing a cart. The windows are shuttered except for one on the ground floor. It is difficult to determine the season. The bright light could be in the spring as well as autumn. Dark clothing with long sleeves indicates cold days, some time between autumn 1941 and spring 1942.

In the town registry, the adult inhabitants of Żydowska Street number between 1,249 and 1,510, the Elefowiczes, the Lisners, the Cyglers, the Bornsztajns, the Flatsors, among others. There were seventeen numbers on that street. Merchants, tailors, sandal makers, artisans, the unemployed, and housewives.

Hipolit Małecki, a blacksmith, the son of a carriage manufacturer, remembered one Jew, Eliasz. He went to school with him. "But he died in the ghetto. Their lives ended there. Those who could have fled to Israel had already fled, otherwise they finished them off. They shoved them into the cars with blows on the head from rifle butts, they massacred them, they weren't even moving anymore. They took them near Koło, to Chełmno nad Nerem. Or they suffocated them with gas from the exhaust pipes of the death trucks. A cousin of my wife's told us that the hair of those who went to work there turned gray overnight.

"As they herded them toward Poddębice, the Jewish women called out to us, 'Mr. Małecki, Mr. Małecki.' And I said to my wife: 'Come, don't look.' We couldn't stop.

"With the divine will of God and the protection of the most holy Virgin Mary, one can emerge victorious from all bad situations. I believe in everything that comes from God. And he looks after man. You have to believe it."

· · ·

Of four thousand inhabitants of the ghetto, a thousand did not survive the first winter. At that point, the Germans still authorized burials in the Jewish cemetery. In March of the following year, they began the killing. They herded the Jews up to the stadium, on Kaliska Street, where they were taken by truck to Chełmno nad Nerem, about fifty kilometers from Łęczyca. Few of them arrived there alive.

Not one Jew appears in the tax register for 1943.

The Germans destroyed the houses on Żydowska Street after the liquidation of the ghetto. It seems that the Poles expected to find gold hidden in the walls. Supposedly they found some. But they also found gold in the building on Szpitalna Street, near the parish church. In the 1950s, they built apartment blocks on the old foundations.

The *kirkut,* the original Jewish cemetery of Łęczyca that is called *kirchol,* must have dated back to the Middle Ages, with the first appearance of the Jews. They most certainly buried more than fifteen hundred victims there after the pogrom launched by the Polish army during the Swedish invasion of 1656. One of the versions affirms that the troops of the hetman Stefan Czarniecki threw the bodies of the murdered Jews into a ditch on the site where the synagogue was raised over a hundred years later. It rested against the old city wall, next to where they placed a plaque commemorating in Hebrew inscription the tragedy of the Swedish invasion.

From 1830 up until World War II, the Jewish cemetery of Łęczyca remained in the same two locations, first just outside of town, and then, in time, on the periphery. It covered several acres of land; it was vast.

In 1943, the Germans disposed of the Jewish cemetery and paved the roads from the train station to the town with the tombstones. After the Liberation, the authorities removed the tombstones from the road and deposited them where the Jewish cemetery had been before. They stayed piled up there for a long time, until people started stealing the stone to use it for sharpening blades and to build foundations. The land of the cemetery was considered unclaimed property. The municipal council decided to dispose of it in 1964. They planned to put a road there and build a square.

The Jewish cemetery of Łęczyca was near to my great-grandparents' house on Przedrynek Place. I didn't realize that it was so close. If you leaned out the window facing the village of Topola, and the fields, you could see the cemetery on the left. Today it is no longer there. They removed all traces of the narrow-gauge rails that passed by there, and the low sheds of the garage and the exercise fields for the drivers. The road has been broken up by trucks. Mirek shows me beneath our feet, fragments of worn yellow sandstone. We can see fragments of *matsevah*, the tombstones, but it's difficult to extract them from the ground without damaging the road.

Farther along the path there is an enclosure of modest parcels of land, simple beds of carrots, onions, leeks, celery, parsley, beets. An old woman is weeding; she is also picking a little of everything, preparing a mix of vegetables for broth. She can't *not* know what was here before the war and why her vegetables thrive here.

I stand for a moment on the rails. They brought them from everywhere, by wagons along these rails.

Sometimes the hollow graves pockmark the earth; weeds grow out of them and obliterate for a while the unequivocal evidence. Fragments of tombstones dug up from the ground. It's been a long time since there has been no smoke.

. . .

I return by the road that was built with the tombstones of the Jews of Łęczyca.

The round cobblestones of Przedrynek Place have been covered over with a new pavement. It's almost smooth—another layer of the past replaced by the following one.

KUCHARY

KUCHARY ESTATE, NEAR ŁĘCZYCA, IN 2000. THIS IS THE FORMER
ESTATE OF MARKUS PRZEDBORSKI, MY GREAT-GRANDFATHER.

I don't know their faces. I have in front of me two doorknobs from the manor house they apparently owned. I
hold them in my hands to try to gain access to the world
that was theirs.

You have to start somewhere; let's begin at the end. And with
the imagined story.

My great-great-grandfather, Marcus Przedborski, landed
proprietor in Kuchary, died in a retirement home in Warsaw.
It was apparently a home for wealthy Jews, on the most elegant Jewish street, Sienna, or Zielna. Marcus died on top of
a woman, a woman called Feniksen, or Gliksman, or something else. The Polish peasants who set fire to his estate brought
about the downfall of Marcus.

I don't know where I dug up this story, or why I believed it. Maybe because of the absence of any family legend. Well, even though it should be evident that everything in this version of his fate is far from the truth, when I think of Marcus it is this picture that first comes to mind.

Marcus liked to introduce himself as a businessman from Kalisz, the provincial capital, but I don't know what it was he sold. Perhaps lace, for which the town was famous; it successfully copied Swiss lace. They shipped it everywhere—to Russia, and even to China. He lived on Złota Street, near the central market, with his wife, Balbina, who signed her name prettily in Polish. I contemplated this signature for a long time; it dates from 1882, the *B* carefully done with imposing little bellies. She gave him five sons. The father of my grandfather, Henryk, was the third.

The manor house of Marcus—that's what they called it, with complete confidence—was located near Kalisz.

Mirek had heard of a Jewish Kuchary near Łęczyca. I had not paid any attention, since my family members from Kuchary had lived elsewhere. But since I was in Łęczyca, and the Przedborskis had lived not far from there, Mirek thought it might be interesting to check it out. The roads were lined with linden trees, the air was clear. Going by Topola Królewska, which was surrounded by fields, it was a few kilometers until Strzegocin.

We couldn't find Kuchary. We somehow lost our way and had to ask for directions. A man pointed out to us in the distance, on the other side of the fields, a structure with red agricultural buildings. He explained to us that the main house at Kuchary had been divided between two proprietors, the Jóźwiaks and the Modrzejewskis.

The big house was squat and clearly divided into two sections. One side had recently been restored with a yellowish stucco, which altered the proportions of the façade; the second half, like the orphaned half of the other side, had been neglected and was in falling-down condition. It was an unbalanced whole. Bizarre. It was hard to imagine the original appearance beneath all that. It had nothing that would evoke a manor house.

In the first courtyard were a few agricultural buildings that had a prosperous air of ease. Pots of geraniums lined the steps. The mistress of the house was tall, corpulent, and energetic. She had a silver tooth and dark hair with an old-style permanent wave. We asked her about the history of Kuchary. She knew little more than what everybody repeated: that the proprietor ran through his fortune in all sorts of sprees. But there was her grandfather, in his nineties, who perhaps would remember more. The mistress of the house went inside and a moment later invited us to enter. The grandfather was going to speak with us.

The walls were thick. From the entrance hall we walked into a light-filled room with high ceilings and a pair of windows in deep recesses. Modern furniture, clean. The grandfather, small in stature, with sparse gray hair, was seated on a sofa, his pants held up with suspenders. His large hands were still and resting on his knees. Crutches were placed next to him. He had a long, sad face. His eyes looked at us from afar. It's not that he didn't hear well, but between the question and the answer a certain amount of time elapsed, as if words had a long way to go in one direction as well as the other. And it was the same thing each time.

"Who lived here before you?" I asked.

"Grabski, a big landowner. The family of Prime Minister Grabski.* He led a merry life with his fortune, he drank and danced in France. He got deeper and deeper in debt. And afterward, there were Jews here. He had taken loans from the Jews, but he couldn't repay them. Thus they had to appropriate his property. They were here for twenty-five years. They made the place work again. The village does not have bad memories of them. They created a day nursery and a school in the next room. Today it is still called 'Jewish Kuchary' even though that

---

* Stanisław Grabski (1871–1949): prime minister of Poland in 1929 and again from December 1923 to 1925. He was president of the National Council in exile in London from 1942 to 1944. (A.T.)

is not written down in the papers. My father-in-law bought a piece of this land in 1912. I married into the Modrzejewski family, who had bought it from the Jews. The grandmother divided her estate between her children, and half of it was inherited by my wife."

The hostess offered us coffee. The grandfather tried to bring the cup up to his lips. I had to help him by steadying his trembling hand. Even so, a little drop of burning liquid was spilled. I brushed it off delicately, as if he were made of glass. He seemed to me inestimably precious, his head, his past, his memory.

Mirek asked, "Do you remember the name of these Jews?"

I am an expert in conversations of this sort. I have had many of them in researching the life of Isaac Bashevis Singer. I know how to circle around the subject, how to change it, how not to press the point. And how to come back to it unexpectedly afterward without arousing suspicion. I don't know how Mirek managed to do it. We had not consulted each other. He was very natural, and he preserved my secret.

The grandfather hesitated for a long time. He couldn't remember. We were already speaking of other things when I heard him say very softly: "Przedborski."

Mirek and I looked at each other, for a fraction of a second. And suddenly, everything from that moment on became important—the thickness of the walls and the height of the windows, the cellars with their arched vaults, and the attic. Everything that the old Jóźwiak, who worked at Kuchary since the thirties, could manage to remember. The ripping-out of the barberry bushes, the price of pigs (fifty złotys) and of chickens (eight złotys), the store for fertilizer and seeds on Poznańska Street, the inexpensive pansies and sweet Jacunda strawberries.

"The Jew who ran everything here owned an alcohol business. He had a wine and liquor warehouse in Łęczyca on Poznańska Street. A good house, old and reliable. I ordered the alcohol from them for my wedding in June 1935. A hundred guests had a good time here on the property. There was good vodka; he didn't cut his stock with water like the others. That was when the national mourning had lasted since May because Marshal Piłsudski had died. The Russian Orthodox church in Łęczyca was razed because not one Orthodox was left, only Poles and Jews, half and half.

"Przedborski was an elegant man; you could never have told that he was a Jew. He was clean shaven and handsome, without any beard or earlocks. An elegant gentleman, corpulent. His conversation with his clients was very amusing. He discussed the films showing at the Oasis, the correct way to tune a piano, or the tools from the Gierlinskis' agricultural store."

. . .

The Jóźwiaks ran a model dairy farm. They had modern machinery, and their half of the manor house was meticulously maintained. They had installed a new roof and redone the whole interior, stripping the walls and the floors. They couldn't alter the windows because of the thickness of the walls. They planned to replace them in time with vinyl windows made to special order.

They couldn't find any old photos. The doors, the windows, and the walls could remember. In this part of the house everything else had all lost traces of the past. The barrel-vaulted cellars smelled of moist earth. And still there was the attic.

Here also order reigned. Some laundry hung out to dry. Against the wall a dust-covered picture in a gilt frame. We looked at a half-naked lady with long, fair tresses, a Mary Magdalene à la Botticelli. The hostess told us this chromo litho hung on the dining-room wall for thirty years and dated back to the old owners of the property. "Do you want it? Take it, please."

Here was the proof. The concrete proof that I wasn't dreaming. Is it also proof that the saint, the woman of ill repute who bathed the feet of Christ, hung in the drawing rooms of the Przedborskis?

It was impossible that my Jewish great-grandparents had this picture in their home. And yet when I look at it now,

in my own home, I have the feeling of owning something
that had belonged to them. I'm incapable of explaining this
phenomenon.

The second courtyard was in disorder. The hostess appeared
in a red sweater and round glasses with thick lenses; she wore a
little braid of what remained of her peroxided hair. Her smile
was distracted and distant. She hires herself out for seasonal
work for several złotys per hour. Her husband delivers milk
to customers. He buys on credit from the stores. He drinks
away everything. At that very moment he was busy drinking
somewhere.

She reluctantly invited us to come in. There were piles of old
things, clothing, utensils, colored cloth—misery, disordered
and frail. It was as if there had been a search, or an earthquake.
On the wall, hanging crookedly, an oval sepia photograph of
the grandmother, the lady of the manor.

Our hostess repeated that the manor had been known as
the Palace. "It's two hundred years old or more. All around
bloomed white-and-pink orchards, and in the autumn you
could pick the fruit. The autumns were beautiful, like a picture. There were beehives, and in the ponds, carp and tenches.
There used to be a park and farmhouses, of which only the
stables remain. During the Occupation the Germans had parties here."

We walked for a long time in the fields. I felt enriched; it was
as if they were giving me back a piece of myself in this Polish
landscape. It was the past. I embraced it closely, as if I had the
right to it.

I felt the great relief that comes from the feeling of belonging. Even if I had only slim roots such as fortuitous memory.
All the same, after many years, something had led me to
Kuchary. A Polish guardian angel? I have returned there again
and again. I looked, I spoke to everyone. Polish village, Polish hospitality, chicken broth and pork chops, coffee served in
glasses, and the hardened hands of the master of the house.
Who were they welcoming with such cordiality? The writer

from Warsaw? Must I tell them who I am in reality, and what I am searching for? How would they react? This thought fills me with embarrassment.

I was given the doorknobs of the manor house during my second visit. I felt it was important to have something from there, and they really wanted to give me something. The brass knobs are inscribed with the fingerprints of my great-grandparents.

THE LITTLE COFFIN

Aleksander Przedborski, the eldest brother of my great-great-grandfather Marcus, was a bookseller. He had studied in England and dressed in the English style, carrying a cane and wearing a black top hat. When he returned to his family in Łęczyca in the middle of the nineteenth century, people used to point him out on the town square as an original character. He had trouble finding a wife.

He knew books the way others knew horses or trees. He spent hours poring over old books and manuscripts, peering through his round steel spectacles. He could read Latin, French, Polish, Hebrew, and English. He was constantly busy with rare books at auctions and foreign exhibitions. He also managed a library.

On his death a top hat was discovered in the cellar, along with a Bible printed in Latin and decorated with hand-painted vignettes, and an ancient Old Testament from the end of the fifteenth century printed in Basel.

In time his son Dawid Przedborski, the same age as my great-grandfather Henryk, took over the management of the bookstore and its paper warehouse with his wife, Chana—excessively pious, but her Polish was irreproachable. The old inhabitants of Łęczyca still remembered the Przedborski store in the town square, near the baker, especially because they always included pencils or colored cutouts for the children. Today those children are preparing themselves to join the next world. Aside from books, the store carried stationery and office supplies. In the documents they had written *bumaga*—"paper" in Russian.

Since 1914 the bookstore has been in the hands of Tekla Chrempińska, from a respectable Polish family. People were startled that they would become partners with Jews. That's when the Przedborski bookstore issued a series of postcards of local sights ordered by the Polish Tourist and Sightseeing Society.

They also issued a postcard that can be seen today in the collection of the Łęczyca Museum. It represents a little coffin containing the remains of a child killed by the Jews to make matzo.

What happened?

On Holy Thursday, in April 1639, in the village of Kamaszyce near Piątek, a beggar named Tomasz kidnapped two-year-old Franciszek, son of Maciej Michałowicz, who worked for the landlady Karsznicka, and murdered him brutally, stabbing him with a knife over a hundred times. After eleven days, they discovered the child in a neighboring forest. During the inquest, the beggar declared that he committed the crime at the instigation of the Jews of Łęczyca. The verdict of the tribunal of Lublin condemned him to be dismembered.

During the trial before the municipal tribunal of Łęczyca, twenty Jews had been imprisoned, among them Rabbi Izaak. Despite the verdict that condemned them, the royal tribunal pardoned the majority of the accused.

The child was solemnly buried in a sepulcher in the convent, and at the front of the Bernardine church they placed a painting of the circumstances representing a ritual murder. At the beginning of the nineteenth century this painting of the ritual murder disappeared from the church. The inhabitants believe that the Jews stole it and destroyed it. The remains of the child were transferred to a small coffin in crystal and placed inside the church of the Bernardines. It seems that steps were taken to beatify the child.

The little coffin remained in the church until the end of the war. In the summer of 1945, it appears, the officials of the Security Office confiscated it. Again, the people of Łęczyca claim that it was the Jews.

The tale of these events still feeds the imagination of the people of Łęczyca. The legends about the ritual murder are deeply rooted and widespread throughout the land in Poland, and you can still find Polish churches with pictures showing cruel Jews victimizing a Christian child.

Aside from a photo in the records of the convent, and the postcard that was published by my great-grandparents, not a trace of the coffin exists in Łęczyca. An inscription describing the murder has also vanished.

THOSE PEOPLE

I spent the Jewish New Year of autumn 1999 in Łęczyca. Mirek and I went to the water's edge, as they did in olden times, centuries ago in the time of the wooden synagogues, to wash away our sins in the Bzura River. That's what is required by the Jewish custom of Tashlik—purification to welcome the New Year. We washed away the sin of forgetting.

Shortly afterward, the blacksmith Małecki, grandson of the owner of the carriage factory whose advertisements were printed by Herman, the Jew from Poznańska Street—"a big fellow, I don't remember what he looked like"—checked my identity. He did it even before speaking to me. Then he spoke unctuously and, by and by, sensing my resistance, with anger. He spoke of the ritual murder by Jews who took children to drain their blood to make matzo. He became more and more aggressive. And I, more and more defenseless.

"There was a little coffin that used to be in the convent. It was the Jews who martyred the child. These aren't just empty stories. They had their reasons for martyring him. It's a true story."

For the first time in years, the primitive Polish anti-Semitism struck me again, the prejudices, the hatred, the aggression. Here before me returned what I confronted years earlier when I was writing my book on I. B. Singer, which seemed to me, without any concrete reason, to belong to the past. The fact that here it was again in Łęczyca, the place I had found that felt like a homeland, wounded me particularly. I could not hide it.

Suddenly I lost a portion of the joy I felt in rediscovering the sequence of my family history. Suddenly my mood darkened, and I fell silent.

The words of the blacksmith Małecki had hurt me. It was the first time that it had been so painful in Łęczyca. I wondered for a moment if it was worthwhile, my digging all that up again. Did I have the strength? Again I knew that I did. How many times have I had this discussion with myself? And yet I don't expose myself, I don't introduce myself as the daughter of a Jewish mother. I have given up on their souls. I could feel the old fear from wartime, somewhat paler, like an echo, but clear.

Mirek also informed me that the municipal authorities considered me a spy; they were surprised that I was so young. I dreaded what was going to happen sooner or later. It would be the notion of "restitution of Jewish property" with all its consequences, including my activities as a spy for the Americans or the Israelis.

It disgusts me. I find it revolting to such an extent that I can't think of the guilt that is the base of these accusations and these fears. Many inhabitants of these old Jewish settlements in my country react this way; they are afraid of visits by people from the outside. They are afraid because those people were once the owners of their homes, their orchards, their farms, their furniture, and their plates and cups. Those outsiders also are incarnations of their guilt, but only among those who have good reason to feel it. It appears that they are more numerous than I had thought.

I am not here to reclaim anything whatsoever; my nostalgia is not for material things. I am looking for what is not there. I am apprehensive about memory.

In this situation, whatever I do I will not escape judgments of this sort. I have to become aware of it. Stop feeling offended. It's Polish. I am Polish. But it's not my way of being. I have the feeling that Mirek is trying to protect me from myself. At certain times, he advises me to wait until I am stronger for the sake of this book. He does not believe that my admitting that I belong to the Chosen People can be of help to me. He is afraid for me. Like Mother.

But I don't want to wait. There will never be the right moment. "This" will always be *trayf,* not kosher, unwelcome. In this land, in my country, "this" has to cause someone to spit on me.

In Poddębice, twenty kilometers from Łęczyca, where there was a ghetto and where we are searching for traces of a cemetery, we are greeted by a slogan in thick black paint along the length of a white wall: "The Jews are looting this country."

Again I become conscious of where I am and what I am doing. In the depth of provincial Poland, where boorishness and contempt for any sort of differences are the norm, the fact that a history teacher is sensitive to strangers who come from afar seems to be a mistake. Is it possible that in me these two strands combine, the Polish and the Jewish?

I insist on finding this cemetery. I wanted to touch something that was them, which belonged to them. I wanted proof that their lives were real and that they did not perish without leaving a trace. After crossing a mound of refuse, the abandoned Protestant cemetery at the edge of the forest, we finally reached a small lapidarium. They are pieces of *matsevah* salvaged and inserted in a brick wall. Remains. I had a feeling of relief. And triumph in the name of Mirek, in the name of Poland, and in the name of those whose memories were preserved. Thus, there wasn't only mockery, aversion, and silence.

. . .

The multicolored kiosk on the town square of Łęczyca was filled with Western merchandise: Fa soap, French hairsprays, name-brand deodorants, Mars bars, *Cosmopolitan, Elle, Playboy* magazines. On the same shelf, right next to them, a half-dozen anti-Semitic booklets from the pens of familiar homegrown Jew haters. Visible behind the window, the titles are clearly legible: "The Jews and the Freemasons"; "Hitler, Founder of the Jewish State of Israel." They cost the equivalent of two packs of Marlboros. The salesgirl tells me they sell like hotcakes.

In a way incomprehensible to me, Mirek feels responsible for all this. I truly believe that he is among those whom the Jews could really trust during the war.

On Sunday, September 12, 1999, in Łęczyca, I remained alone in the town square. A strange feeling of being alone amid a crowd in their Sunday best. Without Mirek I feel like a stranger in this place. At noon the ceremonies begin for the sixtieth anniversary of the Battle of the Bzura, one of the greatest battles of the campaign of September 1939. The sun is out, the beginning of the heavy heat of September. There are already some men who are past their first beers, and couples arm in arm are heading for the town square, coming from all the cross streets. In front of the monuments to the heroes of the war are the memorial tablets to commemorate the victims of the German Occupation. Including the Jewish population of the city, I read on one tablet. A military band plays, amplifying the Sunday mood; people are waiting for the open-air Mass, a solemnity out of the ordinary. I am present, forcing myself to disappear into the crowd but standing out at a glance—a stranger.

I fled. The Jewish city that I saw with Mirek under the veil of night no longer existed. Nothing remains of it. Not even scars. A little Polish town, with its royal castle, its town square, its statue of the Virgin Mary in front of the city hall, a few churches and a convent. How different today from the other one; a little Polish town, not Jewish. My efforts to stop time, change the course of events, restore the memory despite history, the tiredness of humans, the passing of time, despite the despair, the tragedy—all my efforts seem in vain.

OZORKÓW

*I*n Łęczyca, where there was a cemetery, there is no cemetery. Their tombs cannot be found where they lived. For those who were gassed, they erected a monument, in Treblinka, in Chełmno. But that wasn't their home.

Mirek told me it seems that in Ozorków, not far from here, there was a big Jewish cemetery.

Before the war, people from Łęczyca went to Ozorków on outings. The two-hour trip by narrow-gauge rail in a train that whistled and smoked represented an uncommon attraction. Sometimes people went as far as Łódź by tram. Madzia, my grandfather's youngest sister, settled in Ozorków with her husband, a dentist. She had given birth to her son, Henryś, just before the war. She was listed in the register of the Jews of Ozorków during the Occupation. Several Goldsteins were also registered, most certainly relatives of those from Łęczyca.

The cemeteries were generally located on the periphery of town, not far from each other. This was also the case in Ozorków. Next to the Catholic cemetery, the Protestant and the Jewish.

The forest could be seen in the distance. Houses hugged the road leading there. They were all built after the war, which means that before the war this neighborhood had been on the outskirts of town. We asked for the Jewish cemetery. Without a word, people made a gesture pointing toward the forest. It was late in the afternoon, with the sun low on the horizon, piercing through the branches of young acacias and oak trees. The clearly marked trail led straight in front of us. Mosquitoes were bothering us.

At the clearing I stumbled on a stone fragment, pointed, jutting out. It did not seem interesting to us; we continued walking. I hardly raised my head, just enough not to lose my way. Under our feet, this path worn by so many shoes. With the help of a stick, I pushed away the carpet of moss and pine needles, pinecones and fern. But there were no stones, no slabs, nor any *matsevah*. Not a trace of Jews.

We returned to the first stone. With the help of a stick we tried to move it. It wasn't going to budge, or come out of the soil. A fragment of gray sandstone, ordinary. On the back three Hebrew letters appeared. They were the simplest, I could read them: *Shalom*. Word of greeting.

I borrowed a shovel from a neighboring farmhouse. Next to the first triangular stone, there were two others, somewhat smaller. On one I cleaned with a tuft of grass was a sculpted leaf; on the other, flowers. Once the stones marked the presence of someone's body. And the death of someone. They also marked a person's life.

The fragments did not fit together; they were not from one tombstone. The two pieces of sandstone had a clayish coloring; the others were marbled or dark brown. Five pieces, five fragments of a broken destiny, held in the belly of the earth, to survive.

I didn't want to give up. But we found nothing more. Nothing but this, I thought. "All that," Mirek said. We took the stones, wrapped in leaves. It was dusk, but light enough for children to be playing in a patch of sand. One of the boys, a blond child of ten perhaps, asked me what I was looking for— perhaps stones with inscriptions?

A moment later we were again in the clearing of the forest. There was an oak tree in the back. The ground was covered with leaves in much denser layers than on the path, and resembled a cake rising in the oven. It had risen. The children threw themselves on the ground digging with their bare hands. Beige slabs, scarred, cracked, damaged, one after the other. I knelt next to them. After a while I was like them. The ground seemed bottomless.

We couldn't stop. The three boys, the youngest of whom was three years old perhaps, removed the earth sticking to the smaller slabs, rubbing them with grass. A little girl appeared; she showed me lions, coins on bas-reliefs, Hebrew letters from left to right. "Look, on mine there are hands, and fingers, and another hand, two and three fingers." "And I have a lion—look!" "And this little coin, what does it mean?" "A book, can you see, a book . . ." A history lesson.

I returned to Warsaw with the trunk of my car filled. The next day I had the feeling of having committed a sacrilege. As if I had saved life at the price of a transgression of intangible rules. I was afraid of touching these small fragments of *matsevah*. One evening I transferred them one after the other, piece by piece, to my basement, which I had transformed into a library. I washed them, trying not to harm them further, and then I put them on the shelves next to the books.

V

Zamutek

SZYMON PRZEDBORSKI AT THE OFFICE OF CAPITAL'S
RECONSTRUCTION, WARSAW, IN THE EARLY 1960S

SZYMON

SZYMON PRZEDBORSKI ON A BUSINESS TRIP
TO THE USSR, THE 1950S

*M*y grandfather had an unusual first name, as if made from cardboard: Szymon. I didn't know anyone else with such a first name. It seemed artificial to me. It was like a façade or armor—like a banner unfurled during the parades on the First of May.

Recently, I discovered in the archives of the Polytechnic School of Warsaw a request from Samuel Przedborski to change his first name on a diploma dating from before the war, and a certification that the current Szymon is the former Samuel.

In Łęczyca, where he was born at the end of autumn 1903,

the first and only son, his family called him by the diminutive Zamutek. His birth certificate, registered in Russian according to the Gregorian calendar, was burned at the same time as all the other documents of the Jewish community. In the only copy from before the war that was saved are written the first names of Samuel's parents: Henoch and Jachet Gitel, née Herman. At home, where Polish was exclusively spoken, the father was Henryk and the mother Justyna, or Jecia.

Zamutek was the most important man in his mother's life. She strongly believed that he would do something great. She loved accompanying him on the piano when he played the violin. She dreamed of his becoming a virtuoso, even though he was assigned to the double bass in the school orchestra, which diminished the strength of his left hand, and as a result he never played the violin the way he did before. However, he sang very well, especially passages from operas about unrequited love. She forgave him everything; she rarely became angry.

She never reproached him for eating *trefny*, nonkosher food. He was thirteen years old, several days after his bar mitzvah, when he confessed to having eaten piecrust made with lard right after the ceremonies at the synagogue. She only said, "Now, my son, you are sinning of your own will." Her words must have impressed him, because he remembered them to the end of his life, and he repeated them often.

There is only one surviving photo of him from his adolescence. He must be about seventeen, looking timid and very solemn. He is thin, with full lips, high forehead, and thick, dark hair slicked back; he is wearing round glasses. He studied Greek and Latin. He solved problems of algebra and geometry and dreamed of building bridges. He graduated from secondary school with honors. Shortly afterward he began his engineering studies at the Polytechnic School of Warsaw.

· · ·

My grandfather had elbows that were hard, dark like the skin of an antediluvian toad or like the bark of an old tree—rough. Usually he sat at the table near a very decorative cast-iron radiator, playing solitaire for hours on end. Small faded cards, formerly red and blue, with a couple of cupids, which looked really tiny passing through his hands. He was a big, powerful man. Prominently displayed on the piano was a photo of him skiing in the mountains, taken during the forties. His eyes were shining then, and his teeth white. After the war, he had found faith and love, for a short time, but I never knew him then.

Uncle Oleś remembers the day my grandfather returned from the Woldenberg camp to Saska Kępa, that January 1945. Oleś and the family called him "our brother." Tall, strong, in uniform, wearing his round glasses with metal frames, he walked into the room on the second floor of Szczuczyńska Street. In the center of the room there was a small stove, with everyone gathered around it very closely. His sister Frania broke into tears. She hadn't seen him in five years. But he remained silent.

For some time he lived with Bronka, his second sister, on Górnośląska Street. The day after he returned, he presented himself to Stanisław Tołwiński, his former chief at the Warsaw Housing Cooperative, then acting president of the city of Warsaw. He immediately was given a position overseeing the Office for the Reconstruction of the Capital, where his former colleagues from the cooperative were already working. Then he found and brought back his daughter, Halina. He moved to Koszykowa Street in a new temporary apartment he shared with another family. And that's when the great weariness from his five years in captivity became apparent. What was the use of all this, when there wasn't anyone to live for any longer?

According to Uncle Oleś, Szymon's apathy had its roots in the war, from confinement during his captivity, and the inertia of his return. Perhaps also caused by the despair of losing his wife at the last moment, when the war was almost over? Three months—he was three months short of seeing her again.

He had gone inside himself. He remained silent for hours

on end, looking at the wall with a fixed stare. Sometimes he said someone was pursuing him, tracking him down. Absent, apathetic, shattered. It seemed that he had gone through similar states before the war. But now the war had made it worse. He felt more painfully tried than the others. He didn't feel he should explain himself, nor did he have any desire to do so.

His sisters came to his aid. Frania was friends with the wife of the director of the hospital for the mentally ill in Tworki, and she asked for a consultation with a specialist. She explained that her brother had to work but that in the state he was in, he was incapable of doing anything. She observed the visit by peering through the keyhole. The doctor got up from his chair and, placing his hands flat on the desk, he reprimanded Szymon: "You faker!" he screamed. "Son of a bitch, you drive everyone crazy playing insane. Me, I am going to inform the authorities in charge. You are going to jail. Show your face here once more and I'll crack your skull open with this ashtray!"

Szymon was indignant that anyone dared treat him that way. He said absolutely nothing in response. But the next day he went to work. He turned inward more rarely. He only needed to always have a glass of milk in the refrigerator. Hard to believe, but that's what the family legend says. What is more, it put him on his feet.

On one occasion right after the war, he struck his nephew, who had drunk his glass of milk in his absence. He became worried if he did not have his two bottles with their aluminum or golden foil caps in the refrigerator. The milkman delivered them for years early in the morning, leaving them by the front door. Grandfather would wake up then and go downstairs to get his favorite newspaper. It was the *Trybuna Ludu,* the Tribune of the People, the publication of the Polish United Workers' Party. It was his party, the one with which he identified.

He spent hours on the sofa at his sisters' homes. He would return after work and lie down. He felt the life of the house running through his veins. Someone was washing up, flushing the toilet, rustling the newspaper, making tea, noisily stirring the sugar in. Someone was talking; the monotonous rhythm of the words came to him from afar. He would be stretched on his side across the sofa in the room overlooking the garden; the floor creaked, and the house was filled with fragrance. He had known this smell from Łęczyca. Łęczyca was no more, they had killed his mother and his grandmother, his aunts and his wife. Finished Łęczyca. There was nothing but the breath of his sister's house. Boiled fish, boiled noodles, fried liver. He never said "fish prepared the Jewish way" or "Jewish caviar." Chopped liver and onions with hard-boiled eggs had no origins. Like milk, so reliable, white. The milk in sky-blue cans that his mother brought him.

In his first curriculum vitae after the war he had written: "After liberation by the Soviet army in 1945, in the course of evacuation from the camp going west, I returned to my country and was immediately assigned to the first team of professionals for the reconstruction of Warsaw." He was a member of the Party.

"For the first time after six years of occupation, we celebrate May 1st as a free people," proclaimed the manifesto of the Party Central Committee in 1945. "The chains of our cruel enslavement by the Nazis have broken. The Red Army and the heroic Polish forces fighting alongside are at the gates of Berlin. In the West, the Allied armies have marched into the heart of Germany. The world under Nazi domination has perished and with it must perish the obscure forces of reactionaries and of fascism." Those were his feelings.

He marched alongside all the other demonstrators, not far from the balcony of the burned-out opera house filled with the representatives in power. Like all the others, he shouted praises for the glory of the new order and the liberators. If he wanted to live, it was to build a future with justice. The nation needed him. Belonging to the Party gave him support.

He had good and bad days. From time to time he had to relearn how to be enthusiastic; painful specters tormented him. Sometimes he didn't have the strength to fight them off. And when he turned inward, he was violent and unbearable. He didn't look for contact with people. He was incapable of having a conversation. He knew how to make himself understood and then be silent.

That's how his daughter, my mother, knew him after the war—as if behind a glass wall. When they eventually found a home for themselves, he made her the housekeeper. She was fourteen years old, she had lost her mother a year earlier, and before the Occupation she was only a child. She had no one to teach her. Take care of the house, do the cooking, peel the potatoes and vegetables, cook the chops, and fry the pancakes. He would scream at her. When her first dumplings coalesced into a gooey mass, raw in the middle, he couldn't control himself. He made her eat everything, down to the last mouthful: "You will have nothing else until you've learned, and as long as you have not learned." His "no" was categorical, and he would say it only once, leaving no doubt about it. He wouldn't tolerate any objections.

The first spring after the Liberation, the Office for the Reconstruction of the Capital was in charge of building provisional living quarters for those who were rebuilding the city. Wooden bungalows from Finland were allotted to Warsaw by the USSR and were to be built in three locations. The engineer Przedborski became director of the works for the Górny Ujazdów sector. All around was rubble and misery. He would hire anyone who appeared, preferably with his own pick or hammer. For the loan of a tool he would give a day's wage.

In the building housing his offices, water would drip on people after rain; the roof had been pierced everywhere by exploding shells. He hired an electrician who knew how to work sheet metal; he had formerly been a volunteer who had gone to clear Ujazdowskie Avenue of rubble. The electrician recalled the director of the works and the first bungalows from Finland, which they had finished off with a roof of tar paper at the end of April 1945.

One afternoon, a group of workers organized a meeting in

front of the shed used as the canteen. One of them broke open a loaf of bread to show that the inside was moldy. He called my grandfather—the enemy of the workers. He screamed, "Down with the director!" and "Down with the enemies of the working class!" He launched into an enraged, vicious diatribe against Przedborski and his like, who fed them, the workers, with watery soup while they feasted. "Down with Przedborski! Throw him out. He does nothing for us!" he concluded.

He went out in front of his management team. He explained to them that he was conscious of their problems, he went around and he could see for himself that there were problems with the food and the transportation. The bread was moldy because it was wet. Because the roof leaked. But these were temporary problems. "We deplore the lot of the workers dedicated to the reconstruction of the people's Poland. We are with you."

This time he succeeded. They dispersed, perhaps not convinced, but somewhat mollified. My grandfather more than once had to confront the fury of the workers. At home he called them, according to the terminology of the times, "enemy elements who sow trouble."

He was absorbed by the meetings, the visits on location, deadlines. Checking the work in progress, and the failures. The Office for the Reconstruction of the Capital and the Ministry for Reconstruction wanted to see a spacious Warsaw filled with parks and green spaces, with wide avenues bursting with the life of the sciences, culture, and education. He had been deeply moved by the blueprints of the future subway, and the escalators for the stations going in the east–west direction, the opening of the tenth movie theater, the inauguration of a library at the Karol Świerczewski factory in the Wola neighborhood.

Samuel, or Zamutek, had metamorphosed after the war into a Szymon no one had ever heard of in Łęczyca. He wasn't an exception; he did what the others did. In postwar Poland, the majority of the assimilated Jewish intelligentsia took Polish first and last names. The official decrees of 1945 made changing names easier. The law authorizing people to change names that were dishonorable or ridiculous was extended to those that did not sound Polish. People took advantage of this possibility or legally assumed the names used during the war "in order to protect oneself against the acts of violence by the German invaders." He didn't want to be identified with Moses or Baruch, because he didn't want to have to defend himself again, or awaken unwelcome interest. It was better not to stand out, not to be different, and not provoke by being unique.

The Rozenbergs and the Goldbergs became, without any regret, Lipińskis or Sokołowskis. The name of my grandfather ended with "ski," like many Polish names, and presented no problems; by contrast his first name smelled of the Talmud from a distance.

The militant Jews of the Party, the Jews holding positions, the high officials of the state, those could become subject to all sorts of pressures. The others, certainly the majority, had no doubt understood by themselves that they had to conform like everyone else around them. The Abrahams, the Moseses, the Szyjas were metamorphosed into Adamses, Mieczysławs, and Stanisławs. Under the heading "Nationality" they wrote "Polish." The Communists of Jewish origins became all the more Polish because they were less Jewish in their convictions.

Samuel, the Jewish first name of my grandfather registered in his birth certificate that no longer exists, remained on his graduation diploma and in his military documents from before the war. He used it at school in Łęczyca and in Łódź and in 1920 when he volunteered to fight in the Polish-Bolshevik War. That's how he signed himself for six years at the Polytechnic School, and the school for officer candidates in Zambrów, from which he graduated two years after having obtained the degree of civil engineer. He belonged to the Mutual Aid Association of Jewish students of the Polytechnic School of Warsaw. It was Samuel Przedborski, second lieutenant of the 48th Regiment Mountain Light Infantry, who defended Warsaw in 1939, and it was Samuel who was made a prisoner. He spent the whole war with this first name.

Everywhere then, his parents also had Jewish first names. This is perhaps what hurts me the most, the transformation of their genealogy and the past through silence.

On July 4, 1946, in Kielce, thirty-seven Jews perished at the hands of the Poles.

He could not have been unafraid. He could dismiss this information and similar facts, but he could not have been unaware of the situation. They had executed those Jews identified by the newly installed Communist regime, those Jews who allegedly committed ritual murders, but also those Jews who returned to their homes now occupied by new owners.

My grandfather never entertained the thought of leaving Poland. He really believed that the new regime had resolved once and for all the question of national identity. He was convinced that the choice he had made was the right one and remained of that opinion to the end.

In late summer in 1946 he went to be registered in the files of the Central Jewish Committee. Of course he registered himself as Szymon Przedborski, son of Henryk and Justyna, née Herman, but he was registering in a Jewish organization, for the first and last time since the war. Those who registered themselves there were those who had survived.

The birth certificate issued two years later as a result of the approval of the municipal court of Łęczyca contained these same facts, and he used them in all his documents.

Documents reveal no feelings. In the military questionnaire after the war, Szymon's father always bore the name Henryk. He was, according to circumstances, a small businessman, self-employed, the director of a printing press; he did not possess a fortune. As for his mother, Szymon left her only her Polish first name, Justyna; he never added her maiden name. He silenced it the way he silenced his whole past in Łęczyca. And also Dela, the mother of his daughter. The order of the president of the cabinet had authorized these changes also concerning the late parents and the maiden name of the mother when these changes had been motivated by important reasons and special circumstances.

Why am I fretting? It's only statistics. It's all about statistics, because there is no room here for anything other than information! But information can also be useful. What is it that I want: the description of a wagon for Treblinka, a cry, or tears, the sound of instruments in the house on Przedrynek, or the story of the fortunes of the Hermans, the wine-and-spirits warehouse? These are only headings, they have to be amplified, the bricks arranged so that they hold up. It's not about palaces or pleasure parks; this is not a student essay. Nor a lamentation. Facts, irrefutable facts, facts that are grounded.

. . .

He was awarded his first decoration, the Gold Cross of Merit, on July 22, 1948. He felt important—he was one of the directors of the Office for the Reconstruction of the Capital. Then he was involved with one of the employees in the office, Marysia Widawska.

She was originally from the borderlands and made herself appealing. She was warm, open. She was talkative, with the soft, singsong accent of the borderlands area, quick in conversation, in giving help, in bringing cheer. To the life of my grandfather, which was all work and silence, she brought some colorful effervescence. She was good-looking, with beautiful blond hair, a fine figure, and long legs.

They went on vacation together: Szymon and little Halina, with Marysia and her two children. The five of them enjoyed being together. My mother received presents from Marysia: dresses, priceless at that time, which came from packages from abroad, and nylon stockings. But most important of all, she found refuge in her. There are numerous happy photos from this period taken in mountain lodges, in the fields. Mother still speaks of Marysia with great tenderness. Then suddenly, after long years of silence, Marysia's husband, who had been considered missing, reappeared. He had returned from England to find his wife. Was that what caused the breakup with Szymon, or was there something else? I do not know. Nobody really knows. It seems that Marysia, weeping, would confide in Bronka and Frania, Szymon's sisters.

In Mother's album there is a photo of Marysia with her leg on a chair to adjust a garter. Years later, when a tumor developed on her thigh at that place, she laughed, saying that the photo caused it. She suffered courageously.

Her husband died soon after his return, but Szymon felt hurt. I would have preferred his suffering because of her absence, and I would have liked him to have tried returning to her. He would have healed his wounds in her warmth and regained his strength, and little Halina would have had someone with whom she could have cried and laughed. But it was not to be. My grandfather again slammed the door shut, holed up, and withdrew into himself. In the most ordinary way in the world, near the elevator of his new apartment on Puławska Street, which had all the modern appliances and a housekeeper, he became acquainted with a neighbor on his floor.

It could also be, as Szymon's brothers-in-law claim, that he met Żena at a Party meeting. There was, in fact, something of that atmosphere in their relationship. They both had important positions, they were involved in building a new order, they believed in the renewal of the nation by socialism on the Soviet model. They seem to have created for each other two solitary lives after their working hours.

Only later would it come out that he already knew her from his work. At the National Council of the Capital, which served as municipal headquarters at the time, she supervised the building of schools, which were his responsibility as one of the directors in charge of construction. At that time he couldn't avoid all the telephone calls from his comrades pressing him to repair the problems in their apartments. He didn't have a large enough team of workers; he had to improvise at the expense of the schools. That's when she intervened. With her complaints she was always on the telephone to the District Committee, and sometimes even to the Central Committee. She went after him. Years later they would laugh about it.

They met in September, and their marriage took place on December 29, 1949. She was already considered an old maid; she was in her thirties. The marriage was officiated by the mayor of Warsaw, a friend of the bride from before the war, in his office. Their families were not invited.

My grandfather was forty-six years old at the time. Theoretically they were well matched, by their work, their social positions, their taste for music and the mountains. She knew what was what and how things should be. And how they should turn out. What to say to whom, how to behave. In this system she felt important. He did also. She made a home with her Biedermeier furniture, her suits like those of a prewar governess, her piano and her sour faces. Halina had just turned eighteen. From the very beginning they never got along.

· · ·

They often told the following story. I remember it myself. Szymon was in the habit of visiting his sisters during the vacations. Every winter the younger, Frania, went to Zakopane with her husband and children. This time he came to introduce his new wife to them, and Żena greeted them with these words, "I always dreamed of avoiding having to meet families." Uncle Oleś gave proof of his ready wit by answering that this was perfect, because he dreamed of exactly the same thing. The others, however, lacked his sense of humor.

Frania could never forgive Żena. Also, it was in relation to her brother, her beloved brother who deserved something from life. But he never complained. Only, perhaps he visited them more often after his marriage. Szczuczyńska Street and Górnośląska Street offered what he did not have at home. He was used to his little naps on their sofas in the afternoon. He explained to Żena that he was tired and needed a little rest. She was not happy. He hid some of his visits from her.

Szymon loved Frania's sons, and they were mad about visits from their tall uncle. He brought them original gifts: a real military helmet or a revolver. He gave them piggyback rides and lifted them to the top of the armoire, which enabled them to jump down on the sofa. The downstairs neighbor came to complain that her chandelier was shaking, but he never paid attention. I don't know if Żena loved Szymon. I don't know if the fact that he was Jewish had the least significance for her. She insists that she was unaware that he ever had another first name. The change had to have been made before she made his acquaintance, or else she is lying. Oleś suggested that it was she who insisted on the change.

Żena came from a working-class family of Warsaw loyal to the tradition of the PPS, the Polish Socialist Party. Her father was a streetcar driver. He brought up three daughters. All three joined the Underground during the war. Żena had gone into the ghetto several times. One day she had brought a little Jewish girl back home because they couldn't find a hiding place for her. Żena's mother, a devout Catholic, had gone to confession and revealed this fact. The priest told her that she had lost her soul and risked eternal damnation. She walked out of the confessional booth without receiving absolution. Żena's boyfriend joined the Warsaw Uprising and never returned.

Żena completed her studies in philosophy before the war. She had not missed one of the seminars given by Professors Tatarkiewicz and Kotarbiński.* After the war she put her faith in Marxist ideology. First she worked in the education department of the National Council of the Capital, which was really the city hall in those days, then in the offices of the cabinet ministers, dealing with cultural affairs. She spent the next few years at Polish Radio, in the department concerned with education. Under the heading "Profession" on a questionnaire, she wrote "white-collar worker."

Żena was not easy, but Szymon wasn't, either. I didn't realize

---

* Władysław Tatarkiewicz (1886–1980): philosopher, historian of philosophy and art, and member of the Polish Academy of Science. Tadeusz Kotarbiński (1886–1981): philosopher and logician, member of the Polish Academy of Science.

it then. I felt sorry for him, not her. He seemed to me bitter, so different from his sisters, Bronka and Frania. My mother repeats to this day that she chanced upon a real wicked stepmother from the fairy tales. But at the time she did not complain. Her father was just as severe.

Szymon shared the political opinions of his wife. They celebrated July 22,* took part in the May Day parades, each with his or her own organization at the heart of the Party. They booed those responsible for illicit profiteering, the lazy ones, the imperialists. They gratefully acclaimed the buildings of Nowa Huta. They were enthusiastic about the meetings of the workers of the Ursus factory. They lived for the films devoted to Lenin and to General Karol Świerczewski. By mutual consent they avoided films from the West. They were both interested in the blueprints of a skyscraper that the Soviets had proposed building "in the name of friendship." For the one and the other, this friendship was the guarantee of peace and security. They discussed the performances by the Mazowsze folk-dance ensemble in Moscow and Peking.

They never missed the Friday concerts by the Philharmonic, which remained one of their most regular habits. They permitted themselves an extravagant treat sometimes, such as a plane trip to Poznań to see *Boris Godunov* at the opera. They went to Gdańsk by train to visit the restoration of the Old Town.

In their mountain lodge in Kalatówki, Szymon's second wife decided one day to convince her brother-in-law Oleś of the superiority of the new regime over the oppressive *sanacja,* or "moral cleansing," of the prewar government. Oleś, an entrepreneur, had been very prosperous before the war, and during the Occupation had served in the information division of the AK. He remained silent for a long time listening to her arguments, after which he asked her if she did not understand

---

* Date of the ratification, in 1952, of the constitution of the People's Republic of Poland, which would remain a national holiday until the fall of the Communist regime.

that the locomotive pulling her carriage was headed toward the abyss.

No, Żena did not turn Oleś in to the officials of the Security Office. She did not do it, even though she threatened him with it.

My grandfather loved uniforms.

He was seventeen when he volunteered during the Polish-Bolshevik War. He served three months in the army.

He came out of officer candidate school, where he had made "good enough progress." He was regularly called upon for military exercise in the infantry regiment in Zambrów, in Stanisławów, in Kutno. He took part in the campaign of September 1939 with the anti-aircraft defense of the Praga district. That's where he was captured and taken prisoner. He was neither wounded nor sick. The fact that he was an officer saved his life.

Second Lieutenant Przedborski completed his reserve duty in 1948. Despite more than a decade of service and a sound professional preparation, the regional commission overseeing the Polish army judged his military experience "weak." His moral aptitude was invariably considered "loyal."

He had a sense of duty and of responsibility. From his office often came outbursts of shouting. He wanted to build, to serve. Raise the level of productivity, increase production. It was not about his career. He really believed that communism was only just, and that it was necessary to introduce it, even by force. He watched, he verified, he controlled. He did not trust anyone. He telephoned construction sites several times a day and gave instructions by raising his voice. He was irritated that they didn't give their all. It seems that one of his fellow students from the Polytechnic School urged Szymon to start working for Security. Szymon consulted his wife. She told me how she categorically forbade it, how she threatened to leave him then and there if he did such a thing. Did he listen to her or was he afraid of her? In this couple she was literally in the driver's seat. She had bought a gray Wartburg from the transport pool of the office of the Council of Ministers during Szymon's absence. Once, under her very eyes, he had wrecked a Škoda from the office pool, braking too late at a red light and crashing into the trunk of a car. She never again allowed him to take the driver's seat.

He refrained from going to China under contract for several years, even though he really wanted to, because she threatened to divorce him.

They tried to outdo one another telling Jewish stories, apparently only because it made them laugh. She used to say to him jokingly, "What you have that's Jewish, it's not your brains."

He had a sense of humor, and I believe that saved both of them. She had wanted a divorce six months after their marriage. "After six months? Wait at least a year, otherwise what will my colleagues say about me!" He called an admirer of hers "prickly" because he sent her roses, and he always made her take his telephone calls. He played bridge without her. She would give him money to cover his losses and enough so he could bring flowers to his hostess. She then discussed the propedeutic study of philosophy, or the themes borrowed from Tatras folklore in the musical works of Karol Szymanowski, with the only friend she had.

Often he made her angry. He locked her puppy in the bathroom so he wouldn't soil the house; he bought herring, which he loved, although she was allergic to the smell; he had let the teakettle burn; the pigeons were making a mess with their nest on the balcony. She repeated to herself—and repeated to him—words she had heard from someone years earlier: "My dear lady, don't fret about it—a husband is not such a close relative."

He yearned for the home he had lost, a home he had not been able to re-create in that Stalinesque building on the corner of Madaliński and Puławska Streets, even though he had built it himself after the war, over the ruins. He never went looking for old places, he never returned to the real Łęczyca, he didn't go to see Przedrynek. He had shut those doors and thrown away the keys. He refused to give voice to the past; he was protecting himself from it. But he turned to his sisters the way you return to a mother. The taste of the dishes in the home, which he never called by their name—tzimmes or gefilte fish—gave him a momentary feeling of security.

I didn't like going to the apartment on Puławska Street. As far back as I can remember, Żena greeted me with remarks such as: "Does she really *have* to run?" or "Who ever saw such a hairstyle?" or else "There was nothing more horrible left in the shop?" Grandfather remained silent. Often he visited us. Now I think it was an opportunity to escape. He liked to walk. He didn't need a destination; any pretext was good, just to have peace.

He saved writing paper for fear of running out of it, ballpoint pens and pencils, stylographs and drawing pencils, both hard and soft lead. He enjoyed doing crossword puzzles and drawing up petitions. Lined paper, steady handwriting, neat. The *S* starts low on the left, rises boldly to make a little loop, and comes back down slightly inclined, recalling an *L*. That's for the given name. The *P* of his last name starts with a whorl caught inside a half circle like the inside of a shell, or a helmet hiding thick hair. He sometimes helped me sign my notebooks.

He repeated Chopin's saying that music was song. He liked being photographed with high government officials at dedications, which were more and more numerous, of new monuments, new buildings, new housing complexes. He saved the invitation and program for the ceremony marking the donation to the city of Warsaw of the Palace of Culture and Science dedicated to Joseph Stalin. And he repeated numerous times that for that building they had used fifty million bricks, which placed end to end would cover the distance from Warsaw to Vladivostok.

My grandfather was impatient. I was seated at the piano, my legs swinging high above the floor, my small hands stretching to reach an octave on the keyboard. Do, re, mi, fa, sol . . .

"No, no, no!" he started shouting, more and more loudly.

"Try again, don't hurry, listen. Do, ti, la, sol, fa, mi, re, do." He jumped up from his chair and slammed the black cover down over the keys. I was afraid he would cut off my fingers. He left the room without saying a word to me. I remained seated with my hands hidden behind my back.

Żena insists that Szymon's origins had no influence on their life, or their milieu, or their circle. They never experienced any signs of hostility. What's more, she insists that she never heard the qualifier "Jewish" before 1968. Until then, her best friend, the person she was no doubt the closest to besides her sisters, did not know that Szymon had Jewish ancestors.

Then, in that memorable year, he was forced to retire and was driven out of the Party. He was sixty-four years old, and he was as helpless as a child. He couldn't understand what was happening and why he had suddenly stopped being a person of importance or deserving of respect. They stopped acknowledging his presence or soliciting his goodwill. It seemed to him that everyone had turned against him. Those with whom he had worked, built, raised buildings, housing complexes; planned the traffic patterns. His friends, if he even had friends, or his acquaintances—from bridge games, walks in Łazienki Park, personal invitations to the tribunes. His neighbors—who else, if not them?—smeared his front doorknob with feces, left papers under his doormat advising him to run to Israel. His wife would answer the phone to hear: "Still here? When are you off to Palestine?"

"They don't want me here?" Żena said that his first reaction was to go to Israel. He was hurt. But Żena explained to him that it was nonsense. She believed that he wasn't made for conflict or for fighting. He needed a positive environment; besides, he was not in any shape to start all over again.

Uncle Oleś strongly doubts that Szymon had ever seriously considered leaving. He was sure that Żena would have removed that idea from his head. My grandfather never spoke of it. But when his elder sister, Bronka, finally left, he suffered a great deal. He considered it a betrayal. In those days you left for always. He felt hurt and so painfully offended that he never spoke of her again.

His depression returned. He still went downstairs in the morning to get the newspaper and rolls, but on his return he would lie down on the sofa and spend the day there. He would lie on his side facing the wall. I didn't know about it then, but his wife, coldly, had even thought of leaving him. His despair, which she decided to share with him, kept her with him. When he understood that his situation would never reverse itself, in 1970 he joined the PTTK, the Polish Tourist and Sightseeing Society, and started going on excursions. His wife tells me that she pushed him into it. She was already a hiker before the war. At first he protested; he was ashamed. Eventually he became accustomed to it and made new acquaintances, left Żena at home, and went off with them.

I used to cast an indulgent glance at his colored maps, his outings, the PTTK, the backpacks, the canteens, his walking shoes with special soles, and the camping gear.

He would leave in the morning with a group of hikers and return in the evening. Or else he would leave for a longer time.

He always seemed defeated and weakened. With time these excursions of several hours had put color in his face, making him look healthy.

When I sit down at his desk today, more than ten years after his death, I find in the first drawer the tin drinking cup and spoon from Woldenberg.

Underneath are several medical notes with descriptions of his consecutive illnesses in the camp and application forms to the ZboWiD, the organization for war veterans, to have them recognize his time in captivity as war injury deserving of compensation.

The small desk of an office worker. But it has also totally succumbed to time.

It seems that he continued to have faith in the ideals of his youth. In the middle of the eighties, sometime before the ulti-mate defeat of the old regime was proclaimed, he lay down for the third time. A student came to wash him and take him to the toilet. Eventually my grandfather refused to get up. He folded in upon himself, and he waved his arms like oars. He talked about the ghetto, where he had never been, of cellars where he had not hidden himself, of a brick that could fall on his head at any second. His hair and his nails grew. He wouldn't allow anyone to cut them. He wanted nothing. He expected nothing.

Nothing hurt him and everything hurt him. He became irritated when anyone tried to lessen his suffering.

I was at his side when the news of Bronka's death reached us from America. He was lying on his side, with his back to me. He wept. He couldn't calm down, and he didn't want to. I didn't know how to help him. I was not mature enough. I fled.

He stayed lying down this way for several years. He said he wanted to die just like his mother, taken from Umschlagplatz to Treblinka. In filth and degradation. Like his beloved mother.

Żena stayed with him to the end. When he lay down and refused to get up, when he no longer washed himself, and he moaned. When he had refused himself the right to live. She promised not to send him to the hospital. She had promised that she would let him stay at home.

She never put Szymon in the hospital, although she could neither lift him nor stand the smell, which during the months he was laid up in bed penetrated everywhere, the upholstery and the curtains, the furniture, and the books. In her own body. She washed his trousers, with powders, with liquids; she soaked them, she scrubbed them, hung them on the radiators, where they stuck together on drying. There wasn't enough room. Afterward she scrubbed her hands until they hurt. The pestilence persisted, it clung to her face and her dresses, even when she went out, when she fled to the park, toward music, anywhere. It never disappeared, imperceptibly grew fainter, but it was always with her.

His grave is in the civilian cemetery of Warsaw and is indistinguishable from the other similar concrete tombs. Instead of

the formula "In Happy Memory" they engraved MGR. INZ.—
ENGINEERING DIPLOMA CERTIFIED. On it is his Polish first
name, Szymon, by which he was unknown in Łęczyca. But
there's a stone from over there, even though he would never
have said aloud that he was Jewish.

WOLDENBERG

MY GRANDFATHER, SZYMON PRZEDBORSKI,
PRISONER NUMBER 49178/IVA, 1940

*P*rzedborski, Samuel. 49178/IVA. Leutnant, Hohnstein,
Saxe." Name, serial number, rank, and the name of
the camp to which he was transported after the fall
of Warsaw. And a little further on: "Oflag IVB–Königstein . . .
Oflag IIB–Arnswalde . . . Stalag IIB–Hammerstein," from
which he was transferred on the 12th of September 1940 to
"Oflag IIC–Woldenberg." No other trace of the remains of
Second Lieutenant Przedborski in Oflag IIC, prisoner-of-war
camp in Pomerania, aside from several letters in gray-blue

envelopes with the imprint *Kriegsgefangenenpost,* a little steel plate with a number called a dog tag, and a tin cup and spoon, the basic equipment of a prisoner of war. No other mementos.

The first surviving postcard, the first sign that he was alive after disappearing from Warsaw, bore the postmark of Hohnstein (*Sächs. Schweiz*) with the date, January 27, 1940, and the round seal of Oflag IVA. The beige cardboard postcard, addressed to his wife, Frau D. Przedborska, 18 Krasiński Street, was filled from top to bottom in a wretched German. The sender was listed as Engineer Second Lieutenant Samuel Przedborski. He was providing hastily written news of the 27th, 29th, and 30th of December.

The most important information that he was sending concerned the security of the housing for officers in accordance with the 1929 regulations for the protection of prisoners of war. Obviously that's what Dela feared the most, and he wanted to reassure her. She still lived with their daughter in the Fourth Colony of the WSM, Warsaw Cooperative Residence, in Żoliborz at number 142.

He wrote that he needed nothing, he could buy everything, even cake, on his stipend. "Never if it would take away from you."

"Good night, my darling," he ended—"*Gute Nacht, meine Liebsten.*" He would never again be so tender. Perhaps it was easier in a foreign language. They hadn't seen each other for four months.

Everything had just begun. For the moment, despite his being a prisoner, his home was still home, and it seemed that certain rights were still in force. There was something to hang on to.

Oflag IIC Woldenberg was built by the hands of Polish war prisoners during the winter of 1939–40 and the following spring and started functioning as a prisoner-of-war camp in May 1940. According to initial numbers, more than six thousand prisoners were held there, the majority of them officers, from September 1939.

I don't know if I ever heard the name Woldenberg during my childhood and adolescence. Even when he started talking about his time as a prisoner shortly before his death, my grandfather never mentioned that name. He spoke of a German Oflag, and I was persuaded that he had spent the war in Germany. I didn't even try to imagine this place, any more than the state of mind of the young man imprisoned behind the barbed wire. He built a shell that I never tried to pierce.

When he returned from camp, no one here in Warsaw had considered him a martyr, and that had been very painful for him. What's more, someone in the family had even said, "You, you had it easy. You spent five years in a deluxe prison."

"How could they say that? How could they?" he complained to his second wife, Żena.

On the highest shelf of the glass-fronted walnut bookcase, where no one ever looked, Żena had discovered by chance a little darning mushroom made of wood. She gave it to me cautiously with these few words: "That was Szymon's working tool in Woldenberg. You don't have the right to lose it. Or to forget it." That was it.

The little mushroom doesn't look as if it ever served its function. It has a light, shiny cap, and a mysterious, subtle shape. It's hard, made of alder or ash. Linden and pear wood have a different feel. You can unscrew the stem and use it to store needles. I found neither needle nor thread inside.

For a long time I held the mushroom in my hands. I forced myself to conjure up the time and place when it accompanied my grandfather, a young officer then, a German prisoner of war.

They lacked socks. Worn or torn couldn't be discarded. They had to be mended. He had to organize everything, the mushroom and the thread, order them. He was sent a package of thread in different colors, especially strong thread, black and brown, which were the most useful, and needles with large eyes. A metal thimble, charitably offered by someone, was also useful. In time he learned to place the hole in the sock flat on the cap of the mushroom; he made a little knot, a double knot because the wool had a heavy weave, and he started from the right. From the right edge to the left, hook and back, from right to left, like the Torah: *Barukh atah Adonaï* . . . He wasn't praying, he was darning, right, left, right, left, and then from top to bottom between the threads of the weave of the material. He grumbled under his breath. He started angrily and then quieted down.

They brought them to him, clean and dirty, washed or stinking with sweat, worn, smelly. He had to take the filth of others and bring it up to his face. He did not see well with his glasses for myopia. He could bear the hunger less easily than the humiliation. They paid in cash or with food. He also accepted cigarettes, even though he didn't smoke. It was practical for trading.

I was convinced that a visit to the place required a trip to Germany. I never suspected that this Woldenberg with its menacing sound was Dobiegniew, an old fishing village at the edge of the Drawa Forest in Pomerania. They had located the camp a kilometer beyond the nearest urban buildings. But the present town is nothing like the old one. It was almost totally leveled during the war. And rebuilt in the sad shape of the socialist dream.

To its prisoners, its Slavic name, Dobiegniew, became the secret pseudonym for Woldenberg. They used it like a code, strongly believing that a promise was hidden in the name. They thought *dobiegnie my* meant in Polish "We will reach the finish line."

I stood at the entrance to the destroyed camp, almost half a century after my grandfather had crossed it for good and for the last time, and I felt that I was doing something that I should not be doing. I came here to reverse the course of forgetting. Entering a place that already did not exist beyond a closed-off past, even for my family. Perhaps without reckoning, but also impossible to contemplate. I entered the barbed-wire circle of the damned in an attempt to decipher its rusted message.

They had surrounded the camp, which covered an area of

twenty hectares (forty-nine acres) with a double fence of barbed wire two and half meters high. And they had filled the space in between the two fences with loops of barbed wire. There were eight watchtowers armed with machine guns, and this warning on the fence: *Jence woyenne stoy*—"Prisoners of war, halt." This was where the shooting started.

The barbed wire marked the limits of the world accessible to them, sharing it with the narrow daily necessities, and the unreal dream reinforced by nostalgia. The censored letters on war-rationed paper linked them to their homes and their families, to what was left of them. They were not tortured. They were not pressed into forced labor. They were simply locked up. They were fed fourteen hundred calories a day, of black bread, leek or green cabbage soup, barley coffee, and fear.

They lived behind the screen of the Geneva Conventions, as wrote a poet in the camp. Protected by the strength of international laws, always conscious, nonetheless, that they could be disregarded at any moment. Heinrich Himmler became interested in the prisoners of Oflag IIC. He was planning to strip them of their status as prisoners of war and to send them to concentration camps. Many perished by throwing themselves on the barbed wire. Others cut the wire with shears, or dug tunnels underneath for months. Any means were valid to pull them from their weakening circle. Escape or death. Sometimes, each signified the same thing.

"At Woldenberg," wrote the historian Marian Brandys, who had been interned there, "people didn't die under the heel of the SS as in Auschwitz. The treatment at Woldenberg consisted in reducing the inmates to madness."

Twenty-five barracks of unglazed red bricks, spread on either side of a central road: East Camp, West Camp. In the middle were located the canteen, bathhouses, and the administrative center. The low roofs of wooden planks or cement slabs were once covered with tar paper. The double doors in their frames were thrown open with a certain violence; the little dormer windows, once closed for the night with shutters, now formed small shattered openings. The wooden watchtowers evoked the dream of German power; the remains of an inscription in gothic letters above the entrance attempted to bear witness to a past, but this battlefield has disappeared from the memory of history, for the defeated as well as the victorious.

After the war, on the grounds of this biggest of the German prisoner-of-war camps for Polish officers, they built a model pig farm. Its first manager was a former prisoner, a commander. Today buried under cement, half wrecked and half pillaged, these barracks and the pig troughs seem to baffle history.

This place is broken up by the hands of time. With its inflexible law, life has overrun the past, has dominated it, stifled it beneath the weeds. In Dobiegniew, unemployment rules: "The most difficult thing is finding a job, anything at all. Even stealing is out, my dear lady, there's nothing left," said a town official. The door and window frames have been ripped from the majority of the buildings that formerly sheltered Polish prisoners of war, "the flower of Poland's intelligentsia, madam." When they started stealing the beams, the roofs began to fall in. They ripped out the main doors for the bricks. They had no scruples; they dragged them off, like their own possessions, and continue to take them. Despite the pigs and all the chemical products, the brick is still solid. The inhabitants remember the pig farm warmly; they could make a living from their work. They raised fourteen thousand pigs. It was clean work, no butchering, only fattening them; one tinned ham out of five shipped to the West came from their pigs.

The mayor of Dobiegniew proposed leaving only one building of the camp standing, the one in which is located the little museum dedicated to Woldenberg, and to demolish the rest to start an agricultural project.

What good is this piece of land that doesn't belong to anyone, this piece of memory in ruins? This place is of no use to anyone and thus has no reason for being. I walk carefully between the barracks, outside and inside, I pass by the pig troughs and the paths of the prisoners of war. I walk so that I will remember.

The first trees—birches and ash trees—were planted here in the spring of 1941. The poplars must be more recent, although they have grown very tall. I locate barrack number 12A. This was his barrack. There's nothing to differentiate it from the others. Empty, it seems spacious. By the entrance were the latrines, which they could use only at night. Farther in was where they lived, that is, their bunks. Bunks with three beds, a scaffolding of beds wedged one next to the other. A hundred to a hundred and fifty, a company, on one side. I make myself measure the barrack because I know he certainly did; I know his obstinate obsession with minutiae. Sixty meters by ten. That means there were three hundred people on a surface of six hundred square meters. There was no way of moving without disturbing your neighbor. Plus their belongings—suitcases and bags, backpacks and boxes—plus, in the corners, benches and tables. And a tile stove. Plus the cigarette smoke. The uninterrupted sound of voices. The constant presence of others. They never stopped being there, even at night. Even in their dreams.

I step out with a sense of relief.

He was sent to three successive Oflags before arriving at Woldenberg: at Hohnstein, Königstein, and Arnswalde. As a consequence of the registration process of Polish war prisoners subject to the racist laws of Nuremberg, he had been transferred to a transit camp with other officers of Jewish origin, Stalag IIB in Hammerstein (today, Czarne), where according to the Germans they were all going to be set free. Effectively they prepared transport for them toward the ghettos planned in the countryside, or toward concentration camps. It's not known why this plan by the Nazis was abandoned at the last moment. After several months these prisoners were sent back to their original camps or, like him, to Woldenberg. In September 1940 a group of eighty-six Polish officers of Jewish origin, prisoners of war, found themselves in Oflag IIC. They were placed in barrack 12A, henceforth called the "Jewish barrack" in the vocabulary of the camp. Jews were forbidden to enter the other barracks.

The mood of hopelessness after the downfall of France, the end of all hope of a rapid end to the war. Increasingly bad news came from the country. Despair. The first case of madness and suicide. That's when the idea came to form a theater group. He had to know, like the others knew, that the war would last; they had to try, then and there, to organize themselves one way or another. Create a structure that would help them to hold on, do something constructive. To improvise and not let oneself fall into a sense of defeat.

Of the six thousand or seven thousand prisoners of war in Woldenberg, 90 percent were young officers, more than half of whom were second lieutenants. The majority were reservists—teachers, scientists, writers, engineers, politicians, actors. In Oflag IIC there were a captured general and three hundred superior officers. There were university professors, a former prime minister of the Republic, real-estate magnates, and small farmers. The average age of these prisoners of war was estimated at thirty-seven, which meant that 70 percent were under forty. They were all still in good condition and skilled. The fact that they knew their captivity would last for years increased the necessity to do something.

He was in his berth—I can't decide if it's the upper or the lower one—a dim light, penetrating cold, a pervasive rotten odor. He no longer knew where it came from: dirty feet, sweat, chapped skin, cracked, raw, or else the humid walls, rotten bedding stuffed with straw or shredded paper. You could hope to bathe once a month.

In time each of them had two blankets. There were no sheets. Some had received pillows and blankets from home. They built little cases and hangers and stools out of materials stolen from the Germans. Twilight reigned despite six 25-watt bulbs that remained on for half the day. Spiritualist séances multiplied.

It was cold. There were maggots, not only fleas and lice. The disinfectant did nothing. They disinfected with cresol, which was called the "holiday for fleas." They couldn't resign themselves to the fact that they were defeated. It was as unbearable as the hunger, the uncertainty of what would come next for them and for their families out there.

He kept everything to himself, the vermin, the filth, the lack of water in the faucets, the mattress smelling fusty and damp. The stifling rottenness. Hunger. The painful hunger of the first two years.

He waited for packages and he feared for the packages— that they wouldn't arrive, that the noodles would be reduced to crumbs, that they would contain nothing sweet. How could they contain anything sweet when his wife hadn't seen any chocolate since the outbreak of war? Other people received packages containing sugar, sausages, canned meat, and dried fruits. He waited a long time, and he wondered. Only later did packages from America start to arrive. The most important things they contained were margarine and Nescafé coffee, which soon became the most precious currency of the camp.

The norm was two packages a month, which they received with labels of authorization. Only packages with this label were given over to the person listed as the receiver. The aid packages and gifts were shared by everybody. Sometimes they held up the delivery of packages, and the food would spoil and rot. Something would be spoiled when in faraway Warsaw they had deprived themselves of it in order to send it. The beans arrived mixed with the sugar, the tobacco with the oatmeal, the spools of thread split in half, and the noodles all crushed.

In the middle of each barrack was a little stove. On it they prepared the food received in the packages. They also could use a cleverly devised heater: the *kręciołka* of Woldenberg, made up of a compartment for coal and a mechanical blower attached to a pipe, was ingeniously built of sheet iron, plywood, and old shoelaces. It was used to make the coffee, heat the soup, prepare the spinach and the hulled barley. It was truly a life-saving invention, because thanks to it, in matters concerning their housekeeping the prisoners were independent of the Germans. You couldn't imagine camp life without it.

The smell of other people's food irritated him.

The clothing storehouse of the camp outfitted them according to Hitler's conquests. It provided the most visible proof of the power of the Wehrmacht. I don't know with what outfit they disguised Second Lieutenant Przedborski. He could have worn the dark green shirts of the Norwegian mountain troops, or else the navy-blue uniform of the Danish police, but these had a red collar. The least demanding were the khaki shirts of the Dutch Customs officers. The trench coats of the Belgian Royal Guards were more suitable for parades. A little later they brought out the uniforms of the French army. A whole range of blues came from Verdun, and the olive green in which Paris was surrendered.

People chose clothing according to their size, and it was difficult to find big and tall sizes. Then, these incongruously disguised figures scattered throughout the camp. Officers out of a circus. They broke out laughing when they first saw themselves, and then they stopped paying attention. The most important thing was to keep warm.

The first inspection of Oflag IIC Woldenberg by a delegation from the International Red Cross of Geneva took place on October 23, 1941. According to the report, the camp appeared to be "very pleasant" and the barracks seemed "particularly clean and well maintained." There was enough clothing, but there was an urgent need for blankets. Two hundred persons daily had access to a shower.

The camp was divided into two sections: eastern and western. Each section had its own library, composed of five thousand volumes, humanities and the sciences. The majority were in Polish, with a small section in English, French, and Russian. A well-organized university with separate classrooms. A large number of prisoners participated in the theater.

They needed a ball to play kickball. The conclusion was that the Woldenberg camp "revealed nothing out of the ordinary." It was deemed "average"; they thought that the morale of the Polish war prisoners was particularly high.

He was lying on the bed. It was easier that way. That way he could isolate himself from the others. That's how he manifested his refusal of that reality, the fact that he was a prisoner of war inferior to the others. He felt it since the beginning, and he had felt it painfully. He was learning again the word "discrimination"; he tasted the sound and the meaning. Once again this bitter taste in his mouth.

Had he pledged an allegiance different from the others? What was the difference? The pledge was adapted for the different religions. All, except for the freethinkers, began in the same way: "I pledge before God . . ." After that began the differences. The Christians said, "I pledge before God almighty, one in the Trinity . . ." The followers of Judaism said simply "God the almighty." The Moslems called their God "unique." But after that they all said the same thing: ". . . to be faithful to my homeland, the Republic of Poland . . ." They had repeated and once again would repeat: "my country, Poland . . . never to abandon the flag, to maintain the honor of the Polish soldier, to obey the laws and the Chief of State, to faithfully execute the orders of my chiefs and my superiors, to preserve military secrets and fight to my last breath for the cause of my country, and in general to conduct myself in such a way that I can live and die like a true Polish soldier."

Sometimes before the war, for his grandmother's sake, he would attend the synagogue for the holidays, never by himself, and always out of necessity. His father did the same thing, exclusively to oblige his mother-in-law. As for his mother, she lived on good terms with her God. Her God had never suffered on the cross. He was from another stock—another, really? His grandmother Salomea, née Herman, claimed that she was a Cohen, from the priesthood. At times he feared God. Sometimes he prayed for his mother, worried about her health; he would suddenly awaken in the middle of the night afraid that she might die, would abandon him.

Where was his mother now? He was lying down here, rotting away, stretched out, and thinking, where was she? The last address that she sent was in Lesznos, in the Jewish quarter.

The Jews are together in Warsaw, and she went to her family and they are all together in the same apartment. And other Jews, their neighbors, are nearby. Together, nothing bad can happen. The Germans gave the world Beethoven and Handel. Dela teaches children, as she did in Łęczyca, and they dine together. Her mother combs her long hair, and she braids it for the night. And in the morning, as usual, she combs it and puts it up in rollers or a chignon. But how were they locked up, how can one be locked up with a section of the city, its streets, its boutiques, its inner courtyards, its bakeries, and shoemakers' workshops? Where does the wall pass in the middle of the street, along the houses, how was the wall built, of bricks? A wall for the Jews, against the Jews, a wall.

"Mobilized with the third reserve in September 1939 with the rank of second lieutenant," wrote Samuel Przedborski in his military form after the war. "I participated in the fighting as a deputy to the commander of the aerial defense of the Praga neighborhood, with the Thirty-sixth Infantry Regiment of the University Legion. After the fall of Warsaw I was taken prisoner by the Germans."

Of the five hundred thousand Polish soldiers taken as prisoners of war in September 1939, 10 percent were officers of Jewish origin. The segregation within a national group of soldiers from the same army designated for special treatment was contrary to article 4 of the Geneva Conventions. Despite this, the Germans had recourse to it all during the war. The origins of Jewish ghettos in camps for prisoners of war remains obscure.

I can picture him lying down, heavy, immobile, gigantic. His black hair shaved, to reveal the crown of his skull. Shaving every day was not required, or daily washing. The way he appeared could be frightening. That's how I remember him almost half a century later: in striped pajamas lying down the same way, he was silent in the same way.

They had time on their hands. Four hours to kill before lunch and as much afterward. They lacked vitamins and razor blades, paper and shoe polish.

He was stretched out on his bunk or else he was darning. Others took courses, read books, played checkers and card games, prepared artistic programs, participated in sports clubs, wrote letters, carved ram's horns, played the accordion, weeded the vegetable beds, or socialized without caring about what it signified. There were more than twenty thousand books at his disposal in the camp library, and more arrived all the time. He had the time, but he could not make himself read. He envied those who read.

In the winter, the barracks were closed at 5:30; in the summer a little later. Twice a year only, for Christmas Day and the New Year, they could stay out in the open air until dark. Once the door was locked, life followed its course. You could learn what was really happening in the world. There was a camp paper published by the prisoners and a little clandestine gazette. People talked, they told stories: words, words, words, endless words.

A Lieutenant B. from the cavalry barrack had stolen a twenty-gram portion from the margarine on the shelf of a colleague. He had eaten it. An honor-code tribunal banished him from the Officer Corps. After his third appeal and his third condemnation, he slit his throat with a razor. He was buried with honors.

In barrack 15A, housing the officers of aristocratic birth, they planned a Christmas reception with invitations in French and conversation obligatory in that language. They maintained the rituals still honored at the residence of the elites in Łańcut.

In the Second Battalion, they had organized a booth to sell boiling water for making coffee or tea.

For a second time an illegal distillery was confiscated within the perimeter of the camp. The price of a liter of bad vodka reached one hundred deutschmarks. They made the alcohol with sugar, but they also tried to use marmalade taken from the Germans.

In their barrack there was a second lieutenant, Stefan Askanas, who was full of ideas. He had started a private bathing establishment. For two lagermarks, the camp currency, a customer could take a hot bath at any time in the afternoon, every day except holidays. Numerous were the volunteers who wanted to fetch water from the well, despite possible punishment. Finding wood or coal briquettes was more difficult.

He wanted few things and he got used to everything. Everything except the fact that they had decided on his racial origins and they had housed him in a barrack that was marked—so what if it was only metaphorically so?—with the Star of David. He felt stigmatized.

He held himself apart from everyone even though before the war he would most assuredly have wanted to be on friendly terms with a number of his bunkmates in barrack 12A. The majority of them were assimilated intellectuals, sons of newly converted families whom Hitler reminded of their origin. They had been Polish for generations, profoundly rooted in Polish culture. They showed their liberal opinions as much as their ties to Poland, and even with the Church.

Second Lieutenant Natanson was a physician. The Natansons were always considered Jewish elite, even though they had been baptized for generations. Lutek Cohn belonged to the Deuxième Internationale; Stein, a psychiatrist, studied Spinoza and Kant; the philosopher Walfisz studied aesthetics. A few engineers he knew from Polytechnic School; one or two lawyers and economists he remembered from prewar Warsaw.

Along with them, under the same sign and in the same space, they had placed Jews from little hamlets who were attached to their religion and the language of their ancestors, who considered Poland as a diaspora of exile, a way station on their road. They kept kosher in the world of Moses's commandments. It was their synagogues that were being burned throughout Europe. They smelled of garlic, even to him.

Those who were marginalized from the army by the Nuremberg Laws were strangers to one another, without anything in common. They were marked by their attitude toward the world and their place in the social hierarchy. They were marked by their religion and national origin, the lawyer's office as well as the group from the shtetl. No other group of prisoners of war was as heterogeneous.

What they had in common was only their great-great-great-grandmothers.

Every Friday the bathhouse of their barrack was transformed into a Jewish house of worship. He couldn't believe in the strength of the obstinacy on their part. They sealed the windows tightly with blankets, and on one of them they placed the Star of Zion and lighted candles. They stood on the concrete floor, rocking back and forth. Second Lieutenant Natan Cyrank fulfilled the duties of the cantor and invoked God with a prayer in Hebrew. It seems that on holy days they found something that served as the tallit, the prayer shawl. Colleagues kept watch in case the guards approached.

In this same bathhouse, the Catholics prayed during the week, the members of the Brotherhood of the Rosary housed in this same barrack.

He never joined in conversations, but he listened to what they said. Many agreed to come and give talks, about travels, the stars, philosophy. He remembered one radio reporter who often improvised accounts of athletic competitions, or Olympic Games. Among his favorites was the report of the ten-thousand-yard race in Los Angeles in 1932, in which Janusz Kusociński had triumphed. He would make a detour to avoid the distinguished barrack 15. It seemed to him that for these cavalry officers, an elite corps for the Sapiehas and the Potworowskis, the Czetwertyńskis and the Mycielskis, he would always remain a gabardine Jew. They made him feel it. By waving their hands they mimicked the accents of his colleagues and their way of talking. They repeated that Jews were always born on the left side of the barricade, and they knew how to provide for themselves. He felt just as awkward in the company of the naval officers. They looked down on him from the height of their unattainable treasures, the packages of uniforms and tobacco that their colleagues from England sent them. They received as much in one month as the others in a year. This just strengthened their pride. Attempts had been made to make them share their packages with the other barracks, but they had intervened with the highest-ranked officers in protest.

No, he did not really feel that they were equal. Even if the lice devoured them all the same way, they could in the same way run, study, write letters—the time given them was the same. They attended the same performances and the same athletic meets, answered the same roll call, and received the same orders.

At a certain time, when there was a rumor that they were going to put bars on barrack 12A, the highest-ranked officers firmly opposed it, and it was never done. They also protested against other rumors, such as the transfer of Jewish officers.

The Polish administration of the camp steadfastly maintained its position: all officials without exception were officers of the Polish army. They tried to put an end to the special standing of barrack 12A by introducing Polish officers. The leader of the barrack was in turn a prisoner of war of Jewish origin, a Knight of the Order of Virtuti Militari, and a Polish officer who was a renowned fencing champion. The barrack held a particular fascination for the German administrators, who visited it like a "zoological garden."

He heard the epithets expressed by the people from the right, calling for a boycott of their barrack. He wouldn't look them in the face. Sometimes he felt a physical hatred for others. It wounded him. A certain second lieutenant, a member of the ultranationalist ONR (National Radical Camp) in Woldenberg, was caught as he was about to place in the mailbox a denunciation addressed to the *Abwehr-Abteilung* against a colleague who was hiding his Jewish origins from the Germans. The honor tribunal did not consider the offense sufficiently egregious to expel him from the Officer Corps.

At home he had played the violin. Apparently he had talent but lacked patience. He had taken his violin to Warsaw when he went to pursue his studies at the Polytechnic School. When he went off to war he had left it there in his room on the second floor. I wanted so much to find a mention somewhere that he had played in the camp, a mention of the music he loved and the violin. I never found it. There were so many possibilities there: two symphony orchestras and a chamber orchestra.

Maybe he did try, but perhaps he was incapable of concentrating and didn't know how to make himself do it? Or perhaps he had already given up. He wanted neither to read nor to study, practice his vocabulary, draw plans for the extension of the cooperative housing. Perhaps he tried. Maybe there was no inspiration? Or perhaps his hands sweated and his eyelids trembled? Or his heart beat at an accelerated rhythm and he had to lie down? Perhaps that's how it all began. These were all typical symptoms of "barbed-wire syndrome."

What was he busy with, when he could have practiced with the others, be surrounded by them, and feel protected?

He could play cards; he liked bridge, for example. Some played through for the five years, hoping for four spades and a slam. He could play chess. He could have given lectures on bridge and road building, classes in construction and statistics; he had experience as the director of construction sites.

He turned toward the wall, and that's how he remained, with his back to the world. He was challenging existence, that was his objective.

In the course of their second year of captivity, the prisoners were given permission to tend small garden plots. They were right next door. I don't think that he ever cultivated a plot, but perhaps he went there to rest and look at all the extraordinary plants growing, tomatoes and radishes, which, all the while belonging to another world, were still, however, edible. That strained, watchful expression would have vanished for a moment from his face. He would breathe differently while looking at the young leaves.

Every month he was allowed to send two postcards and one letter. He reached his limit and never asked for more. In this correspondence he placed great importance on financial questions. In accordance with the Geneva agreement, the officers in Oflag IIC received a stipend. Like the majority of his colleagues, he had it sent to his family. As a second lieutenant he would receive seventy-two lagermarks a month, and lieutenants received twelve lagermarks more. For a money order to the territories of the general government, the rate was two złotys for one mark. He wanted a confirmation that his family had received this money.

His situation was painful at first, but eventually, no doubt, he could have read, studied, memorized vocabulary, drawn up plans and argued about them with others in his profession. He who was so practical, how could he have wasted his time, let it pass so easily, and confusedly? Confusion. They had the important library of Marshal Rydz-Śmigly, seized by the Germans. German publishing firms sent them books and manuals for studying languages. So they studied: Arabic and astronomy, the history of philosophy and economics. Some devoted themselves to their studies obsessively. They were in denial about the disaster and the wasteful flight of time. This autodidact anarchy proliferated unchecked. But their energies were reined in and channeled, and they organized an authentic serious university of prisoners of war.

They found escape into the strangest worlds. One of his fellow prisoners translated the Hindu *Ramayana* in verse, accompanied by his drawings. It was said to be one of the most beautiful things to have come to light in that camp.

They lost themselves in dictionaries and foreign vocabularies. They studied the language of Shakespeare and of Victor Hugo, but also that of Sophocles and Ovid.

They escaped into what was closest or was the easiest.

I took a walk along the barbed-wire fences. In the section reserved for prisoners of war, and in this way excluding the German buildings, the camp had an almost square shape, with a perimeter of approximately 1,700 meters. That represented, on the average, the itinerary of the daily walks, with the more resilient and those who craved more exercise in the open air doing it several times. One tour of the grounds following the wire fence was a complete round, an obligatory ritual before the evening roll call, just before shutting down the barracks. They called that "making the round." What distance did he walk in five years minus three months? One thousand eight hundred days, and each day an average of more than one kilometer, sometimes more, sometimes less. Almost two thousand kilometers, which is seventeen times the distance from Warsaw to Łódź, or six times up to Kraków.

The moment I try to resolve these questions I become irritated. And before my eyes appear all the times when my grandfather tried to explain mathematical problems to me. In proportion, it is simple; the worst was with several people starting at different speeds from point A walking toward point B. For example, they came out of barrack 12A at four o'clock in the afternoon and went to the theater for a performance of *Revenge* by Aleksander Fredro, the Polish Molière; the speed of *x* did not vary, he never hurried, he always left early. Besides, he took large steps, as if regulated by some machine installed inside him. His colleague Danek was still playing cards, he wanted to tidy himself up, and he left the barrack a quarter of an hour later. How fast did he have to run to arrive in time for the five o'clock performance? Whew!

I could multiply the examples. In camp they performed *Revenge* thirty-four times, and each time only so many spectators could attend. Several came many times over. How many times . . . etc.

I walk between the remains of barbed wire, what's left of the pigsties, and piles of bricks. Mine is a clumsy mental reconstruction. I compare the doorways with the aisles, the partitions, and interior walls, all the obstacles they had to overcome then, those that I have to overcome to arrive at their experience.

I am cold. But I continue on my way because I have to feel cold.

One day one of the prisoners gathered all the photos of children everyone had. Amateur photos, often worn pictures of the sons and daughters of the prisoners. There were many, perhaps two hundred or even three hundred. He hung them up on the walls, one next to the other in one of the rooms. One next to the other. Small heads and faces, figures on their knees, or holding themselves straight upright, among others on bicycles, in baby carriages, wearing bonnets, berets, and hats. These photos were on them when they left home, they received them in letters or in packages, and they kept them in trunks or in lockers and pinned them up on their bunks. Seven thousand men, a little town; thousands of children playing ball, hide-and-seek, learning to write and read, listening attentively to letters from Woldenberg, which the mothers or older brothers and sisters read several times over so that they could better understand them. Prisoners ran from that room. They wept or maintained a stony silence. Did they still have children? My mother had not seen him for five years. She was eight years old when he left the apartment on Krasiński Street, and she was fourteen and wearing a bra when he came to fetch her in the summer camp in Wilga. She did not want to leave with this dark giant who said he was her father. Calling him "Daddy" wasn't suitable, and never again would it fit him.

There were radios in the camps, and underground newspapers. What did they know about the Jewish situation? To what extent did the information about the ghettos, the policy of liquidation, the transport to Treblinka and Bełżec, Chełmno and Auschwitz reach them? Did they know a lot, and what did they make of the information that came to them from the outside? That must have been the worst of all; being powerless. It was like being on the other side of the wall and watching the ghetto burning, the ghetto where the family remained. What did they know about the month of April, that spring of the year 1943? Holy Week in the Warsaw Ghetto, the Jews of Warsaw.

At the beginning of April the prisoners in each barrack received from the Red Cross a little sugar, tea, seventy cigarettes, and one additional package for each barrack. On the 10th of April the sky was overcast and drizzling. On the heater someone had prepared an exceptional dish: crêpes with cheese. They were a success. They marked the afternoon roll call by the sound on a horn. On the 11th of April, it was sunny followed by overcast skies. On the 15th, the German press continued to deplore the bestial brutality of the Bolsheviks against Polish officers in Katyn, where an estimated four thousand were slaughtered. Rumors circulated in the camp that it was Jews who committed this crime. The German fleet sank twenty-one Allied ships. The 18th of April, Palm Sunday, Mass at 9:30. Spring had come, the wheat and the grass had started showing green, and the trees were leafing out. Those who were tending their allotment gardens were waiting for seeds of radishes, carrots, and other vegetables; they used the time to prepare. They gathered horse manure for fertilizer. Two powerful purebred Mecklenburg dray horses came every morning pulling the garbage cart. On April 22 they received a crumb of halvah, some cocoa, and milk that came with the donations from the Red Cross. The prisoners on duty had their hands full distributing it. On April 23, the trees in the orchard came into bloom. The 24th of April, they visited Jesus' tomb, and in the afternoon they took the dried crackers and the salt to be blessed.

During their fourth year in captivity they received packages from Canada, English cigarettes, and excellent tea from Tel Aviv; rice from Cairo, invaluable for stomach problems; raisins from Turkey and chocolate and cocoa from Venezuela. They were provided with notebooks of scrap paper, a rare and valuable gift. They enjoyed sunny weather that year and got a tan. They organized athletic competitions. The camp record for the high jump was 1.65 meters. At times violent storms shattered the windowpanes of the barracks. Water started leaking in during torrential rains. Violinists played Paganini's Caprices, quartets by Mozart and Schubert. They were satisfied.

In the fourth year of captivity the Germans electrified the barbed wire.

Who was he in this herd divided into companies and battalions? An engineer? A husband? A father? A son? Nobody. He had nothing to give anyone, he took care of and protected no one, he took no risks for anyone else. The feverish activities of the others disturbed him, the courses, the lectures, the competitions. What was the use of this game of imitating life, what was the use of not suffering, what was the use of pretending to be someone, pretending to believe that there remained something of the self: knowledge, feelings, pride? We are no longer there, colleagues, there's nothing to pretend. Write plays, translate Shakespeare, study Sanskrit. Weave kilims, carve wood, construct philosophical systems, play circus, or the Olympics, if it's of any help to you, if it effectively distances your fear. Only me, leave me alone, don't touch me, go away. Leave me alone.

Keep on playing. Chess and checkmate. Checkmate. Yesterday, again someone threw himself against the electric fence.

In the International Red Cross's inspection reports to Geneva, officers of Jewish origin are mentioned only once. The report was dated February 25, 1944, according to a confidential conversation with a confidential source. They learned that eighty-six Jewish officers had remained without any contact with their families, who had no information about their fate. The Red Cross undertook to send to Geneva a list containing the names and addresses of these families for verification.

. . .

American uniforms with underwear and shoes began arriving in the camp by the middle of 1944. They had buttons as shining as gold twenty-dollar pieces. Now men were busy sewing on the stripes of a Polish officer.

At the end of August the Allied armies liberated Paris. By September the fighting had reached Antwerp and Brussels. On October 20th, one hundred officers from the Warsaw Uprising arrived in the camp. They were received with honors. They told of the fighting and the conditions in the occupied country. Warsaw was in ruins. Lorraine was liberated as well as the major section of Alsace. The German army launched an

offensive in the Ardennes. On November 30, Samuel Przedborski, my grandfather, turned forty-one years old. Without
acknowledgment.

In January 1945 the aerial bombing of the Reich was in full
force. Nuremberg suffered heavy losses. By mid-January there
was talk of evacuation. The prisoners gathered their belongings
and started sewing backpacks with whatever was available.

In the barrack museum they gathered documentation, proof
that everything that occurred behind the barbed wire really
occurred. There are the tombstones from the camp cemetery,
barbed wire, and inscriptions carved in bricks. There's a heater
for heating water, and the stove called *kręciołka*. A little mirror
made in Woldenberg. Metal dog tags. There's a piece of a beam
with a hiding place for a radio. There is a cigarette holder artistically carved with a hiding place for passing messages. There
are manuscripts of plays, and theater posters, a little souvenir
notebook with a drawing representing the characters played by
each of the actors in *Revenge* by Fredro.

There are puppets and masks. There's a bone letter opener.
Silver signets. A wooden model of a boat with two sails. Some
lighters. A little box decorated with a clover, money boxes inlaid
with grapes in marquetry. The cross with the figure of Christ
that hung above the entrance to one of the barracks. Hundreds
of wood carvings and also illustrations for *Don Quixote*.

There are thousands of photographs. Exhibits of crèches,
Brahms and Offenbach concerts, performances of *The Barber
of Seville* and of *Marie Stuart,* always with men in the wom-
en's roles, acts of the Neumann Circus, and numerous athletic
competitions. Nowhere is Samuel Przedborski to be found. His
photo isn't there. His name is not there.

He is not a member of the circle of building experts. His
library card has not been preserved, or any certificates for completing courses. There were classes on engines, and on apiculture (the life of bees, raising the queens, diseases of bees,
products of apiculture), courses on navigation and commerce.
According to the records, 90 percent of the prisoners took part

in these activities. The index of lectures, the homework, the colloquiums, and the tests and final examinations have been preserved. There are the notes from a course on Egyptology.

He is neither among the athletes nor among their supporters. He didn't try to obtain the certificate for the physical fitness of prisoners. In the category for under forty years old, the test was composed of walking along the perimeter for nineteen minutes; throwing the medicine ball seventeen meters; shot-putting thirteen meters; jumping three and a half meters, and running.

There are countless caricatures, but not of him. It's as if he had not existed.

There were orders given by the Germans forbidding officers of Jewish origin to participate in the cultural and educational life of the camp. However, these were ignored. It sometimes happened that the Germans crossed off the Jewish names from the programs of lectures and classes. Nevertheless, they tried again. In fact, the favorite actors of the prisoners' theater, their favorite pianists and violinists, were artists of non-Aryan blood.

I don't want to explain away everything by fear.

It was at the end of January 1945 that they received the order to leave. The winter was glacial, the evacuation was on foot toward the interior of Germany. That's not what they expected. They had waited so long, liberation should have been different. They didn't sleep that night. They spent their time packing their bags. The backpacks couldn't hold all the prisoners' belongings.

They built sleds. They destroyed, without giving it any thought, the tables, shelves, stools they had obtained with such difficulty over the years. Now their sleds would enable them to carry the maximum. Suddenly those who had nothing were in a better position than those who had something. Those who amassed reserves for hard times had to leave them with a heavy heart: a fortune wasted again—bags of kasha and peas, canned meat from the beginning of the war, some damp cigarettes. Sugar and powdered milk were stuffed on the top of the backpacks, over the books and warm clothing. It seems that manuscripts in sealed glass jars were buried in the ground.

They packed all night, feeding the stove as they had never done until then. They burned almost half of the planks from their bunks. There was heat in the barracks, which was rare. Outside the windows, the dry air was icy and the stars shone brilliantly. They were ignorant about where they were going, but the prospects of movement, of a change of place, seemed promising to them. Anywhere, as long as it was outside the barbed wire.

They were not used to walking. For them, who had been squeezed into such a limited space for years, the road seemed endless. They were short of breath. It was windy. At the end of four days, the East Camp was scattered for the night over the estate of Dziedzice, near Barlinek. They spread out as they could in the barns and pigsties. The next day, toward noon, they saw the Soviet tanks approaching Dziedzice.

The Germans attempted to engage them. An artillery shell from the Soviet tank exploded in a barn filled with prisoners of war. It wounded about ten and killed a few.

They were buried in the local cemetery.

Among more than three thousand war prisoners, Szymon was one of those who gained his liberty on January 30, 1945.

ŻENA

EUGENIA (ŻENA) GADZIŃSKA,
STEPMOTHER OF MY MOTHER HALINA,
WITH MY MATERNAL GRANDFATHER,
SZYMON PRZEDBORSKI, 1960S.
ŻENA WAS HIS SECOND (POSTWAR) WIFE.

I think of Żena, my grandfather's wife, this August 16, 2002, the day of her eighty-sixth birthday. Grandfather died at that age thirteen years ago. Ever since, without letup, Żena has been preparing herself for the next world. She has written her obituary, which is waiting in the right-hand drawer of the desk, underneath the bills. Żena doesn't believe that Mama, her stepdaughter, will know how to equitably settle her affairs after her death.

There are many things she did that Mother cannot forget, but above all, half a century later, she remembers a pair of wooden coat hangers, which used to be called portmanteaux then. When she moved out of her father's house after her marriage, to a sublet room, Żena told her not once, not twice, but several times not to forget to return them—fifty years have gone by, but her stepdaughter still cannot forget this rebuke.

Żena stayed on alone in my grandfather's apartment on the corner of Puławska and Madaliński Streets, in this apartment I hated going to because of her. And to which I return so often, so many years later, for her. She has a serious case of asthma, and heart problems, vertigo with fainting spells, and strange allergies, for example, a sensitivity to the odor of fish.

What perfume were they using in the families of the employees of the tramway system coming from the working quarters of Wola? Blood sausages with gruel, or cutlets, or cauliflower, or green cabbage must also have produced odors. My grandfather, who loved carp and herring, could never eat any at home. Neither with oil, nor with cream, nor with potatoes, nor marinated. Without chopped onions, either, which also nauseated Żena. Sometimes his sister secretly brought him some portions in a hermetically sealed jar, or the heads of sweetened carp in aspic like at home. He would eat them standing, taking all precautions, without making any noise, but she always detected traces of the smell. She would then stop talking to him.

She ruled the house even though he was the big one and looked distinguished in his suit. She had about her an offensive sense of superiority. I didn't understand why she treated him like an intruder or someone who had to be constantly reprimanded. Dressed with care, elegant, suit and hat, generally on her way to a concert or the theater, she made everyone feel from the height of her grandiosity that she was doing them an honor in speaking to them, which she really did reluctantly as an exceptional favor. She had the willful face of those who were never good-looking even in their youth because of their coldness and lack of charm. To this day I still don't know the color of her eyes.

She had shapely calves in nylon stockings and high-heeled shoes, usually brown, with short laces. I was surprised, such a body on such legs. She could have taken flight on those legs, but she chose dry ideology and the principles that turned her into a sort of modern witch. Her food had to be nutritious, her clothes practical, her man committed and useful.

She had a sting like a wasp. All the annoying things she did I remember as anecdotes. After a ceremony at the PEN club, where I was awarded an important literary prize, she came up to congratulate me afterward and said maliciously, "Even the Queen of England doesn't smooth her hair so often during one ceremony."

For years I was kept away from the wife of my grandfather; it seemed to me that she had no feelings. I don't remember her as someone who taught me to respect old age. But now that she has no one, she cannot simply be abandoned.

I make myself visit her, hiding it from Mother, who is incapable of understanding how I can devote time to such a person. Sometimes she doesn't open the door even though we agreed I should visit. She wears sweatpants and blouses that seem to float more loosely from month to month. In this house the moths are well fed and surfeited. The suits, dresses, housecoats progressively lighten and lose weight. The hats and berets she used to love she now wears rarely. She darns everything, in an effort to keep it from disappearing. For herself, she can't help reading a few pages of Plato or Kant every day. She had begged her father to let her continue with her studies, and then she devoted years to fighting illiteracy. The workings of our gray cells are in direct proportion to the severity of the discipline we impose. She hasn't missed the concerts at the Philharmonic for half a century. She has only changed her subscription from Fridays to the Saturday matinees, because she is afraid of returning home alone after dark. As long as she is conscious, as she put it, she will not stop attending. She can't change her habits; she has no one to help her in case of emergency.

Formerly she collected rings. She made a gift of one of them, a gold one, a large rectangular ring with a blue stone, to Halina, my mother, just after Żena and Szymon were married. Mother remembers that she was studying for her baccalaureate, and her friends had not liked the present. They had said the stone was an aquamarine, so she asked her stepmother. Then, for the first time, she had the experience of how it feels to be considered someone inferior. "Do you think that I would have owned something so ordinary? You only have to look at it to see that it's an authentic sapphire." She purchased her jewelry from the cooperative ORNO, and what she loved most were sets: rings, bracelets, necklaces. Especially silver. She chose the models herself. Decimated by time, lack of interest, and theft, they lie in a heap in a box of Zakopane wood. She doesn't take them out, she doesn't even look at them, or with covetousness slip a ring on her gnarled fingers.

The last years have changed her. She shows a sort of solicitude. She is anxious about my travels. She who before the war had taken flying lessons is afraid of finding herself alone. She always says goodbye to me with some emotion and always repeats, "Take good care of yourself." With me she softens, but I still won't touch her for fear of being wounded.

The apartment hasn't been repainted for forty years. It's gray and has suffered the insults of time. The paint and the plaster are flaking in chunks, there are grease stains from hands, and dirt; it is crumbling from within, full of dust and paper. She is sensitive to dust but doesn't have the strength to fight it. She won't let anyone touch what belongs to her. She won't let go of what she had.

The apartment swarms with a mass of things. Swarming as if some hidden process were operating here. Clothing and objects in dismal wrapping paper are piled against the walls. Vases everywhere, wooden bowls, paper cutouts, little glasses, each filled with its portion of the past. Books multiply, they increase, spreading along the shelves, taking up more and more space. The shelves seem to stir; perhaps it's an illusion, but it is clear, and the plants in the pots seem to be muttering. Even the playing cards lying on the walnut table are not inert; they seem imbued with a mysterious energy.

For many years I believed that all this occurred uniquely in the realm of the metaphor, conveying a sense of anxiety. But recently I walked into the kitchen. Insects came straight toward me in a line, they were in ranks of four, whole companies, battalions, as for a major holiday or a parade. I fled.

She is always seated on her Biedermeier sofa, more worn in some places than in others: the places where her head and body rest. Her body, the corpse, ever lighter, still wrapped in the gray skin. On the table a book with a bookmark, and cards similar to those used by her husband, my grandfather, for solitaire— perhaps the same ones. She remains seated this way for days on end, really half lying down. She is afraid to stretch out, because if the pain in her chest comes on, she wouldn't be able to get up. She lets her pots burn on the stove, she scorches items from her wardrobe one after the other, using an iron from the time of Stalin. She won't part with it, any more than she would from the propaganda brochures that add up to yards of bulletins and circulars, and laws that date from the time when she was always right. American imperialism still disgusts her. She meditates on the disastrous failure of the system, powerless in the face of unemployment, broken plumbing, and the smell of paint in the stairwell. Going down to the basement, where she stores the prune preserves, is already far too painful.

The next room is my grandfather's bedroom. It's crammed with papers, stuffed in corners and also piled on the sofa on which she has recently spread out her clothes, piles of clothing of a peculiar cut and color, perhaps dating from the thirties. Spread out like an exhibit, just waiting for moths. Two-piece suits with worn collars, pleated woolen skirts, boleros and jackets, and heavy coats. No sense buying anything new; she only has to air out these things, to freshen them, so they won't be smothered, like her. There are photos on the piano. Szymon sometimes tried to play it, but it irritated her. He irritated her with his silence, the silence with which he hid his despair, and a world to which she had no access.

Against the window, facing the balcony, there is a little oak desk, my grandfather's desk, that I consider mine. I am eager to know its contents. Next to the identity tag from the prisoner-of-war camp lies the medal, the Polonia Restituta for service to the state.

She doesn't want to die in the hospital. She made me promise not to send her to the hospital. I promised, although I knew that she would be sent there if I was out of the country, and she would not return.

She doesn't want to die away from these yellowed walls on which reflections trace the contours of familiar mountains she loved formerly, away from the brown kilim with folk designs hanging above the bed, away from everything she has accumulated and which, in any case, will remain as it is for others. They have no value; she has no illusions. She was always a realist. Let the dust gather; after all, it's hers, accumulated in the course of years of a life shared with Szymon, with him and the pigeons he fed secretly on the balcony. She couldn't stand the pigeons, they destroyed her begonias and they smelled, this odor also a trace of every day. She caught him, when he spoke to those obese gray birds she would chase every time they alighted on her railing. He lost himself in long monologues using words she didn't understand. They listened. They scratched in the empty boxes, scattering the fertilizer she brought from the florist, losing their feathers. Sometimes they destroyed her flowers: grape hyacinths, pansies, geraniums. She couldn't stand it, she started screaming. He let her carry on, he didn't defend himself, he withdrew in his silence.

Her will is in the sideboard, on the third shelf from the top, under a Chinese porcelain cup. She revoked the last one, changing it to divide her remaining jewelry, and replaced it with this one. There are days when everything slips from your grasp. When she fell in a corner of the entrance hall, for example—she doesn't know how it happened. She forgot the moment; in the entrance hall near the stacked shoeboxes where you can clearly hear the noise of the elevator, she had to drag herself for a long time to reach the light. All the windows were far away, and she had the feeling that she would never find them.

It's like being in the sewers during the Uprising. She wasn't in the sewers, but she often has the feeling of being there, and with difficulty she catches her breath at the end of her ordeal. The night is the most difficult, but she knows that she has to get through it, to the light, more light, if she has to live again. She has decided to live even if the others are dead. She doesn't feel well, worse than she will admit, because they would then and there send her to the hospital. Who are "they"? She doesn't know. Sometimes they move her plates, and the yogurt in the refrigerator.

She and Szymon had met by the elevator on the ground floor, when they came home from work separately, each to his or her apartment. It was responsible work that they left with the feeling of duty well accomplished. The engineer Przedborski had a bandaged finger—she remembered that it must have been the thumb wrapped in a checkered handkerchief. She asked him what happened. He had jabbed himself with a paper clip. What moved her? The instinct of an older sister, the nurse from wartime, whatever it was, she made sure that he soaked his finger in boiled water.

She boiled the water in a small pot with two handles. She looked on amused at this tall man trying to avoid the treatment; he had barely skimmed the surface of the water, then pulled away his hand with an expression of great pain. She grabbed his hand, once and then again. For his own good, to disinfect it . . . she doesn't remember anymore. Three months later, they were married. It was a moment of weakness, because she had vowed to remain single. When her fiancé never returned from the Uprising, she had explained to herself that things would stay that way: work, music, service to society, rebuilding the country for which he had perished. I don't know who he was, and if he really existed, her man, her rebel, so passionate about the music of Szymanowski, her love. The word is so alien to her that even here on the page, it's out of place and wants to disappear. For more than half a century, she visited his grave once a year. She made a life for herself; she had to. In her rigorous agenda of hours and days, there are no surprises, simply routine, systematic work, a series of habits. Me, about me, for me. The rest was obligation.

Sometimes Blanka telephones from Paris. It irritates Żena because her school friend doesn't condone self-indulgence. She is curious about the world and people, and she doesn't understand how Żena can waste her time thinking exclusively of herself. They are of the same age, but Blanka still manages her leather-goods store, where she caters to successive generations of customers. I know from her that Żena was the only one of her Polish friends—and there were many who danced at her wedding under the chuppah—to show her any sympathy after the war, after she had lost her whole family. I was going to write, to show her "any heart," but I hesitated, even though Blanka, Polish Jew from Warsaw, said "heart": "Żena was the one and only who welcomed me with her heart."

Żena had told her secretary—she was working in the cultural department at the time—that a friend had returned, by a miracle she had survived, and now she had to take care of her. Blanka will never forget this, she won't forget because others greeted her with these words: "How come you survived, they didn't burn all of you?" And even though Blanka had left Poland, where her world had crumbled, for more than sixty years she had maintained contact with Żena. She sends her presents and money. She always defends her because, in the end, she is hardest on herself.

Lately Żena calls me more often. Her voice on the telephone is very irritated. Very humiliated, because she can't manage and it goes against her principles to have to ask—ask what? Help, attention, a favor. She has never asked. She tells me how many times she has to go out to buy milk, bread, cheese, and the newspaper. Or that a glass has slipped out of her hand, that she grows disoriented and bumps into things, and afterward she drags herself to bed and lies down until it passes. It doesn't pass. She doesn't want anyone looking after her, neither part-time nor live-in. She categorically refuses to discuss the subject and all attempts to get her a paid helper.

Once when she called me, sobbing, I thought that the hour had come, and I said: "Don't be afraid, I'm coming. I remember, no hospital, wait for me." I couldn't believe that it was all about her beloved master of the boys' choir, who was arrested because he had been molesting those in his charge for years. "It's impossible," she repeated, "impossible, everything ends up in the gutter. Why do I have to know this?"

Several times she has called me urgently. When I arrived, it was because she had to dictate to me the manner in which she had to be dressed to be laid out in her coffin. "Write faster"— she impatiently slides a piece of notebook paper over to me— "and don't make any mistakes: the navy-blue two-piece, the white silk blouse, they are over there on Szymon's sofa . . . the black shoes." I remember that she had prepared two pairs of shoes because feet swell and she doesn't know if her dress shoes will be too narrow. So, in that case there's the other, more worn pair.

She takes a long time to walk from the gates of the cemetery to her husband's grave. Leaning on a cane and on my arm, she drags her feet in the copper-colored oak leaves. It reminds her of her childhood. The rustling sound evokes a carefree mood she no longer expected to feel. Down the central path, the rows follow one another. In front of the grave, she becomes old again. She wipes with a cloth the flowers from last year, old gray groundsel, still usable. Next to a round pebble she places a pine wreath. She lights the candle on the glass saucer. Then with a sudden gesture she hugs the headstone of the grave, as if she wants to lean against Szymon's chest, against his living body. She rocks monotonously, as if she were trying to extract some warmth from the sandstone block, and asks of him: "Say something."

When we move away, she makes a sign to him with her hand, a slight gesture, almost bickering, as if they were going to see each other in a moment. Undoubtedly she has been delayed, but it really won't be very long now.

• • •

A gain she is lying in the entrance hall; the last thing that she remembers was the sun of an unnatural red, but she doesn't know where she is. A pile of newspapers, Tuesday, September 20, 1970. Szymon must be in the next room. She calls. But what's the use, he won't get up anyway. Is he sleeping? How many years have they not slept in the same bed? Each one always had his or her own bedroom, but sometimes she let him come to her. If he deserved it. She knew that it was her conjugal duty. This newspaper is the color of toast. She is hungry. She cannot get up, there is something wrong with her right arm.

The telephone must be around here somewhere, she only has to raise her hand, but whom to call? She doesn't want an ambulance; everything ends that way. Her last electrocardiogram reminded her of the final fragment of a Beethoven sonata. She looked suspiciously at the lines rising and then falling, forcing herself to remember the position of her left hand on the keyboard. In her baccalaureate class she knew how to play it. She can't open her hand. These fingers already don't have the reach of an octave. What's the name of that sonata? Les Adieux? The Moonlight? The Pathétique? It's not possible she forgot.

She doesn't want any priest. She wants to join her mother. Yet over there, there's a cross. But she's not a believer, just like her father, the old militant of the Socialist Party. She was proud of him. He worked hard to earn his daily bread, and he asserted social equality. As soon as she could string together the letters of the alphabet he asked her to read Marx and Engels to him. She remembered the way he listened, his head resting on his hand, making a sign of agreement. She remembered the way he ate his potatoes with buttermilk, and then wiped his mouth with the back of his hand. She remembered his rough beard, and his certainty of what was right. She inherited it from him.

Smoke. Where is that smoke coming from? The smell of burning. Something is burning. She was no doubt warming some baked apples filled with the remains of the preserves. She had left everything for a moment to fetch some medicine. A glance in the mirror, she's afraid to look. From the kitchen to the bathroom, there's an L-shaped hallway. At least she has to try to get up. Lean against the wall. It tumbles down upon her. The shoeboxes fall over, spreading everywhere, spilling so many pairs, so many years. Misshapen, worn, cobbled together, so many times resoled at the shoemaker on the corner. Out of fashion. She has never approved of fashion. She has traveled so many roads with them; they were always useful. Slipping on her shoes. It's easier to walk with shoes. Pumps, boots, walking shoes always laced with a pair of new shoelaces. In shoes she will climb the mountain. She remembered the itinerary.

What will happen afterward? What difference would it make if she gets up? Make some tea, you need a glass, cover it with a little plastic cover, sometimes something is floating in it, don't forget. In a little piece of glass she sees the face of her mother, with a scarf on her head, like when she went to see her father in prison, in the visiting room. She would like to kiss her hand, as always, as she did every day before going to school. "Kiss my knee," call out her sisters, repeating what her mother said when she was disobedient. They are making fun of her running around the table: "Kiss my knee."

What's the difference whether she gets up or not? What difference would it make for whom? Those philosophers' books in her home library will not change places for years. The starry sky will continue. And the moral conscience between the covers of her books. Someone else will occupy her seat at the Philharmonic, in the eighth row center. That dotty woman whose "shhhh" constantly demanded silence did not arouse any sympathy. Her neighbor will stubbornly ring the bell until the end, and then she will open the door with her duplicate key. Her obituary is ready.

VI

Dela

ARYAN PAPERS OF MY MATERNAL GRANDMOTHER,
DELA GOLDSTEIN. HER EMPLOYEE ID CARD BEARING
HER POLISH NAME, ZOFIA ZMIAŁOWSKA, WAS ISSUED
SHORTLY BEFORE HER DEATH IN AUTUMN 1944.

THE GHETTO

*D*ela Goldstein. My grandmother.
Everything is uncertain and inconclusive. Her first name, her last name, her fate.

The moment they started talking about her they called her "Dela." Dela, Adela Goldstein, like one of those poor Jews from the annex at number 9 Przedrynek Place in Łęczyca, those from the coal warehouse. But when she married Samuel, the son of prosperous neighbors, they immediately started calling her "Mrs. Przedborska." She stood under the chuppah in a borrowed wedding dress, and she bore with pride the name of one of the prominent families of Łęczyca. She was a schoolteacher, the wife of an engineer graduate of the Polytechnic School of Warsaw. In reality there never was any Dela Goldstein. Neither in my memory, nor in the existing documents. The war further disguised her with another role. Then nothing more.

Not all the registries of the Jewish communities were burned. The one in Koło, the one where my grandmother Dela was registered on June 2, 1902, was spared. She was the daughter of Chana Rauf, from that community, and of Jakub Goldstein from Łęczyca. They gave her a name that I had never heard before: Udel Sura. For years she appears in the tenant registers of the house at number 9 Przedrynek Place. In time, she was listed as the eldest of seven Goldstein siblings. I had to get used to Udel and to Sura.

It was difficult to create her from the bits and pieces. For me and for my life. For a long time she didn't have a face, and then the photo on a wartime document had appeared deceptive.

This woman with harsh features, a large nose, her black hair with a center part, pulled back, looked out at me with eyes that seemed unguarded. Not empty, but vulnerable, disarming and cold at the same time. A mouth that was too thin, eyebrows surprised at the world. She was a stranger.

I never knew her gestures, or the sound of her voice. I don't know how she spoke, if she spoke little or much, what words she repeated, which diminutives were hers, if she was tender. Did she ask many questions? What did she want to know? Was she patient or did she have to exert self-control? Did she gesticulate or laugh a lot, when it was still possible to do so?

In 1931 Dela gave birth to her daughter, Halina, my mother. Eight years later war was declared.

The first of April 1940, the Germans had begun building a wall in Warsaw. It was the boundary of a "zone threatened with an epidemic," the Jewish quarter. The last days of April in Łódź they sealed the ghetto. In May, rumors were circulating in town saying that the Jews were going to be transferred to Madagascar. Paris fell on June 14, and the same day the camp at Auschwitz began operating. Dela remembered precisely because her brother-in-law Oleś, the husband of Frania, Zamutek's sister, had told her. He foresaw the darkest future and spoke of extermination from the beginning. "You mustn't allow yourself to be locked up for whatever pretext," he would repeat. But no one in the family agreed with him. Dela's sister arrived from Łódz, where there was the threat of a ghetto. Madzia, Zamutek's youngest sister, came from Ozorków with her mother and grandmother from Łęczyca. Together, nothing could happen. In June the linden trees were already in bloom in Łazienki Park. Someone said that she was afraid of going out in town, but where they lived on Wilson Square, there was the promising smell of summer. The Germans finished the building of the wall.

Two months later the family moved to the ghetto.

All Jews had to go behind the wall: they would be safer there. Zamutek wasn't there. He had been taken prisoner during the battles defending Warsaw. Since autumn she regularly received cards from the Oflag. She didn't know anyone in Warsaw, she didn't have any friends. As for the family, the family wanted to be together. Temporary troubles would pass like many other things that passed, moving, changing homes; the most important thing was to find a good apartment, big and, as far as possible, comfortable. And work. When one is working it's less difficult.

Would the presence of her husband, Samuel, the father of Halina, my grandfather, have changed anything? He was zealous, he liked working with ruler in hand, carrying out orders, even giving them, but always in the framework of a defined structure and ideology: don't give in, don't get carried away, don't shoot for the moon, no rifles against tanks. But perhaps I am being unfair; perhaps he would have felt responsible for the family and might have seen danger coming. He wasn't one of those who fail.

My grandmother was nearly forty years old when she moved to this sealed quarter, the Jewish quarter. With a ration card for bread: fifty groszy a kilo; it would nearly double in time. Without the card: seven to eighteen złotys. A bowl of soup: from twenty groszy to three złotys. The doctor charged fifty groszy a visit. She kept the accounts, long columns of numbers added up. The ordinary inhabitants of the ghetto received two and a half kilos of bread a month, of increasingly bad quality, mixed with more sawdust and bran. Some meat. Taken from whose mouth? One's own, that's the easiest. Or the black market. In the ghetto, all the essential provisions came from smuggling. That was still in place, it was sufficient, without taking risks.

Daily coming and going: the crush, crowds, so many people wearing the star. So many strangers. In Łęczyca she was at home; here everything had to be learned again. Pańska Street: the medical warehouse, the corset maker, the laundry, the fortune-teller. Śliska Street: shoemaker, phonograph repairman, secondhand dealer, accountant. Easy to get lost, easy to hide. She still didn't understand.

Dzielna Street: baker, carpenter, drapery maker. Not much farther were several hairdressers. In the ghetto they had a lot of work: bleaching hair, photographs, touch-up work. Especially after January 1942, when the obligatory *Kennkarte* (identity card) was introduced. Dela did not dye her hair, as shown by the two surviving photographs. Neither one seemed to have been touched up.

My grandmother was a teacher. They organized clandestine study groups in dormitories, in communal kitchens, orphanages, and in the schoolhouses that now were shuttered. She certainly took part in it. They had closed the schools for Jewish children in December 1939; the first only reopened two years later, in the autumn. As a teacher, she also had to assign essays on the subject of the changes that occurred in the family because of the war. She had to read on pages ripped out of a notebook that "Mommy" had to sell her own coat and, when conditions worsened, also the wardrobe and the table—since the wardrobe had become useless. And that wasn't enough for very long. They lay like corpses on the beds. But perhaps she only played games with the children: "Here we go round the mulberry bush" or "Old brown bear is sleeping soundly." Did she model funny characters out of clay, did she embroider cherries and wild strawberries, did she make drawings of dreams? She certainly showed them how to fold paper to make a boat or a bird that could fly through the air. In the secret archives of Emmanuel Ringelblum, saved from the ruins of Warsaw after the war, the part dealing with education in the ghetto, the accounts by those in charge of the classrooms, were preserved. They're written mostly in a dry, bureaucratic style at the end of 1941. One of them, for the homeroom located at number 3–5 Bagno Street, near Grzybowski Square, is signed S. Przedborska.

I have no doubt that it is she, even though she rarely used the name Sura. I don't know if it's her first teaching position. CENTOS, the organization that supervised Jewish children and orphans, continued its work in the ghetto during the war.

During the third winter of the Occupation they oversaw thirty-five homes, providing a supply of food for thirty thousand children.

She washed, she nursed, she dressed, she fed her children, "naked, barefoot, suffering from itching and smelly." Some wouldn't eat at school. They were afraid of being punished by their mother. Dela wrote that mothers hit their children, grabbed them by the throat because they had eaten and didn't bring them anything. She saw to it that they were warm, attended to their hygiene, to their education. She made sure they had shoes, shirts, and gruel. This occupied her more than reading works by Jewish writers—Bialik, Sforim, Sholem Aleichem. The preceding fall she had been sick with typhus for six weeks.

I would have liked to have overheard a conversation of my grandmother in the ghetto. But not on the subject of soap, which she made herself: two kilos of tallow, seven liters of water, two hundred grams of rosin, three hundred grams of caustic soda, cook for two hours. Nor her way of doing the laundry, with grated potatoes. All the dirt came out of her silk handkerchiefs, but she no longer had silk handkerchiefs. For her woolen shawls she used chestnuts soaked in water and strained, or they had to be scrubbed with wheat flour. She didn't always have it and had to search for it in these closed quarters. She had to sew, to transform old clothes, turn them inside out, to dye them. I would like to hear her yearning for a new hat: modest but in good taste, straw with a plum-colored ribbon, and a suit to match. And also a summer handbag. A pair of gloves. All this for a stroll in Ujazdowskie Avenue. She could walk for kilometers, even from the distant neighborhood of Żoliborz, walk without stopping, everything returning to life with the first buds coming into leaf, so delicate and light. I want her to have believed in the life to come.

I see her in the ghetto, my grandmother who didn't have time to become old, or even the time to see her daughter as an adult. I see her in the apartment on Sienna Street. As if the others were being erased in the background, becoming less and less distinct. I see her making noodles, with flour which was still available, using eggs obtained by some miracle. For seventy groszy, for one złoty, for 2.40 złotys by the third spring of the war. She never paid more. She works the dough on the wooden board, long and patiently. She sometimes got additional eggs with a special coupon that had an oval seal and the signature of Adam Czerniaków. Several times she bought Erika powder, imitation egg, for which she apologized. But if you didn't know there wasn't a great difference. And the few groszy she saved she could send to Łęczyca. With a worn wooden rolling pin she spreads out dough as thin as a fine piecrust. She sprinkles it with flour, she cuts it and she dries it. After drying it she wraps the noodles in little cotton bags she sews in the evening by a dim light. Noodles for her husband in the camp.

She never cried. Hence perhaps the particular expression of her glance, as if she had passed the limits of grief.

She had different addresses. I have two in the ghetto: the first on Sienna Street, the other on Leszno Street. They called Sienna Street the Champs-Élysées of the ghetto, an area that was quiet, green, and clean. The black marketeers and the demimonde of the ghetto met on Sienna Street, the pianist Władysław Szpilman performed in the café of Tatiana Epstein. At the restaurant on the corner of Sosnowa Street, the price of a dinner reached two hundred złotys, the monthly salary of a worker. There were still elegant women walking their little dogs on a leash.

To number 16 Sienna Street, the same building in which my family lived, they had transferred the Janusz Korczak Orphanage. The old doctor sometimes told stories to the children. They collected two złotys at the entrance. My mother was nearby. She doesn't remember hearing the stories by Korczak. She never saw the puppets, or the adventures of the clown Buratino. The doctor with his children left 16 Sienna Street and went to Umschlagplatz.

I understood only recently that I have heard stories about

that place. The orphanage building had survived the war and was only pulled down to make room for the foundation of the Palace of Culture. There they opened a puppet theater, the Doll, the first theater of my childhood. Thus all roads lead to the ghetto. I don't know if my mother realizes it.

Leszno Street was also an elegant street for the ghetto. It was the equivalent of Marszałkowska Street, filled with the hustle and bustle of crowds and businesses. Answering a questionnaire about the Occupation, after the war, my mother gave her address as 58 Leszno Street. It was that of the emergency room, a very respectable address in the Medical Center. Located in the same building was a big café with a small summer garden. Not far away also, on the even-numbered side, was the Sztuka, "Art," a café with music and other attractions. Further on were other establishments with exotic names—Splendid, Esplanada. In the afternoon Leszno Street smelled of perfume, strong tobacco, fish, and sweets. Just like in former times.

· · ·

The neighboring house had three courtyards and a mill for grain. During the blockades people talked about money, and the heroes in Dickens, sometimes also about the ways to disguise the doors. There were hiding places everywhere—under the floorboards of an old antiques shop with piles of Meissen plates, candelabra, and paintings; in a walled basement where the entrance was hidden by an enormous bakery counter. There were elegant hiding places with light, water, and bedspreads. My grandmother hid children in baskets of dirty laundry, or behind the armoire and under the beds. They always managed to hide just in time.

My grandmother sent a fur coat to the Aryan side; she really believed that she would live. This fur coat that had to be aired comes back many times as a detail in numerous anecdotes. It was safe for furs, but not for people. A fur coat on the Aryan side was inconceivable to me. All the same she had to have sent it, she couldn't foresee that in the closing days of 1941 the

Germans would order the Jewish population to surrender its furs. Since then, she had to live in the ghetto; she had to think about the coming winter, as icy as the preceding one. All the Jews had to turn over their furs in a matter of days, regardless of what kind or size. Large or small, mink or Siberian gray squirrel, fox, astrakhan, coats, wraps, even if it was only a collar or lined bonnets or muffs. Not to surrender them risked the death penalty. The Jews did not want to give up their furs and did not want to hand them over to the Germans. They gathered every piece they could haggle over, coats, dresses, slippers. They called on Poles who lived beyond the wall to sell them. Some liquidated everything, others hid them, and still others destroyed them.

Collecting the furs was the responsibility of the Jewish Order Service. Thousands of people hurried to their offices from morning until night to get their voucher. Once they had the voucher, the piece of paper seemed very important. Only a few people, before turning over their furs, spilled boiling water over their coats and then dried them. After several days the fur fell out by the handful.

The furs went from Umschlagplatz toward the Eastern Front, for German soldiers.

Did Dela know that her father's brother, Zelig Goldstein, was in the Warsaw Ghetto with his wife, Chava? His *Ausweis* (passport), with a photo and a Star of David and a thumbprint, survived. Their fate is unknown.

The oldest brother of Henryk Przedborski, Bernard, died in the ghetto. He lived with his wife and three children on Twarda Street. He died in July 1941: the death certificate mentions his lungs as the direct cause, but he also had a heart condition. Buried by the funeral home called the Last Path.

Dela always needed eggs for the dough to make noodles. She went to the market spread along Gęsia Street. She brought back carrots and onions, sometimes cooked fava beans, horse meat, or horse blood, to give the child strength; sometimes she found *sztynki,* small decaying fish, at one złoty per pound. Little Halina didn't want to eat them. Rare were apples and eggs. She can never forget the policemen, their policemen, our policemen, Jews in uniform, their pockets full. Their pockets were filled with eggs—obviously someone had tried to bribe them. The eggs broke, dripping, down to their feet, a viscous strand, disturbing. The broken shells suggested dreams of sweet-smelling cakes, or at least *Kogel-mogel*. Thirty złotys for a pound of sugar. So many eggs for making dough wasted this way.

Later still, everything was permitted. Not only burning Jewish prayer books in the stove, imploring forgiveness from every holy book; not only working on Saturdays. It is written in the Torah that human life is what is most precious. A wedding band against a bottle of milk. A gold ring against weak milk, thin as water. Psalms and commentaries, coffins, and then doing without shrouds, and then up in smoke.

On Leszno Street they lived across from the courthouse. They had been looking for a large apartment. They were actually still all together. Dela with little Halina; Zamutek's sister Bronka, with Bolek Kuszner and their son, Maryś—that made five; Madzia, Zamutek's youngest sister, with Olek and Henryś, made eight; Grandmother Jecia and her brother Bronek, with Gienia and Adaś, made twelve; and Babunia, their mother, was the thirteenth. The eastern section of Leszno Street, renamed Gerichtstrasse, was within the ghetto. The courthouse remained on the Aryan side. An entrance on Biała Street gave access to the building.

Inside the courthouse was a money market doing business; they sold American dollars at the base rate of a hundred złotys, Swiss francs, and gold rubles. They sold jewelry and gold. In time there was less and less to sell; the price of false papers rose ever higher. In the beginning, to go through the courthouse cost a few złotys, like two pounds of potatoes. The price increased.

She didn't decide all at once. Oleś, her Polish brother-in-law, had to explain it to her, and persuade her. Months passed, punctuated by typhus epidemics and despair. A decree of the death penalty for Jews beyond the walls. Work permits still guaranteed your life. She was certainly still there during the summer of 1942. On the 22nd of July notices were posted on the walls of deportation to the East. Were they deported earlier or during that great deportation, the *Grossaktion*?* It was during that time that they deported the mother, the grandmother, the sisters and brothers-in-law, Henryś. The suicide of Adam Czerniaków—did that make her conscious of what awaited them?

Everything indicates that they left on a cold day at the end of July or the beginning of August. My mother has the impression that the Uprising started shortly after they left the ghetto, but that seems impossible. It doesn't seem probable that they could hold out until 1943. Besides, at that time it was no longer possible to leave by the courthouse.

I don't want her near the ghetto on April 19, 1943, when the Uprising broke out. I won't accept that she went to Krasiński Square. I won't allow that she heard the echoes of music from the fair, and the joyous cries of the populace on the merry-go-round. The explosions and the bursts of automatic weapons that intensified and then were silenced, in the flames. Let her be as far away from it as possible, let her never learn about it.

Dela must have rehearsed her itinerary in her head and imagination, become imbued with it before it became a reality. The staircase, the great staircase filled with a tide of humanity like the breaking waves of an ocean. The door didn't resist. She constantly had someone in front of her, near her, next to her, moving, always accompanied by the clamor of the crowd. It must have been tumultuous, whereas I always see this scene in absolute silence, like a silent film, in unbearable, suffocating silence. The imposing entrance hall on the ground floor, a glance to the left and to the right, two staircases on either side, and in front of her the hallway leading to the other side of the building. Which way to turn? Above all remain calm.

She thought about her husband constantly, although they

---

* The "Great Deportation" was carried out from July to September of 1942.

managed to write so little in their letters. Beyond the essential that she was alive, safe and sound. But the courthouse and the fear, the telephones, blessed telephones in the ghetto, contacts, arranging meetings, purchases, the daily struggle for food, and human considerations—all that occurred without him. As if they had stopped being husband and wife. She shared her table with her husband's mother, she peeled potatoes with his grand-mother, she commiserated with his sisters over the letters and the lack of letters. There was no news from Łęczyca. Her sisters and her parents were silent, like the parents of the brothers Kuszner, Bolek and Aleksander, the dentist. They still had a store of gold teeth that they could use. For the moment she had inherited her husband's family, since she had lost her own. For the moment.

ŁOCHÓW

ŁOCHÓW ESTATE, WHERE MY GRANDMOTHER, DELA GOLDSTEIN
(MIDDLE IN WHITE APRON), WORKING AS A MAID AT THE
FARM, HID AFTER ESCAPING THE GHETTO, 1942

I want to go to Treblinka. It's my birthday. I will go there by Wołomin, Tłuszcz, and Łochów, where my grandmother spent some time on the Relin estate. No one knows exactly how much time, or exactly where it is, but a photograph remains and a sheet of paper with an address dating from sixty years ago.

I saw it for the first time in an album of my mother's, and I didn't pay attention to it. Someone must have saved this photo, with its scalloped border; on the back is written in the hand of Halina: "Łochów 1943." She is standing in the middle against a background of trees, smiling, not confidently, but distinctly. She has round cheeks. The same dark hair pulled back with the same part, visible despite the white scarf on her head. For the first time I can see her full figure. She is small and plump. She wears an apron but doesn't seem to fit into this late-summer scene—in the background green trees, on the side a haystack.

If truth be told, the composition of the photo is different; it's not my grandmother who has the important role. It's a photograph of the mistress of the house with some of her servants.

The mistress of the house has a confident peasant face, with her hair braided in a crown on top of her head. She is the mistress of the place and of the afternoon. Her dress, decorated with braid around the open collar and little pockets on her chest, doesn't add to her femininity or soften her look of determination. On her left hand, a wedding band.

She doesn't like to waste her time on useless things, and without a doubt she considers having her photograph taken as such. She is looking askance, unwilling, without sympathy. As if she were saying: "There's nothing unusual so why this fuss?"

The woman standing on her right, my grandmother, Dela Przedborska, née Goldstein, is embarrassed. Of course she is smiling, showing her white teeth, but she seems bothered. Worried. As if she were afraid of something. Of course, she is standing in full sun, in a dark dress with a turned-down collar and an apron that confers on her the dignity of a servant, but that is not her real identity. She has strong legs and broad shoulders; her stomach is covered by the white apron, she does not look hungry. She seems tired; rather, perhaps, resigned. You can't see the expression in her eyes.

The blond young man beside her in a light shirt with rolled-up sleeves, the personification of carefree vigor, seems to be saying something. The camera caught him as he was speaking.

The farm is opulent. No trace of war. Thick grass and leaves. One child is in a carriage. On the side, a boy a few years old, wearing only underwear, his bicycle thrown on the ground, a well-kept wooden fence.

I don't know how much time she spent in Łochów. I don't know how she found her way there, and thanks to whom. Who helped her find this address? How many others failed to materialize before this one? There are many missing weeks and days in my grandmother's time during the Occupation. Even if she left the ghetto with the little one during the summer of 1942, after months spent in Warsaw with Aryan papers, and arrived in Łochów by the following spring, as the date on the photo indicates, it still seems that she stayed a long time in the countryside. Weeks have disappeared, and with time it has become more difficult to follow her traces. At half a century's distance it is impossible to reconstitute her chronology. Especially since everything was done to prevent anyone's being able to do it. She was excellent in the art of erasing her traces.

I try to penetrate my grandmother's world as an intruder and an undesirable.

Wołomin Plain is a settlement of some five thousand inhabitants on the Liwiec, a tributary of the Bug. It has several centuries of history, a palace with a park dating from the beginning of the nineteenth century, a patriotic page in the January Uprising of 1863. The forest of Łochów, called the Heron's Site, is covered with pines and alders, highlighted by two types of birch trees.

Łochów itself is like a Turkish bazaar, plastered with advertising, and oriental carpets, shirts, bras, shoes, artificial flowers, and plastic toys sold from hand to hand. The neighboring forest gives it a feeling of greenness. At the police station I learn without any difficulty how to find the Relin estate. A few houses on the outskirts of Łochów, not far from the mill, near the brick house for sale. You can't miss it.

The meadow that I cross on the right side of the path, a field of a lush green, this field of brightness brings back the past. My grandmother brought cows to pasture in this field, and perhaps she also milked them at times in this field, where my

mother again knew the smell of grass and rain and the sense of
freedom she had. It seems she had been afraid. Of the cows,
their hooves, their humid muzzles, their udders that weren't
easy to take hold of, but most of all she was afraid that someone
would come along and point her out. That someone would
come, that she would be led again to the basement, or behind
the wall, that they would take away her mother. Of Relin she
remembered the son of the owner, Adam, and the farmhand,
Jasiek. She remembered Kasia, with whom she played house.
Storks and green woodpeckers, small titmice, and bullfinches.
She had known nothing about them beforehand.

I push open the gate with a determined hand, so that I can't
back out. I call out, but I don't see anyone. On the porch too
small to hide anyone, there is a jumble of things. I knock on the
open door. In the kitchen at the end of the hallway, a woman
of indeterminate age whose perm has lost its freshness, like so
many women in the countryside. She wipes her mouth with
her apron, inviting me to enter. I hand her the photo and ask
if she recognizes the people. There's more light in the kitchen,
but she needs her glasses. Her hands are sunburned, hardened,
and strong, making the photo seem fragile and out of place.

"The one on the right is my mother-in-law," she said without hesitation, "and the little blond boy near the haystack is my
husband, Adam Sadomski." She asks where I got this photo. I
don't know who gave it to my mother, when and how. She is
surprised, worried that her husband is not nearby, but clearly
pleased to have a visitor. "I'll ask my husband, he will certainly
know who are the other woman and child and the young man."

We go together to look for him in the neighboring house.
It's on a larger plot and the courtyard is much wider; the big
house is incomplete, cluttered with old things in front of the
building, tools scattered about. The man who comes toward
the gate is tall, well built, imposing, wearing a hat, his shirt
open and pants worn. He carries himself with a certain dignity and natural elegance. Dressed in a suit he would appear
quite respectable. Sunburned like his wife, who, next to him,

appears old. I hand him the photo over the gate. "How you have changed, it's unbelievable! But how did your photo find its way into my family album? Is it really you?" He holds the photo to the light; he needs his glasses, we have to go back to the house.

"Me and there, my mother, Maria Osóbka, Sadomska by marriage. Albin, the father of Maria, and Marcel, the father of Edward Osóbka, were brothers; the family was from Bliżyn, near Skarżysko-Kamienna. But maybe you are related in some way or other to the Osóbkas?"

My grandfather, the engineer Samuel, or Szymon, Przedborski, was an employee of the Warsaw Housing Cooperative in Żoliborz before the war and was a colleague of Edward Osóbka-Morawski.* My grandfather was taken prisoner defending Warsaw. In the autumn of 1939, Osóbka-Morawski crossed to the other side of the Bug, where he returned after several months. Without his help, we don't know what would have become of the wife and daughter of the engineer Przedborski during the Occupation.

Osóbka-Morawski was a born social activist. He didn't finish university, and he had worked as an organizer of the cooperative movement for community and municipal rule, and then as the administrator of cooperative housing. I don't know what he looked like, but I know that for my grandfather's family, he was an important person. During the war he was the vital reference point outside of the family. They could rely on him and his colleagues. I assume, although I was never able to verify it, that they arranged the successive hiding places for Dela. They provided refuges, they gave her and other Jews hiding in Żoliborz, the papers they needed, the documents, the addresses. Thus this place was also part of it.

Wisła Morawska, his wife, took care of children during the

---

* Edward Osóbka-Morawski (1909–1997) was prime minister of the provisional government and first prime minister of the Polish People's Republic. (A.T.)

Occupation. Halina remembered that in the summer camp at Borów, they prayed to Wisła as you would to the Virgin Mary. She promised that the Russians would soon arrive and then, most assuredly, nobody could hurt them in any way. In one of the letters to her mother in Otwock, Halina told her the happy news that Osóbka had become the prime minister of the new Poland—"and you know him." Perhaps she was right in asserting that her mother should go to Lublin to look for work. Perhaps if she had gone . . . In her notebook she had written an address: "Lublin, 62 Krakowskie Przedmieście Street, the head office of Polish Radio."

Half a century later, I had met the people who, with many others, had saved my grandmother.

"The photo must have been taken by my father, Leon Sadomski, an amateur photographer, an engraver by profession. My father was deaf and dumb. He was born in Warsaw and until 1942 he lived in the Mokotów district. Later my parents-in-law purchased this farm, thirty hectares, and we left the city. They bought it from the Kowaliks."

Related to the Kowalik sisters? Of course. The Kowalik sisters, the maids in the Fourth Colony of the Warsaw Housing Cooperative, 18 Krasiński Street. Before the war they worked for the Rydygiers. It was in the Kowaliks' home that Dela found herself hiding with Halina in the alcove in the kitchen. Who found her this place on the Relin estate, and how? Did the sisters watch over her from afar, and had they acted as go-betweens to find this address also? I will never know.

"That's me, the one in front of the haystack, skinny, I was eight years old; that's my little sister, who died of diphtheria in 1945; and that's Mrs. Zofia, a Jew—she was called Brandau or something like that, the one my mother was hiding. She came to work as a maid. She was the wife of a doctor, a great lady from Skarżysko, a great lady. She thought that my mother should have served her. Standing there is Jasiek, the farmhand who helped my mother work.

"She remained with us for a long time, supposedly working

for us. They also sent us a little girl for a while. She used to take the cows to pasture, and she slept there in the next room. As for learning anything, she learned nothing except for prayers in case anyone asked her. One day, after some time, a Polish policeman in blue uniform came to warn us: don't hide any Jews in the house. She left. I don't know why or how, but she left and she never came back. My mother also hid Węgiel, a Jew from Łopianka. In the barn.

"What was the use of doing all that? Why did my mother put her whole family at risk? Why all that? What are they doing to us now? It's a shame and disgrace how the Jews have dominated the whole world. I don't know why we had to save them. They came back through the windows and the doors, yet it seems they killed so many, and they want to govern here, over us, to make their Judeopolonia."

His anti-Semitism is violent, aggressive, and crude. He knows what is the cause of the evil in the world. He hates. The Jews have taken over the whole of Poland, they won't let the Poles have any peace in their own country.

It's unending, his monologue of accusations and insults. To such an extent that his wife tries to calm him: "You should be ashamed." His daughter, even his daughter who went to Canada and works at the airport, works for Jews, who have taken over the whole world.

Dela knew that she had to live, to save the child. In the fields, several times a day she heard the trains passing. At first she was reminded of home, Łęczyca, and afterward the confusion at the Koluszki Station, where she tried to find her husband, mobilized to defend Warsaw. The anxiety at the start of the war. But immediately after, the trains meant nothing more than the wagons leaving the platform at Umschlagplatz. Madzia had gone with her son, Henryś, Aunt Liba with little Izio, her mother, Babunia, and her mother-in-law, Grandmother Jecia. She didn't know how they had taken her parents from Łęczyca.

In the handbag my grandmother had on the day she died, there were three letters from her husband, Szymon, sent from

the Oflag to Leon Sadomski, 51 Żelazna Street. The first is from
May 22, 1944, the last from the 13th of July. Addressed to "Dear
Mr. Leon," they give information that can only be understood
by Szymon's wife, for example, the real treat he is preparing
for his afternoon tea on June 2nd (Dela's birthday), because he
has a sweet roll and powdered milk, some chocolate, and other
good things. It's also for her that he comments on his good
health, of which he was convinced recently thanks to a new
identity photograph; and in another, that he was cheerful and
in good health, but rued his absolute laziness. He wasn't studying, read very little, and satisfied, really satisfied his stomach.
Effectively, he lay about, got fatter and older. But he was over
his problems with his digestion.

Several times he discussed financial questions with Leon:
How much did Praska pay? See Mrs. Stasia or Trzcińska, or else
the cooperative office. He mentioned Helena and Inka, who
are not there; Mietek, to whom he is grateful; and Antoni. I
don't know who they were.

He always sent expressions of his "utmost consideration"
along with "kisses to the ladies." Or he sent a sincere hand-
shake, counting on being able to soon express his thanks in
person for everything. Did it happen that way? I don't know
that, either.

Janina Kowalik, one of the young maids on Krasiński Street,
sent money to Łochów in the spring of 1944 and during the
summer, from 500 to 1,800 złotys each month. Another time
the receipts were signed by a neighbor, Helena Karolewska,
from number 45. Was it a money order from Woldenberg, via
SPB, the Enterprise for the Construction of the Capital, in
Żoliborz, or payment for hiding Dela?

The cost of boarding a child in a Christian family was
between 2,500 and 3,500 złotys a month then. Dela kept in
chronological order the thick oblong paper postal receipts.
Next to them there is still today a ten-złoty bill with the Chopin Monument in Warsaw, and one for fifty złotys with the
Cloth Market in Kraków.

Maria Sadomska risked her life to save Dela, whom she

knew as Zofia, the wife of a doctor, and the Jew Węglel, exposing her family and equally risking the life of her son, Adam. He hadn't learned at that point how the people his mother helped to survive were despicable. The little boy in the photo, Adam, so proper, inspiring confidence, a playmate for the little girl with dark braids. Perhaps he never played with her, perhaps he never even said a word to her. The farmhand, Jasiek—that was something else. No doubt he tried to make a pass at her. I have the impression that she was afraid of him. And yet she was nostalgic for Relin. In a letter to her mother on June 22, she wrote, "I often think of Relin. I imagine that the grass has grown tall there now. But the flowers have surely faded because there is no one to water them."

The farmhand Jasiek is still alive. His name is Jan Grenda, and he is no longer a farmhand. He lives right next door. Why try again? Now I know. I went, I couldn't help it. Thin, old, with some remaining hair and teeth, in a navy-blue Sunday waistcoat, he kissed my hand, for a long time, to greet me and to show his pleasure in having a visitor. Still spry with his cane, he crossed the courtyard to fetch his glasses. It's only the moment he examined the photo that something happened. As if the life went out of him. "It's me." He points at himself. "That's the mistress . . . I don't know, I don't remember." He sent away his children and his grandchildren, he was seated on a bench against the fence, he placed his heavy hands on his knees, he lowered his head and toyed with his eyeglass case made of cardboard. He raised and lowered the photo, raised it and lowered it as if he were still going to say something. Shrunk into himself, with his missing teeth, he repeated as if in a loop: "I don't know anything." As if he wanted to say: "It wasn't me."

It wasn't panic but a crumbling, not out of anxiety, but from the conviction that it had happened—here he was crushed, hit, found out. "If Adam, who was so young, remembers," his wife insisted, "then you should also remember."

Had he been afraid of this moment all his life, the moment when someone would come to question him about Mrs. Zofia?

Asking him what he did, if he did it? Had someone effectively denounced Zofia? Perhaps this is only the product of my imagination? What provoked my grandmother's departure from the Relin estate? No doubt she had the possibility of staying there until the end, to wait for safety. There would have been no going back, uncertainty, panic, new addresses. There wouldn't have been Otwock and working in the boardinghouse, and the shelling on a market day. What did the photo from 1943 remind him of, the farmhand Jasiek?

OTWOCK

*T*o Otwock I went to visit the cemetery. As long as I could remember, with Mother and my grandfather, I went to the grave of a grandmother about whom I knew nothing. I didn't like Otwock. I avoided it. Instinctively. This lasted for years. Otwock came back to me when I stopped being afraid.

There is no Jewish life in Otwock. There were photos of it from before the war that I saw in the museum. A theatrical setting in nature. Quiet evening among the scraggy pines. Verandas, mansard roofs, turrets, Jewish sanatoriums: Atlantic, Beatrice, Europa, Regia, Savoy.

They said that the dry air was "brawny" and "mahogany." The sandy soil breathed differently, "like in Egypt," and the forest tempered the whims of nature.

A blue Star of David shines from a piece of tile, the floor of a bathroom, a fragment of the reality of the old boardinghouse of the Nusbaum brothers at 42/43 Warsaw Street. During the Occupation the Germans made this house the *Kommandantur* of the town. Did they smash the tiles before killing the people or after?

They set fire to one synagogue right at the start and completely destroyed the other one in 1941, and death struck the cheder, the baths. The yeshiva and the Jews. They already weren't giving out ration cards to the Jews. Neighbors took over the unoccupied houses, because there is nothing like an empty house. And the "irreplaceable" people.

Their sewing machines, their pots and pans, their dishes,

their tables, their beds, their pillows, their windows, and their doors were now used by others, and no one was in the wrong. And in the end, the tiles on the floors no longer raised fears at every step with their Stars of David. Was my grandmother afraid of trespassing on his Jewish suffering? What do you think when you continue to live despite events and the fact that others died? "You, you will live," she repeated to her daughter. "You, you must live." How many mothers have said these words in vain?

Dela Goldstein—Zofia Zmiałowska—found herself in Otwock at the end of May 1944. She seemed to have in fact come from Warsaw on the train. On a sheet of paper from a notebook was jotted the address of the boardinghouse of Mrs. Czaplicka, 17 Piłsudski Street. She came to work. Someone, I don't know who, found her a job as housekeeper. Far from the station, in the resort section, the Jewish quarter of Otwock. At a rapid walk, about half an hour.

What could my grandmother Dela know about the Jews of Otwock? She wasn't from there. She didn't even know Warsaw very well; the summer places around Warsaw were unknown to her, Miedzeszyn, Falenica, Michalin, Józefów, Świder, the summer landing places for the *starozakonni*—Israelites from the Old Testament, as they were called in those days—the less well off, burdened with eiderdowns and cloth diapers, from May to September. Her own family couldn't afford to take trips, even for cures, so what's the use of speaking about lack of appetite or nerves; the dwellers of boardinghouses on the outskirts of Warsaw suffered from it as often as from tuberculosis. There came people with lung ailments, heart disease, or disorders of the nervous system; or convalescents, who wanted to improve their digestion and their appetite: guaranteed a weight gain, on the average, of eight kilos a month. Hydrotherapy and a cure with fermented mare's milk.

What did Mrs. Maria Czaplicka know about her new housekeeper? I don't know. No one knows.

Dela had to go to the market. Did she know, or when did

she learn, that the market of Otwock was located near the place where on the 19th of August 1942, in full daylight, they had taken all the Jews of the town to Treblinka? They had organized with their own hands their place of departure. They had enclosed it with barbed wire the length of Górna Street, up to the corner of Orla Street, near the railroad junction, according to orders received. From there it was easier to load them into the wagons. The Jewish police with uniform caps, armbands, and truncheons drove them in that direction. Seven thousand, plus four thousand shot in place.

The night came. A Jewish policeman who had escaped, who had himself loaded his family onto the transport, described feathers floating in the air, old ration cards, photographs, identity cards. The Polish mob smashed the doors with axes and pillaged everything they saw. In time the fence around the ghetto disappeared. The life of Otwock, the summer place, hadn't stopped.

Other people settled in the empty houses. They sat down at other people's tables and slept in their beds, and ate from their plates, and turned their armoires and their drawers inside out. Their lives didn't stop the moment it was denied to others; on the contrary, they had briskly filled the vacant places before other people did the same thing. The fabric of daily life cannot stand a void.

According to the records, the population of Otwock for the year 1943 was thirteen thousand. Half of what it was before the liquidation of the ghetto. Before the war all the boardinghouses on Piłsudski Street belonged to Jews. Of medium size, they resembled each other: about ten rooms, a drawing room, large dining room, servants' quarters in a separate building in back, stoves for heating. Running hot and cold water. The boardinghouse of Mrs. Czaplicka at number 17 was one of thirteen in business in the town in 1944. The seasonal tax was calculated to be 39.6 złotys a month.

"In any case, when they take you away, you'll have to leave it behind," the Poles said to the Jews in the ghetto, there and elsewhere. At first they didn't want to sell, to give in finally to an unfair price. Anything the others wanted to take, anything for a piece of bread. To live, live another moment. Very quickly they began to understand these new expressions: "end up as lard" or ". . . as soap." They themselves even used them, up till the end, without realizing the horror of the situation. Death awaited them on the other side of the wall, this is how the Germans and the fear of Poles taught them to think.

"The Jew is the mortal enemy of the Church and of the Greater Poland" was written in the Calendar of National Self-Defense. "The misery of Poland today has its roots in the Jews." Brochure of 1939. "Evacuate the Jews from Poland and the misfortune afflicting us will disappear." Sometimes Jews read these in the homes of Poles who were hiding them. It happened that the Poles who hid them did not know how to read. That was the case of the Polish lady in whose home a Jewish policeman from Otwock was hiding.

. . .

What did Dela do after her working hours? Whom did she meet? I see her in an easy chair under the stairs, not far from the dining room on the second floor, near a lamp casting a pale light, a bulb of low wattage, and golden shades with flaps— for hours leafing through the old registers of clients from before the war in the boardinghouse of Chanon Cetlin, 17 Piłsudski Street. Now the boardinghouse of Mrs. Czaplicka.

Registers in large format with covers of marbled cardboard, blue-gray, brown-beige, six, eight, twelve, perhaps even more of them, with greasy corners, softened, worn, marked with traces of the hands that touched them.

"Miriam, daughter of Izrael and Sara," she read. "Rachel, daughter of Moszek and Raca . . . Lejzor, son of Abram and Rajzla." I don't really know what happened—she, that is to say, me in her place, me looking through her eyes, she who was laid to rest in the ground ten years before I was born—I am not sure what occurred during these rituals she went through in the evenings. What guided her in this world whose extermination she was witnessing?

She looked at the dates of arrival and departure, the declaration of residences, the addresses, the professions, the dates of birth. She was searching for anything that they might have in common. She found it. An address at 37 Leszno Street—in the ghetto, she had lived at 58 with her family. An address in a better street, Marszałkowska Street, right next to the house where the brother of her father-in-law, a doctor, had his practice. Several engineers. Mrs. Lankierowa, a housewife, whose first name was Halina, just like her own daughter, and her mother was named Salomea, like their grandmother. Rotsztejn, Bronisława, like her husband's sister, dentist at 18 Muranowska Street. Clock maker, salesman, cashier, nurse. Where are they today? Leszno, Chłodna, Trębacka Streets, Grzybowski Square. Ruins. She noticed few people of the Roman Catholic faith. Nearly all the servants had other names: Zofia, Marianna. Only a few Jewish women of the upper classes had names like that, very few. A milliner, the wife of a lawyer on Trębacka Street. The last mention dates back to autumn. Schon, Ewelina, office worker, thirty-one years old, 3 Sienkiewicz Street, spent three months in Otwock in 1940.

By the end of 1942 there were no boardinghouses listed in Otwock. A note saying this with the signature of the mayor is on the last page of the clients' register. No one knows the fate of the Cetlin house from the moment when they were loaded onto the wagons to the moment when Mrs. Czaplicka opened her boardinghouse.

She spent much time in the kitchen. Light gray walls. Bars on the windows. Of course she didn't do the cooking, but she supervised the replenishing of supplies, she checked on the delivery of *koumys* (mare's milk) and the mineral water destined for special afflictions, she carried back her purchases from the market, bags of staples: flour, sugar, kasha. Fate was mocking her. She had access to kilos of food that she could not share with her mother and father, with her sisters who were begging for a crust of bread, with children who couldn't remember what red currants or cherries looked like. She took each apple, each pear in her hand, this is for Halina, this for Henryś, she will grate it with sugar, and for little Izio, raspberries with cream; for cousin Adaś she will stew prune marmalade, for Maryś, she would bake an apple tart. Would she see them again?

After years of being afraid, the fear was gone. She knew that she had to survive for her daughter. She had no other goal. It appears that the *fildekos* stockings were pink. *Fildekos,* a funny word, as if from a cabaret from its sound and its construction, whereas it was a cotton thread used in hosiery. From the French: *fil d'Écosse,* thread from Scotland. Bloomers or stockings are made of *fildekos,* defined with the adjective "respectable" from the end of the nineteenth century. In the summer camp, the girls wore stockings of *fildekos* in turn when they went shopping in Garwolin. She had also bought other warm clothing because it was the end of summer and Halina had come to Borów, like the others, for only a few weeks.

The Germans left Otwock the night of July 27–28, 1944. At the break of dawn detachments of the Red Army entered the town.

On the 19th of September 1944, she had received a new document, in Polish but still under her false Aryan name. An identity card with a photograph stating that she was employed by the National Council of the town of Otwock. "National Council," that was now the new terminology. Perhaps someone remembered that she had managed a day nursery, or she had directed a Polish Red Cross aid station, where she distributed food and clothing. It was about supplies. And if that was the case, was she still living at Mrs. Czaplicka's?

With the coming of autumn 1944, Otwock was systematically shelled from the other bank of the Vistula. In a bloodied, burning Warsaw, the Uprising was coming to an end. The German artillery attacked Otwock every thirty to forty minutes, paused, started up, paused, then started up again. They targeted the places with the most people: the train station, the bazaar on market day. A German pulled the trigger, God carried the bullet. If someone still believed in His existence. The missile shattered into pieces, wounding directly or by ricochet. That is what could have happened to Dela. Crowds all around, market, panic, people running in every direction, the shriek of the missile, falling on the ground. Pain. Could she have gone any farther or did they pick her up in the street, and where did they take her? The most important sanatoriums had been converted into hospitals.

I was told earlier that on that autumn day in 1944, she was running around in the neighborhood of Praga, on the right bank of Warsaw, liberated recently from German bombings. For a long time my mother told a version in which her mother died by a German bullet during the Warsaw Uprising. I know today that the other version is more likely. She was hit by shrapnel in Otwock, also on the Vistula, and equally on territory liberated from the Germans. Perhaps she was going to the market, perhaps she was distributing clothing or food.

In the autumn of 1944 my grandmother Dela, Zofia Zmiałowska, with impeccable papers, had survived the war.

Almost survived. She had succeeded for so many years. Alone with the child. The downfall of Warsaw in 1939, the road to the ghetto, the moves within the ghetto, the decision to flee, her escape, crossing the wall, her wandering life with Aryan papers, going from one place to another alone with her child, and the noodles for her husband in the Oflag, and the thought that the others had perished, had disappeared, were killed, the ghetto in flames that she could see from the windows of her successive hiding places in the town and the countryside, the absence of letters from home. When everything was coming to an end, and everything had been accomplished, and she had to work; if not, if without work, what would happen? She had to remain in Otwock, not let go of Mrs. Czaplicka, not lose her grasp on life, that's exactly when she was struck by the shrapnel of Big Bertha, also called "the Cow." Neither hunger nor the wall had killed her, nor the blockades in the ghetto, nor her appearance;

nor had her glance betrayed them, nor the child with dark hair. People had not deceived her; she was felled by Big Bertha.

She had fled, she had run like everyone else on hearing how near was the shell. She was wounded in one leg. Where on the leg, on her thigh, or calf, or ankle—and which leg? Why had they amputated it, and where did it happen? If she was taken to a hospital, why did it end this way? They lacked anesthetics and bandages; did they do without them? Was there an infection? Was it her heart that couldn't hold out? My mother says today, "Her heart was broken."

She was buried in the Catholic cemetery of Otwock; it never occurred to anyone to do otherwise. She rested under a pine tree which in time masked her false name and the cross dedicated to her "blessed memory." During all the years following the war, Samuel Przedborski did not transfer his Jewish wife to another cemetery. He did not change the plaque on her tombstone. And I also visit my grandmother today in the Catholic cemetery.

THE BLACK HANDBAG

THE BLACK BAG BELONGING TO MY GRANDMOTHER,
ADELA GOLDSTEIN (ZOFIA ZMIAŁOWSKA), GIVEN BACK
TO HER HUSBAND IN JANUARY 1945 UPON HIS RETURN
FROM A GERMAN OFLAG. HIS WIFE HAD BEEN DEAD
FOR THREE MONTHS.

Zofia Zmiałowska's black handbag with its contents was returned to her husband during the winter of 1945 in the parish of Otwock.

When I became an adult, Mother passed it on to me. It contains everything I know about my grandmother. Not very large, almost all of it fits into my open hand. A little black leather handbag. It would look good worn to a dance. Vertical stitching, a little flap, a fold under which was the snap. Only one part of the snap fastener remained. The top, a small stiff roll with a white metal button at each end. It looks like silver.

On the back, a sort of handle, a leather strap on a slant. I don't know if it was ever carried that way. The rounded upper part fits perfectly under the arm.

She carried it every day during the Occupation. Prominently displayed in her wartime handbag, my grandmother kept a religious picture in sepia, with artistically scalloped edges. It's of a shepherd with bare feet, Jesus in a white robe. Bathed in a halo of light, he is knocking at a wooden door. Where did she find it? Perhaps she entered a church alone, when she was still in Łęczyca, and got it in the sacristy? But in town everyone knew her. It seems unlikely that the daughter of the Goldsteins from Przedrynek, who accompanied her parents to the synagogue every Saturday, could have decided to do such a thing. Besides, she still was not aware at that time that an accessory with the Sign of the Cross could be helpful to her.

This happened only after another raid, when she hid the children—hers, and those of her sister and sister-in-law—in a basket of dirty laundry, trembling with fright that they might be smothered or that the dogs, huge German shepherds, would sniff them out. She didn't know which death was worse than the other; it was only then that she understood she had to flee. Get herself on the other side of the wall at any price.

Thus, she may have received this picture from her brother-in-law Oleś, who organized her flight from the ghetto, passing over to the Aryan side through the courthouse, and who came to help her several times later, when the *szmalcowniks,* the traffickers, blackmailed her and when she didn't know where to turn next. He knew how to behave so as not to draw any attention, how to recite the prayers, make the Sign of the Cross with an ample gesture from the left to the right, then with hands joined ". . . world without end, Amen."

Next is a large document folded in two, a baptismal certificate. In case of an ultimate confrontation, it could constitute irrefutable proof of innocence. The best were the authentic papers obtained from the parishes, generally in the name of people who were absent or dead—on condition that their death certificates were located in the same place. Priests signed and delivered papers without asking any questions.

There were several ways of obtaining false papers. Polish friends took care of it, members of the Resistance, or, most often, numerous intermediaries handsomely rewarded. Sometimes these papers cost exorbitant sums, up to five hundred dollars in 1943, during the liquidation of the ghettos on Polish territory. In the space of a few months, the dollar rose from 100 to 360 złotys, and with it the price of food.

The following advertisement was preserved in the archives of Ringelblum: "False papers, perfect counterfeit with seals, professional printer, each document: 3,000 złotys." A hundred złotys was the equivalent of more than three kilos of white flour, four of pearl barley, a kilo and a half of sugar. The price of a hen plus a loaf of bread, the price of a pair of women's shoes, and of nine liters of petroleum. A worker earned three hundred złotys and managed to live a month on it, even two.

A *Kennkarte,* that is to say, an identity card, and an attestation of employment cost several times the price of a birth certificate.

Testimonium nativitatis et baptismi. In February 1942 the priest of Stanisławów, Józef Rzeczkowski, made out this authentic birth and baptismal certificate. In Latin. Made in Stanislaopolis. He certainly didn't know who it was for.

Now she was named Zofia Zmiałowska, daughter of Hipolit—son of Mieczysław and Zuzanna Rymarkiewicz—and of Agnieszka Hożelska—daughter of Józef and Wiktoria Mękicka. She was born on the 10th of April 1902 in Stanisławów. Stanisławów? Galicia, the eastern borderlands, Ukraine. Southeast of Lwów, capital of the Stanisławów district. A city founded by the Potockis, hence their magnificent seventeenth-century palace. Perhaps she should know more about the château. After all, she had grown up in its shadow.

Only the year of her birth was authentic, and she had to imbue herself with all the rest. She wasn't allowed to make a mistake. Even during the night. Daughter of Hipolit. Hipolit could repair shoes or work in a circus. He resoled shoes and could walk the tightrope. But they had shut down the circus, a sign of the times: the animals had been eaten. Better he be a shoemaker, he could make a better living, people had to walk. Agnieszka, his wife, her own mother, was a seamstress at home. She was sickly.

Dela had to make this story her own. Always on the alert. During the day. Because in her sleep she still and always had two sets of parents. Her father, Szloma, was turning gray and kept shrinking. In his long, threadbare frock coat he was sitting on a low stool in the coal warehouse. He was speaking to the pigeons while rocking forward and backward. She was frightened because he spoke Yiddish, and looked ill. She motioned for him to stop, she put a finger to her lips. And suddenly her mother, her mother, Chana, saw her: "Dela," she called out and opened her arms to her. Dela wanted to run toward her, and she heard her own words: "Mom, now my name is Zofia, and I have another mother."

All this was drowned out by circus music. Her new parents, dressed in loud colors, came running into the ring. Applause. They took their bows, ready for their star performance. With a whip used ordinarily to guide horses, from a huge bucket they started splashing holy water. "Praised be He, *Spiritus Sanctus, with God . . . ,*" they bless everything that is impure. Everything that is not theirs. Everything that smells Jewish. Drops of water are sprinkled on her mother and father. Father is the first to disappear. The pigeons disappear. And she also disappears. It doesn't hurt.

Second Lieutenant Engineer Przedborski, Samuel, no. 49178. Barrack 12A, Woldenberg. *Offizierlager* IIB. She arranged all the cards from her husband stamped with the German seal of the *Kriegsgefangenenpost* like playing cards. The first one is dated January 27, 1940; the last one, July 3, 1944. A few are in German. As much by form as by content, it is reminiscent of the writing on an industrial drawing blueprint. Monotonous graphics, sharp, concrete, firmly grounded on the paper. He

sent them to several people at several addresses. He began them
with "Dear Madam."

Or "Dear Sir." He informed them of his health, the weather,
and asked if the money had arrived. "With me, everything is
fine," he invariably reported. There's not much to read between
the lines.

Actually, it's painful to me that he wrote in such a way. It
can't be explained either by censorship or by how discourag-
ing it was to see months and years succeed one another in his
immobility within an enclosed space. I understand the precautions and the need to cover his tracks. But the Poles also loved
one another during the war, and they didn't forbid tenderness,
and solicitude was not punished.

They passed each other at the Koluszki Station on the 30th
of August 1939. Second Lieutenant Przedborski was joining his
unit; Dela was leaving the house in Łęczyca for Warsaw. They
had not been able to say goodbye. During the next five years
she could find support only within herself. She alone made all
the essential decisions.

My dearest, my love,

Thank you for your package. It smells good of home and
your hands. It has that unique scent for which I am nostalgic every day and every night. Especially at night. I look
for it in vain around me. It's your scent, my darling. Do
you remember the place on the banks of the Bzura where
we used to sit in the afternoon when I came home for the
summer from Polytechnic School? There everything was
first. Ours. Unique. I talk to you at night when no one can
hear me.

It was a letter like that she was waiting for. He never wrote
her any letter like that. But he regularly sent her his birthday
greetings on the 2nd of June.

She had two stamps left over from a large sheet. They both
had a portrait of Adolf Hitler on a red ground: 24, Deutsches
Reich. The best proof that she had nothing to do with the

ghetto. It was forbidden to use stamps with his "effigy" in those quarters. They could send only those that reproduced "any sort of view of buildings or landscapes."

A little agenda book for the year 1941, with a dirty orange cover that was becoming unglued. Notes in pen or pencil of different colors, often crossed out as if these things were completed. Addresses: Śliska Street number 15, Pańska Street 69/5, 67 Dzielna Street. Addresses that reveal assistance, help, life, or which are the successive stages of her path. Elsewhere, the address of Dr. Rosental in Istanbul. And the telephone numbers of family and friends, especially in Żoliborz. All this prudently coded. Long columns of numbers added up. Cost of packages sent to Łęczyca in the spring of 1942. Notes about lard. She noted down summer shoes on Madaliński Street, an appointment with G. in a little café. A new stage in her war transit. The name of Janina Kowalik, the young woman working in the Fourth Colony on Krasiński Street. In her home behind the curtain hid Halina on escaping from the ghetto, and it was through her acting as intermediary that Dela received the money from her prisoner husband. Some receipts—proof of payment with a mention of the month. It was a complex network of people taking part in the transfer of money. Who paid whom and why? The Jews paid the Poles. They paid for their lives and the courage of others. They paid strangers and their relatives.

On a sheet of paper torn from a notebook, my grandmother had recopied in pencil the song about the loving heart and the soldier. Taking pity on the amorous heart, he took it with him in his knapsack. For him the war was not so terrible, because he had a heart in reserve. A popular Polish melody for soldiers. Did she also have to learn this song, so new to her? Yes, certainly.

Before the war she taught children how to read and write. In Polish. In the Jewish school in Łęczyca. She spoke about nature and friendship, she spoke about *Heart* by De Amicis. On her orange *Kennkarte* in the name of Zofia Zmiałowska, under the heading "Profession" was written "salesperson." Her working card was dated July 1942. It waited for her on the Aryan side.

She had never worked in a store. She didn't have a knack for business. She had a way of reciting the poetry of Tuwim and Pawlikowska-Jasnorzewska.

She didn't know how to cook. It explains all the recipes for dessert in her handbag. Toward the end of the war her work entailed composing menus. A quart of wild strawberries sorted out, simmered with a spoon of butter, passed through a sieve, and chilled. She now learned to solve herself the complexities of the stove and oven. Dessert of wild strawberries, and cherries, yeast cake and shortbread, veal and cabbage dumplings. She jotted down how to make bread pudding on a small sheet of graph paper with a fountain pen that had ink the color of overcast skies.

. . .

My mother remembers Dela's warm voice and the certainty that nothing could happen to her when she was with her. Her mother was always with her, and always came to get her. In every lodging outside the wall, in each basement, with the people, the men and women who changed all the time. She was with her mother in an empty room facing the ghetto in flames. For the first time she didn't hide behind a curtain. From the fourth-floor window she saw everything. Beside her on the table was broth with noodles that a kindly neighbor had just brought for them. The vapor from the two steaming plates slowly misted over the window. Dela was not crying.

The boardinghouse of Mrs. Czaplicka, Otwock— underlined—17 Piłsudski Street, for Mrs. Zmiałowska. Deep red stamp with the likeness of Hitler, 24, Deutsches Reich general government. Round postmark. Summer 1944. Envelopes formerly blue, now faded, a gray-yellow, like a worn-out coat, pliant with time and handling. Address in pencil, a childish handwriting. My mother, thirteen years old then, was called Alicja Szwejlis, had long dark braids with navy-blue ribbons.

She wrote having just arrived at the home of exceptionally kind people, although strangers. She wrote that everything was fine for her, and she played with Hania, two years younger than she, an orphan who lived with her grandmother. She compared the house and garden to another one certainly known to both of them, that of Mr. and Mrs. Stanisław. Only here the garden was bigger and the house as completely elegant as a candy box. Not the least trace of dust.

She would never have believed that she could be so comfortable with people who were strangers. She didn't give the address because she had to leave again in a few days.

A week later, on half a lined page torn out of a notebook, she remembered Relin. She tried to remember the fields and the flowers there. "I can guarantee," she wrote, "that all the hens lose their eggs." She asked to send her greetings to Papa.

How many times did she change houses and apartments? At Hanusia's, Zosia's, Janka's, Grandmother's, aunties', cousins'? She learned to wait. She learned never to complain. It seemed to her sometimes that her rag doll—which didn't belong to her, borrowed also like everything else—was her own little daughter. "Don't be afraid, don't be afraid," she repeated. But the doll trembled and wept. She promised her that when the war was over, she would never again be afraid. For her birthday in 1944, Halina received a journal. It has been lost somewhere, like the ring that had turned out to be too small.

On the 7th of July her letters took on a serious tone. She was really worried that she hadn't heard from her mother. She used adult words and repeated several spelling mistakes. It was summer vacation and she wasn't learning much. She practiced her French vocabulary. With the same pencil, on the same piece of paper now turned yellow, she informed her that she had grown and had gained weight. Her head was now clean because "Auntie" had killed all those dirty lice with *cévadille*. What is *cévadille*? She knew; children from wartime should know it. I looked it up in the dictionary because it could also happen to me.

In fact, *cévadille* is the seed of the sabadilla plant. They made an extract from the seeds of the sabadilla, added water and alcohol, and used it as an insecticide and against skin infections.

She rarely received letters; the last one was from July 11, 1944.

Shortly afterward Halina went to Wilga, near Garwolin, to a summer camp for orphans organized by the Warsaw Housing Cooperative, which helped the families of employees from before the war. She stayed there longer, several months, because the Uprising had broken out in Warsaw.

Her friends envied her being able to correspond with her mother. "They will certainly never see their parents again," she wrote in a letter. She wrote how she was the most studious in her class and helped Lila, older than she. That the sweater was too warm, and even her pants were hot. The bra was her size. She had told the house monitor that she had returned it, so now she hid it from her. A bra. She was wearing a bra. The chocolate was great.

"My dearest mother . . .," she wrote. She wrote that she was in good health and was feeling very well, which was the most important thing.

Dela visited Halina at the end of August. She went from Otwock to Wilga partly on foot, partly by riding in military vehicles. The right bank of the Vistula had already been liberated. She brought her warm clothing and some underwear. She had to return to work; she promised to come fetch her as soon as she could.

Five days later, in a letter, Halina told her about the distribution of warm clothing—flannel nightgowns ("I didn't receive any because I have mine"), dresses ("Those who didn't have any got one; me, I had my pink one"), stockings ("I didn't get any either because you brought me some"). But she had also managed in other ways. She traded her short ribbed stockings for those another little girl had received, brown, in Scottish wool, going up to the thigh. Now she had enough to be able to change.

"Clothing, it's very important. Isn't it?" She wanted to be sure. She asked for a letter, a letter, a letter.

Her mother remained silent. She did not answer the news her daughter sent on the 15th of October, or on the 20th. The whole long autumn passed without any news from her. October passed, thirty-one days, parents began to fetch their little girls. In November, thirty days, she had fewer and fewer friends. December, a month of holidays, passed. They certainly put up a Christmas tree for the children, and the children sang Christmas carols. Perhaps the first that Halina had ever heard. How she must have worried. The new year 1945 began, the war was ending.

An envelope from October is open, even though Dela had never read her letters. A piece of lace for cuffs, a little piece for small wrists. The obligatory reading of my grandmother: Alina Gniewkowska, *Contemporary Cooking at Home,* fourth edition.

A handbag with Aryan papers. A bag made sweeter by Polish desserts, Jesus Christ, to whom it was permitted to pray, and the love of a little girl. The bag of big and little things that kept her alive.

VII

Remembering

WITH MY MOTHER, 1963

*I*n the beginning there was a little girl—my mother, who doesn't remember. Sometimes we would have a session called "What She Is Sure Of."

She is sure of the armband, the white armband with a blue Star of David that her mother had to wear on her right arm, but she is not certain that it was on the right arm. The armband meant one was an adult. My mother celebrated *her* birthday in the ghetto, once certainly; twice, she can't recall, but my mother never wore the armband.

She didn't have a doll. And she never played Wall. She doesn't remember having ever played it. At the beginning, she wasn't alone in the apartment, there were Adaś and Marian, her young cousins, and afterward Henryś and Izio. Maryś used to speak about a god, or more precisely, two gods. She heard him explain that they stood with feet planted on earth, they had huge shoes and pants and beards. The Polish god also had a face, but the Jewish god, better, touched the sky. The Jewish god, that one must have been ours, the true one.

She could talk about green trees with or without needles. Of the forest, of pinecones, even about the sea where she had been with her parents before the war. Of the pier in Sopot—that is to say, the place where you stroll on the water like the wooden overpass over Chłodna Street that links the "little ghetto" to the "big ghetto." They had taken a photo of her holding a big, fluffy teddy bear. The photo has disappeared. She remembers few things, but apparently she learned to swim then.

She is sure of remembering the meadows just behind the house on Przedrynek Place, full of dandelions, poppies, and cornflowers. Behind the field, on the other side, was the river Bzura, where her aunt Bronka sometimes took her to the park; her mother had told her that she and Papa used to go there, before they were married.

At home for holidays, there was always broth. In the ghetto her mother was constantly making noodles, drying them and then wrapping them in little linen bags. She sent most of them to Halina's father in the camp; the rest they ate themselves. "I don't want any noodles. They are twisted like snakes." Wounded horses ran through the streets. "I don't want to eat horse's liver. I am afraid of eating entrails, Mother."

"Calm down. You would prefer the little fish?"—that's what she called those cheap, foul-smelling little things, yellow, brown smelts. "You'd prefer these fish?"

"No, I prefer the *makagigi*."

She had learned the word and the taste in the ghetto. She had never tried it before and would never again afterward. They were sticks of poppy seeds, a mixture of poppy seeds with something sweet, grilled on a stone. With sugar. "Surely not sugar? Sugar in the ghetto? What are you talking about?" But it had a sweet taste, sweet like nothing else. She ate it slowly to make it last longer.

She is certain she never played Wall.

She is sure the mailboxes in the ghetto were yellow.

She knew how a raid was different from an armed guard.

She was anemic. She was able to describe a coupon. A ration card.

She doesn't know when she will forget all that.

In the ghetto, she changed addresses several times. She doesn't remember any one of them. They were together for a long time: her grandma, her mother, the aunts, Bronka, Madzia, Liba, the children. They moved from one street to another, from one floor to another. No time to get used to it, they didn't own anything. They had to be ready to move on at any moment.

Still another apartment, open like the preceding ones, gutted by the greedy hands of the Germans. The drawers on the dressers and the armoires wide open, the doors on the sideboards and linen closets ripped off their hinges, generations of photographs mixed together, stomped on, torn, coats, dresses, pants, tablecloths and napkins, chandeliers, plates, candles, saltshakers, tea kettles, hand towels, receipts, buttons.

In the photographs spread along the floors formerly waxed the color of honey or oak, there were clean prayer shawls, and long beards ready for the holy days. She had never seen so many photos and so many religious Jews. Only in the ghetto. But here the Germans made them sit on barrels and, doubled over with laughter, cut off their beards. They also kicked them and showered them with blows.

She remembered the eyes, tens, hundreds, thousands of eyes, in the photos, looking upward to the ceiling. Eyes, living eyes.

She heard it said that the trains filled with people left Umschlagplatz for the ovens. For a ten-year-old it is hard to believe that there could be devised an oven in which to burn you.

When she first heard the word "courts," she associated it with the Day of Atonement the Jews observed in the synagogues. Even assimilated Jews like her father or her father's father, even they went to pray on that day. Therefore Judgment Day. The Day of Reckoning.

A person could work in the courts. Or have business in the courts. Have something to do in the courthouse, business to settle or to pursue. You are pursued when you do something bad, stealing, for example. In the streets children steal bread, rip packages from your hands, grabby, famished little children, they swallow in a second even though sometimes what they have taken is not food. It looks like a piece of bread or cake, but it's soap or a sponge. Can these children have anything to do with the courthouse? Who is to judge their misdeeds? She was convinced that it was the Germans, they had complete authority over everything. The Germans locked us up in the ghetto, no one thinks anymore that it's for our own good, but everyone forces himself to work. Work gives us life. My mother also works, and my uncle, and my second uncle who manages a carpentry shop; only Grandmother Jecia doesn't work and neither does my Babunia, and I don't know what will happen to them.

Their last lodgings were on Leszno Street, almost opposite the courthouse. She was sure the courthouse building had four stories, three of them identical, and the top floor's cornice was set back. After looking at the wall a long time, the brick rectangles were reminiscent of chocolate bars. She couldn't remember the taste of chocolate. She tried to remember all the sandwiches with cold cuts that her mother prepared that she surreptitiously threw down the toilet. She was convinced that what happened to her was her punishment. She certainly would never again throw away even a crust of bread.

From the window she could see an eagle wearing a crown, the Polish eagle of which she had been taught to be proud. He stood out a little from the wall, and he was shining with the whiteness of his outspread wings as if he wanted to fly away somewhere. Birds don't fly over the ghetto, and this one had also been turned to stone. From afar you couldn't distinguish either the beak or the crown, but she knew they existed; she had seen them before the war.

She is certain that she left the ghetto through the courthouse. The imposing building on Leszno Street swallowed up all the people who entered there, from one side or the other. It looked anonymous, like all administrative buildings, and because of its high function. The confusion of its hallways turned out to be a salutary labyrinth. She wanted to believe that she was safe in the belly of the courts. It was once past the doors that the light hurt the eyes with its particular brilliance.

That's how they were identified.

Her mother, by the hand, her worn shoes closed with buckles. Under her feet a green floor. A floor cannot be green. It was linoleum. Under her footsteps it was green, nothing more.

Years later she remembered the staircase. Big steps that were difficult for her to climb; she did everything she could, she was perspiring, pulled by the hand, but they were still there, and new ones always turned up. They increased as she climbed, as in the story of Cinderella. And as in the story, it seemed as if she didn't have enough time, that the spell would be over at any moment, that the truth would come out, the cock would crow, and everyone would learn who she was. She didn't lose any slipper. Her shoes were not magical. And they learned everything. A little later.

She's not sure when all this happened. Was it during the first action in the ghetto, perhaps in August 1942, or was it already during the Uprising in April of the following year? Sometimes she thinks that she remembers little baskets with eggs that people were carrying in the streets, just before or right after. Someone explained to her that the baskets were blessed and Christ was resurrected. But she could have heard it elsewhere, when the ladies from Żoliborz taught her the prayer and explained to her what to do in church and how to receive Holy Communion. She was already called Alicja then, and she knew that there were things she was not allowed to remember.

She was not allowed to remember Grandfather Jakub, because he wore a yarmulke and prayed while rocking forward and backward. She wasn't allowed to remember Grandfather Henryk, even though he looked like a Polish gentleman, with his curled mustache, and he read only Polish books. She wasn't allowed to remember Papa, whom people before the war called "Mr. Engineer," or Mother. Mother, who ran around the round table in the large room overlooking the front yard here in Żoliborz, and who begged: "Halusia, eat a little something, Halusia . . ." It's especially about Mother that she's not allowed to remember.

Not the chairs either. They gave the chairs to Uncle Oleś to keep in Saska Kępa, as soon as she and her mother moved to the ghetto. The chairs and the oak table, and perhaps also the sideboard. Uncle Janek, the brother of Grandfather Henryk, habitually sat in the chair with dark green trimmings. He was called "the pediatrician," which meant that he took care of children, and he was always urging Mother not to force Halina to eat. But her mother didn't know how to do otherwise: "A child shouldn't go hungry!" Uncle tried to persuade her: "When she has fasted for a while, you won't have any more worries—try, try it just once." He mopped his brow with his right hand, and smoothed his dark hair. "A child mustn't go hungry," Mother repeated, and that ended the discussion. Uncle Janek always wore an elegant suit and a hat that he would tip forward lightly as a greeting. He always visited them in a carriage, and he was usually in a hurry.

On September 1, 1939, she didn't go to school. Even though everything had been made ready; the maid, Józia, had starched her collar and ironed her navy-blue dress. Her shoes were next to the bed. Her father was still sleeping in his room. Mother had gone back to Łęczyca a few days earlier; her students were waiting for their lessons. By the time she returned to Warsaw, Halina's father had already gone off to war.

She is sure that the two maids who had let them stay in their place on the ground floor for some time in return for a sum of money, the very same ones who had the kitchen cupboard with a curtain, were called Hela and Stasia; one of them had come as housekeeper to Mr. and Mrs. Rydygier. They made apple pancakes and enjoyed their day off.

They used to go out dancing, which they would recount with laughter. Helenka had met her fiancé there, the one who liked his soup salty.

Formerly, they never left their hiding place until nightfall to go for a walk in the courtyard of section 4. She remembered the name of the concierge, Pawlowski, because they were always looking out for him. He would harangue the children who made mischief, who threw pails of water on passers-by on Easter Monday, and he would scream when they broke branches or trampled on the lawn. Then she wanted to be invisible again. Dela didn't even have a veil to hide her face. And she never dyed her hair. Why? She walked cautiously, keeping close to the walls; she checked that the way was clear, and they didn't speak to each other. She knew that he couldn't see them. And he never did.

"My name is Alicja."

I curtsy and I recite a little poem about trees like I did in the ghetto.

"My mother worked with the RGO. You don't know? The Central Welfare Council."

"Your mother was not in the ghetto, Alicja. They locked up Jews in the ghetto."

Some children didn't know what buds are. I could explain to them. About pinecones and heather; I had memories of the forest. Peas have white blossoms. Weeds grow more profusely. Some had never seen flower beds, or ponds, or swans. Swans are difficult birds to describe. Like giraffes.

Onstage we sang the song about the sun—"No one can take the sun from us."

"Our mistress wears paper shoes"—it's better that you sing that one, it's an Aryan song. Certainly Aryan even though Grandfather Henryk sang it, and then Grandmother Jecia in the ghetto sang it on the telephone for Frania's son. "She had shoes made of paper"—Frania stayed on the other side of the wall and everybody worried, believing that the Germans would kill her. They would kill her because she had a Polish husband and she had not gone into the ghetto as had been ordered. It's good that she didn't obey. Thanks to her, thanks to him—as Babunia used to say: "Goy, this goy—thanks to this goy we are alive." All those who allowed themselves to be saved are alive. Why did the mistress have paper shoes? Halina never gave a thought to this song. Was her husband a poor Jewish shoe-maker who could not afford shoes for his wife? They didn't have the means to buy shoes but they wanted to dance. "Wear-ing these shoes, with her husband she will dance."

. . .

The first empty apartment seemed gigantic to her. The floors squeaked at every step. She forced herself to stay still and to move without making any noise; everything echoed. She took up little room. Ladies came to see her, and then these same ladies decided that now she should go down to the base-ment. The basement was located at the opposite end of the courtyard with which she was familiar. All this occurred within the precincts of the cooperative housing on Krasiński Street, where she would go by coach with her parents, wearing her fin-est coat to go visit her aunt on Wilanowska Street.

She is certain that the basement was dark. A dim light filtered through a small, boarded-up window, but she couldn't go near there lest someone catch sight of her. During the day, through a crack, she watched legs passing by. Shoes went by on the sidewalk, to the left, to the right, a lot of shoes, and for each pair there was a story. Big shoes with buckles like those worn by young maids passed by and returned several times in one direction or another. Perhaps they were going to the market, or shopping, or perhaps going to pay a visit at the hospital, or else to the library to fetch new books. Short white felt boots, closed from behind with three loops, and others with the pattern of spotted fur. It seems that a neighbor in the Third Colony made them. She learned that after the war. Sandals and running shoes—boys ran and jumped, played tag, or played ball in the neighboring square. Once a ball fell very near her; for a second she saw close-up yellowish leather scuffed in places. But hands reached out to it instantly, and again, nothing happened. She saw a bicycle. Someone was beating a rug with loud, monotonous blows. Roller skates resonated. A newsboy walked by. The big boots of the concierge, and the twig broom sweeping up the remnants of the daily chaos, leaves, rubbish, scraps, the remains of the ordinary.

After several days she asked the lady who brought her a roll and some milk for something to read. The candle wasn't big and had to be saved, and above all kept at a distance from the door and window. She made a place for herself, near the coal pile, on a dark blanket which she used to cover her head. She felt smothered. She read *Uncle Tom's Cabin*. In the book the sun continued to shine. She couldn't remember much else.

One fine day, at dusk, they moved her from there. She walked with a new lady in the streets of her neighborhood, which she didn't know well since they had lived there only briefly with her father before the war. In an apartment, by a yellow lamp, her mother was waiting. "Mother, don't leave me." "Remember that I will always come back to get you."

She could count to a hundred. She didn't know how to keep

count of the number of places where she was left. Seven, twelve, twenty and some? She doesn't know. She didn't have anyone to talk to for days on end.

She dreamed about packing. A dream she continues to have. According to dream books, packing means moving, and moving means upheaval and confusion. She is eleven years old and she lives behind the wall. She is alone and she tries to take everything remaining.

She adds new things that multiply, swell up, she tries to close the lid. The suitcases overflow with clothing, plates, linen, towels, shoes. She wants to take everything, and she can't fit them in. It's confusion: the shoes creak, the pens push aside the pencils and spill ink on the white sheets, the comb expels the brush. The skirts chase the pants. Panic. Crockery cups crumble under the weight of the pots, the silk stockings shrivel up next to the fustian pants, hats and fingernails are crushed. Panic about selection. New suitcases appear, new wagon trains whitewashed, disinfected with chlorine, step inside, faster, faster. There's more and more. And still there's Peter Pan and Nastasya Filipovna, Lord Jim, King Lear and the Montagues, and Grandmother Jecia's favorite, Meir Ezofowicz, a young Jew who rebels against the obscurantism of his people and ends up cursed and chased out of his home. Make room, I need a place for him. A scream. No air.

She made herself say her prayers, "Our Father, who art in heaven, hallowed be thy name. Thy kingdom come *my name is Alicja Szwejlis* thy will be done *diminutive: Alisia* on earth as it is in heaven. Give us this day *do you think that I can sleep peacefully with these papers?* our daily bread, *I am Aryan, do you hear, it doesn't matter that there is no daily white bread* on earth as it is *my mother also has a Polish name, Zmiałowska, Zofia, remember,* Amen. *Good night.* Amen.

Mama and Papa were married under the chuppah, you have to forget this word; Mother had to borrow a dress, because she didn't have the money to buy a new one. She had borrowed it from Bronka, the sister of her future husband, my papa,

Zamutek. Bronka had gotten married earlier, perhaps under this same canopy. Dela was the eldest child, and her parents were proud of her because she had been to teacher's college, and she taught school in Łęczyca. Me, what I liked most was that other children had to listen to her. She had long black hair swept up in a special way. But now it's bad to have shining black hair, that's why my mother's hair has lost all its shine. Now it doesn't remind me of challah bread. Nothing should remind me of challah.

Nor the candles in the silver candlesticks. No doubt I am not allowed to mention the holidays. Now I know about other ones: Christmas when Jesus was born, and Easter when he was resurrected. To celebrate Passover there was a special set of dishes in the house, there was matzo and "Dayenu" was sung. The door was left open, because we were waiting for the prophet Elijah. Stop. Instead remember Grandfather Henryk's small coffeepot, the one with the portraits of the emperors. Or the demijohns of red beet soup in the storeroom.

"And a scapular, you don't have a scapular of the Virgin Mary?" "I don't have one." "Blessed are you" as words of greeting. "What little black eyes you have, miss, exactly like—excuse me, I am not making any allusions—like a little Jewess . . ." Blessed. Our bread.

She remembered having cried with joy when, on the road to Garwolin with the other children, they greeted the Russian soldiers.

She is sure that if her mother had lived she would have come to fetch her in Wilga. She is certain that everything then would have taken another turn.

VIII

Frania

FRANIA PRZEDBORSKA WITH HER BROTHER, SZYMON,
MY GRANDFATHER, AFTER THE WAR, ON VACATION

FRANIA

In the family she was called Aunt Frania, or Franuchna, even though in reality her name was Celina. They always spoke of her with lowered voices, with a solicitude or an embarrassment that was inexplicable. I felt that they wronged her. As far back as I can remember, I had heard the sentence "Franuchna spoiled her life," but for a long time I didn't understand what they meant.

Frania, the sister of my grandfather Szymon, seemed old to me. She was like an echo of those with whom she lived. Wearing hand-me-down clothes, in secondhand shoes. Always solving other people's problems as if they were her own. There wasn't enough room for her. Between her husband and her children, between breakfast and dinner, between the laundry and the housekeeping. No one heeded her needs, nor her dreams. In time she shed them as useless reminiscences of her youth.

I have few memories of my childhood visits to my uncle and aunt Majewski. A narrow entrance hall into which my mother and I barely fit. Taking off a coat was a sort of dance between the wall and the armoire—armoires, there were many—in the darkness, or only the impression of darkness. An enormous tarnished mirror. I have always been afraid of figures coming out of the darkness toward me. The witch in the kilim rug hanging in the dining room belonged to a cruel fable, a boy and a girl reaching for a poisoned apple.

An uncle and two aunts I didn't like to kiss waited for us. There was no one to play with. Their sons were grown up. I was wearing my best dress, and Mother told them of my accomplishments in school. Because education was the most important thing.

I never wondered why one uncle had two wives. It was simply like that. I had always known that the one who was ours, truly ours, was Frania. The other one, Regina—I called her "the other one," but only in private, to myself—she was the one with pretty dresses, who smiled sweetly and spoke French. I politely accepted her show of affection and waited until we could leave.

Years later, Frania sometimes showed up in our apartment on Kasprzak Street. Always tired, carrying several heavy net bags that she barely set down, and then only for a moment. Right from the threshold she rushed to the telephone to learn how they were managing without her at home. She felt guilty of having taken too long, enjoying her liberty unscheduled. She called me "Fifille," darling daughter, and asked when I was going to get married, because the most important thing was to make a family and have children. I wasn't in a hurry about either one. I was adding to her worries. She knew to remain silent about herself. She became animated for a moment when she gave my mother her recipe for carp in aspic. She repeated that once the fish was ready, it should not be washed too thoroughly, there should remain a little blood. "Do you understand?" she asked, lowering her voice as if sharing a secret. On these occasions she mentioned Łęczyca, but I didn't pay any attention. I didn't think that one day it would become important.

Frania never finished her tea; she was already in the entrance hall to take her leave. Before going outside, she checked on her purchases wrapped in a newspaper, carefully arranged the vegetables, leeks, celery, carrots, murmured something about apples and plums apologetically, looked to see if the cottage cheese was still intact. Alongside, covered in gray paper, were books from the neighborhood library. Above all she liked romances with happy endings. She closed the door behind her noiselessly, taking with her the confused feeling of the need to suffer. I didn't accompany her to the bus stop, although with her burden she had a long trip ahead of her to the other side of the Vistula.

I was an adult when I started visiting them regularly every year, in their apartment on Szczuczyńska Street. Curiosity spurred family obligation. I wanted to penetrate to the secret heart of their union.

They generally invited me for noon on the dot. At that hour there wasn't the feeling of tiredness from having gone through another day. I arrived a little early, as they were obsessively punctual, and as I rang the doorbell, the Viennese clock in the dining room started chiming its longest count.

That's how I remember them, in the same setting that repeated itself. The clock rang triumphantly. The three of them were seated at the rectangular oak table, becoming more and more rigid with the ringing of the clock. As if before a performance. Curtain.

They have passed more than half a century together: Frania, Regina, and Aleksander.

He is the chief. Of small stature, he has a large head, nearly bald, with the skin on his face flabby, loose. When he disagrees with something, his jowls shake from side to side as with an old dog. He hums constantly. His eyes are no doubt gray, but I am not certain. He rarely makes eye contact with the person to whom he is speaking. He doesn't need affirmation. These days his eyesight is getting worse, which he cannot stand; he has never lost control over anything whatsoever. Extremely courteous, in an old-fashioned way, he tries to use the jargon of the young. He poses questions and answers them, his own as well as those of others, for himself as well as for others. Aleksander Majewski, Oleś, an industrialist before the war, an executive after the war—an absolute monarch.

On his right, like a porcelain doll, his wife Regina Schumacher. Round cheeks with asymmetrical traces of pink, thick glasses, and a wig, askew, the color of autumn leaves.

The face of a cubist portrait. Or else, bad makeup. Hard to believe that men turned around on the street when she passed by before the war. The daughter of a well-known dermatologist from Łódź, she was a brilliant student in law school and became a lawyer. She is a member of what is called the "upper echelon." At the table but absent, perhaps unfocused. Drowsy. Grimacing with a fixed smile.

The woman on his left is also his wife. She has a soft face, wrinkled, framed with gray hair worn in a loose chignon. Frania. Franuchna. Teary pale blue eyes. Heavy shoulders. It's as if she were constantly affirming: You can't change anything, and it's fine this way. Because, after all, it could be worse. Formerly she had dreams. Then she was marked for death. In the end she learned that life is a duty.

On the table, as with every year, cold hors d'oeuvres, roast veal, salted pickles, yeast crumble cake, and a bottle of cognac.

Uncle Oleś is a bigamist. He is also a hero. I like him very much. He impresses me. He speaks with the same verve for hours on end, about his erotic conquests just as much as the Jews he saved during the Occupation. The one and the other come just as naturally in his story. If he is proud of anything, it is rather his virility than the help he gave to people who needed it. He has saved many people, more than ten perhaps; he never expected any reward. Doing good seemed to him a natural component of human nature. It did not need any justification. Besides, he succeeded in doing something that appeared impossible: he lived for years with two wives under the same roof.

In his last will, he asked that three words be engraved on their communal tomb: "Fidelity, Wisdom, Courage." It's only when they had both passed away that he started speaking about them.

Frania, the sister of my grandfather, was the third child of Justyna and Henryk Przedborski. And like her elder sister, Bronka, she had blue eyes. A Jew with blue eyes, big advantage.

In Łęczyca they used to say "the pretty Misses Przedborski." They wore bows in their hair, played the piano, knew how to cook and embroider. Bronka loved to cook. In a notebook of recipes, she wrote down her own versions on how to cook *cholent*, fish in aspic, duck and stuffed chicken. She was constantly laughing. Frania was always poised. Absorbed in her music and her own thoughts. She had learned very early how to read musical scores. She read them effortlessly, like words.

As a child she spent a lot of time in her father's office, at the foot of the mahogany bookcase. They left her alone and generally found her in the same place. She read everything that she could reach. The largest volumes were on the bottom: encyclopedias, dictionaries, atlases, the history of Poland. For novels about love, she had to grow taller. She became acquainted with Anna Karenina and Madame Bovary even before her bat mitzvah, before she was thirteen years old.

She wasn't the most gifted, but she wanted to learn. Like her older brother and her sisters, she had completed her studies at the Polish Lycée of Łęczyca. She had obtained her baccalaureate in May of 1927, and it was in religion that she achieved the highest grade. At school it was the rabbi who taught her the subject; the priest taught it to Roman Catholics, and the Russian Orthodox priest had the fewest students. In a photograph from this period she has her hair cut with bangs in the fashion of Pola Negri, with an expression of determination in her eyes and on her face. Perhaps she had already announced to her parents that she was leaving home.

She felt smothered in this remote little town on the Bzura River. She was drawn to distant places—beyond the fields, the river, the vista of the forest. The great world. She had enough of these concerts by the firemen's orchestra, the films in the Oaza movie theater, the rhythm of provincial visits and holidays. She wanted to learn, study history, become a teacher. She wanted to breathe a different air. She didn't know which of these aspirations was the strongest; each one was enough to make her decide. She wasn't afraid. She left.

She had never been to the capital before, more than a hundred kilometers distant; she had never even seen a large city. She had spent the last few years in Łęczyca with her grandmother, who had eye problems, to whom she read out loud novels published in the popular dailies. Now in Warsaw she lived with her father's brother, Uncle Janek. He was a well-known pediatrician, with an apartment and a practice always full of patients on one of the most elegant streets of the city, Marszalkowska Street. She began her life in Warsaw in the position of the poor relation who looks longingly at the store windows and the people frequenting the cafés, the palaces of old magnates, and the royal residences of kings. Few Jews lived in the very center of the city, not far from the central train station and the Philharmonic, even though one of the main thoroughfares, stretching from the Vistula to the western boundary, was named Jerusalem Avenue.

The majority of Jews in Warsaw had settled in the northern section of the capital. Men with earlocks, dressed in long frock coats; merchants with stalls calling out in Yiddish; peddlers; people selling shoelaces, combs, and galoshes filled the streets and labyrinths of makeshift booths with an exotic crowd. They had maintained the costumes of the old faith, and loyalty to tradition gave them a feeling of belonging and a sense of security.

Nearby, on Nalewki, Leszno, and Sienna Streets lived the wealthy Jews—industrialists, real estate and factory owners, financiers. Half of the businesses and industries of Warsaw were in their hands. Of the million inhabitants of the Polish capital, one in three was Jewish. One private doctor out of two, one lawyer and one notary in three had Jewish ancestors.

Uncle Janek was the fifth son, the youngest child of Marcus Przedborski, owner of a business in Kalisz and of an estate near Łęczyca. He no longer used his Jewish first names, Samuel Janas—any more than his brother Henryk, who didn't use Henoch either. Both spoke a pure and literary Polish, and physically, they did not resemble the Eastern European Jewish stereotype. Janek was the only one of the brothers to have earned an advanced degree, from the Medical School of Kiev. He now took on the financial responsibility for his niece's education.

He made an ostentatious display of his Polishness. He sprinkled his conversation with Polish proverbs, referred to examples drawn from Polish history, and recited bits of romantic poetry. As if he wanted to deny his past and his origins. Aunt

Maria, a cousin who was often in Janek's home, spoke with contempt about the Orthodox Jews of Nalewki Street. She referred to them as the "gabardine Jews." She made all her purchases exclusively in Polish stores. Her great delight was going to the spa.

According to the census of 1931, 10 percent of the Jews declared Polish as their first language. The majority of the Jews lived in a culture of earlier centuries, but a good part of the Jewish intelligentsia followed a progressive process of assimilation. At times, often enough, it brought a denial of their own heritage, a feeling of embarrassment and shame.

The Przedborskis of Warsaw were said to belong to society. Frania didn't know how to be as frivolous and "Varsovian" as they. Not yet. She had the anxiety of an unformed life and the excitement of the adventure. She considered assimilation as a means to a goal, to acquire an education and earn her independence. She could not foresee the traps.

There is a Jewish saying: "To change an address is to change fate." For the moment, that was her sentiment.

She was admitted to the humanities department at the University of Warsaw. The papers dating from before the war proving that she realized her dream are preserved in the archives of the university. During the solemn convocation for the start of the university year 1927–28, she took an oath to pursue her studies assiduously and lead a life that was moral and dignified.

Her professors were authors of books that were in her father's library, the greatest Polish humanists of European renown. She attended their courses in philosophy and culture. She studied the history of Poland during the Middle Ages, and the geography of the classical world. She was curious about Italy, Rome and Venice in particular, two cities where the first Jewish ghettos were created, symbols of imprisonment but also oases to which they had voluntarily withdrawn in order to cultivate their own religious practices according to the letters of the Talmud.

She studied history for two years.

In Poland, the world economic crisis and the great stock

market crash struck in the autumn of 1929. Shortly after the new year 1930, Uncle Janek asked her to step into his office. With great regret he had to inform her that her studies were at an end. He could no longer afford to let her continue them. In any case she would be married soon, she would have children, and she would devote herself to her family. What's the use of spending money without any return?

I don't know whether she protested. I don't think that she asked her parents or her grandmother for help. They had financed the education of their son, Zamutek, who was already working. But a daughter did not have to study; they considered her education a capricious whim. She knew that she had to manage by herself if she wanted to stay in the city.

In Warsaw as everywhere else in the world, long lines formed at the soup kitchens, and for every job that became vacant, there were hundreds of applicants. Through the director of a bank, with whom they were on friendly terms, Uncle Janek found employment for her in the Drago firm, the distributors of petroleum products. The head of the firm was a dynamic young man, full of ideas: Aleksander Majewski—Oleś.

To attend the wedding of a colleague from the office, she had worn her finest suit: a bolero that was in vogue, and a straight skirt that went down to mid-calf, with a slit in back. She had put up her hair like her mother. She had borrowed a pearl necklace to bring good luck. It was June 24, 1930, her birthday. She was twenty-three years old.

By chance they left the reception together, she and Oleś. They were practically the same age, but she seemed young to him, clearly much younger, as if life had just begun to open before her. With his twill suit and his light Borsalino hat, her boss reminded her of the heroes of the romances she used to read to her grandmother. When she told him that it was her birthday, he invited her for Champagne at the legendary Adria, the most fashionable establishment in Warsaw, with a jazz band and a revolving dance floor.

It was her first evening out dancing, her first glass of Champagne. And her first date. First declaration of love. And first night with a man.

Oleś insists that was when she chose him. Although he already had a wife and had had many amorous adventures, which he willingly talked about. He was in the middle of a divorce. With all her sincerity and her fervor, she appeared naïve to him. He gave little weight to his promises, but she was ready for anything; she never loved anyone else. She didn't want him just for a moment, she wanted him for a whole lifetime.

This scene of their first encounter, I often go over it in my imagination. I smile at the thought of Frania as such a beauty and so disarmingly happy, even though I have difficulty in believing it. I look at her once again.

For Frania, Oleś seemed to be an accomplished version of her father. In his every gesture and in every word he spoke, he let it be understood that he knew what he was doing, and everything was going to succeed. Both played the violin and shared the same taste in music. Even the arias were the same, and they sang the same way, he had a rich tenor voice. Oleś's strength attracted her as if she wanted to measure herself against it. She felt safe near him, even though she continued to call him "Mr. Director," even whenever she brought him documents to sign and closed the door to his office. He was kindly and also focused. He was never mistaken and spoke clearly, with conviction.

She asked for nobody's permission. She didn't feel that she should. Polish? Divorced? Of another religion? Her man. She had chosen her fate, just as formerly she had chosen a new address.

Outwardly their daily life did not experience any changes. At the office, they followed the regulations. Each lived his own life. Each one managed his own affairs and followed the principles of individual freedom that they allowed one another. But at the memory of their nights together Oleś, today nearly a hundred years old, glows with the radiance of a lover in the movies. He tells about his passion in language I cannot repeat.

For a moment, Frania becomes related to all those famous temptresses, with their desirable bodies.

His reputation as a Don Juan followed him. She had to have known about it. Perhaps she thought that it did not concern her? I don't know how she took it when she learned about the existence of the others. Oleś insists that she was the one who demanded the story of his conquests. He also affirms that close as they were as a couple, she felt safe and that his numerous adventures had altered nothing between them.

They went out together to restaurants and the theater, to concerts and shows. He spent a great deal of time at the Warsaw Rowing Club, where the Polish elite, the intelligentsia and the embassy staff, came to receptions and dances. Oleś is emphatic about the fact that Celina Franciszka, as he called her—not by her diminutive Frania, as at home—passed everywhere for Polish. He admired her beauty, the peach complexion, her eyes, her figure. Would he have been as popular in this club with a half-century tradition if they had discovered that Frania was Jewish?

He remembered the Jews from his childhood. He sometimes told her about it. He was originally from Mazovia; his grandfather was a peasant, his father had completed his secondary school studies. Over there they were passionate about the socialist ideals, the legend of Ludwik Waryński,* who when hunted by the Okhrana† hid in the family neighborhood not far from Nasielsk. The Jewish merchants were an inseparable part of the landscape in the Polish countryside where Oleś spent his childhood. His mother, a seamstress, constantly needed something from the Jews, sometimes a needle for the sewing machine, sometimes household utensils or coupons for cloth. They sold, they bought, they advised. Often an old Jew with a gray beard would show up in the Majewski household. Wearing his little

---

* Ludwik Waryński (1856–89), one of the founders of the Polish revolutionary workers' movement Proletariat. (A.T.)
† The tsarist secret police. (A.T.)

hat with a visor, he sat down at the table and refused to partake of anything besides the tea. When Oleś, still very young, was wounded in the leg, which became infected, it was this Jewish merchant, to be sure, who saved his life. He took the child, who had a fever, to a doctor's assistant. Oleś, who likes to find a justification for everything in life, insists that it was then, when he was ten years old, that he resolved always to help Jews in need.

He took Frania to the big synagogue on Tłomackie Street, where world-famous cantors, Sirota or Koussevitzky, would perform during the Jewish holy days. They went strolling in the Jewish quarter, Nalewki Street. She didn't like it. She didn't read the Jewish newspapers and didn't enjoy the Jewish theater. They rarely went to cabarets where Jewish parody predominated. It was Oleś who drank *pejsachowka,* a vodka distilled from prunes, and, when the opportunity presented itself, ate kosher food. I don't know if he did it as a tribute to her. She had already distanced herself from her origins. Her brother and elder sister lived in Warsaw, but Frania looked at the world through Oleś's eyes.

Her sister Bronka lived in the Powiśle district. Her husband was Borys Kuszner, an engineer. Zamutek, her brother, also an engineer, built the residences of the Warsaw Housing Cooperative in Żoliborz, where he had a company apartment. Frania's younger sister, Madzia, had married Borys Kuszner's brother. They had moved from Łęczyca but remained with their customary circles of friends. In Bronka's home broth had the same flavor as it did in the house on Przedrynek Place.

The life of the Przedborski family before the war is absent from Oleś's stories. He sometimes mentions the Sunday teas with the cake and the slices of halvah, but I don't have the feeling that he is talking about people close to him.

Despite the crisis, Oleś's business, backed by German capital, was thriving. He crisscrossed the country, spending several days in Łódz, where he had opened a branch of his firm. He was full of enthusiasm, and his ideas for advertising were considered innovative. In time he opened his own large store. His business was doing perfectly well. In his Warsaw office he employed more than twenty people.

Oleś kept his own bachelor's apartment in town, first one, then another; he changed them according to his need. Frania had moved away from her uncle a long time ago; she sublet a room. When Oleś returned to Warsaw, she stayed with him for the night. This lasted a long time—the dinners, the separations, the train stations, the period of time without him, the waiting and the euphoria of what they had in common. Years passed, the birthdays succeeded one another, the twenty-fifth, the twenty-eighth, the thirtieth. Others were married and others had children. She wasn't afraid of remaining a spinster, she didn't think in those terms. She felt fulfilled as she had never felt before.

They never spoke of marriage. He was not in a hurry and she never asked for it. Did she not dare to? For a long time it was enough that they were together.

He was different from her brother and her two brothers-in-law, whom she had known since childhood. On Sundays he came to her house on his black English motorcycle that made explosive noises. He raced across the city, and Frania clung to his back, burying herself against his leather jacket. He took her for kayaking excursions. She was incapable of imagining Bronka with a paddle in her hand, Zamutek on a bicycle, her brothers-in-law in the saddle of a motorcycle.

That's how I see her, but I don't really understand. There were always other women; she was not, in any case, the center of his universe. Yet they stayed together. Finally, after seven years, she declared that she wanted a child by him.

She was thirty years old then, Oleś two years older. It was 1937—in Europe the menacing atmosphere intensified, but war did not yet seem inevitable. The world was just coming out of several years of crisis. Oleś had bought a car, an Opel convertible. He liked speed and the feeling of air blowing in his face. His business had developed a chain of stores. It was time to start a family. It was he, not she, who proposed marriage.

Mixed couples, Polish-Jewish, were not frequent in Poland at the time. Only the Communists, who ignored tradition on principle, thought these marriages seemed natural and needed no commentary. Everywhere else there was a predictable censure from people, as much from the Poles as from the Jews.

In the period between the world wars, civil marriages were not recognized in Poland. Before walking up to the altar, Frania had to convert.

Baptism. I feel the very word should have aroused her resistance, even if Frania would never admit it. A Christian sacrament. Even though she was emancipated, a rebel, and a free woman, she could not have been indifferent to it. Conversion required an effort, the study of catechism lasted a long time, the act of belonging to a new religious community needed a period of immersion in a foreign, even hostile world. She had thought about this decision; it was not just an impulse.

For a Jew, Catholic baptism was generally the expression of a genuine faith and was not merely a means of legalizing a personal situation. Conversions not based upon an actual religious necessity took place among the Protestants or in the bosom of the Russian Orthodox Church. Frania and Oleś chose the Orthodox Church, thus opting for another cross seemed to carry less weight. Besides, in the eyes of the Catholic Church, Oleś was still married.

The Orthodox metropolitan parish dedicated to Mary Magdalene had a beautiful church in the Praga neighborhood, one of two that Warsaw has preserved. In the archives survived the records of the baptismal registry for Celina Franciszka, daughter of Enoch and Jachet Gitel, née Herman, thirty years old, of Jewish origin. She obtained a dispensation from His Excellency, Metropolite Dionizi. She received the sacraments of Holy Baptism, Confirmation, and First Holy Communion at the same time as she took on a new first name, Zofia (Sofija), January 28, 1938, in the presence of the patriarch and two witnesses. I don't know if she believed in God.

As a parishioner of the Orthodox faith this time, three weeks later in the same Orthodox church she married Aleksander

Majewski, a divorced man. She was now Celina, Franciszka, Zofia.

She never spoke about this. He remembered the magnificent choir, the dim light, and the gold crowns. Every one of the ten bells cast in Westphalia had been rung.

The witnesses were Oleś's brother and a colleague from the office. No one from the Przedborski family showed up, neither from Łęczyca nor from Warsaw. The young bride had a mother and a grandmother, two sisters and a brother, paternal uncles and an aunt as well as aunts and uncles from the mother's side, cousins. Not one was present.

What was shameful, and for whom, in the fact that Celina Franciszka, no longer young, had decided to step up to the altar after being united for eight years with a man? Not under the chuppah that her birth had designated for her, not in a synagogue in the presence of a rabbi. Not as the daughter of her ancestors but as a stranger, a convert, a renegade. I understand that this could have upset her grandmother; for her such a choice was a transgression against the commandments. But what about the others?

The same year another ceremony took place. Henryk Przedborski, Frania's father, died in the autumn. I don't know whether he died of a heart attack or of tuberculosis. Both versions are current in family lore. The second evokes the picture of wet sheets in the sickroom to relieve his breathing. In the cemetery, the crowd of mourners from the community. Ironically, there is only one version of the funeral. No one, aside from Oleś, remembers it.

In the crowd of mourners a stranger was noticed. Someone pointed out to the rabbi that a Pole was among the mourners. Oleś states that they refused to let him enter the cemetery, to participate in the funeral of his father-in-law. He waited behind the gates.

This story that Oleś remembers, could it be true? Henryk Przedborski had served several terms as municipal councilor of Łęczyca, he carried on a business with Poles. He belonged to the elite of Łęczyca. Was it possible that his neighbors, his colleagues from city hall, people who had known him for decades, had not attended his funeral? I don't know of any examples of a Jew or a non-Jew who was barred from a funeral. Was this about something else? I don't know.

That day, Frania left Łęczyca for the last time.

TRIO

Frania, Zofia Majewska, was four months pregnant when German troops marched into Warsaw in September 1939. Five months pregnant when the barbed-wire fences appeared for the first time at the entrance of Jewish streets. Shortly afterward, they ordered all Jews more than twelve years old to wear a white armband with the blue Star of David. It marked Jewish businesses and stores. She was seven months pregnant when Jews were forbidden to change residence without special authorization, and they were forbidden to take the train. That's when talk of creating a ghetto started.

I don't know if she allowed herself to be afraid. She carried in her womb a child for whom she would have given the whole world. The ration cards for Jews were different from the cards for Poles, and in March, a month she had dreamed of, when she was due to give birth, and she did, signs appeared in the cafés of Warsaw that Jews were forbidden to enter.

Until then she had never asked herself what was meant by "having a good appearance." She was like other people, she was not in any way different from the Poles. At least according to her. She analyzed every aspect of her face. In turn: lips too full, as if sullen; well-shaped nose, although slightly too big like her mother's; black hair, but there were black-haired Poles, her hair was luxuriant and shiny; only her eyes drew no criticism. Blue eyes, like Polish eyes, they didn't express too much fear. She knew that. Nothing to be frightened about.

In June when Paris fell and the camp at Auschwitz was put into service, they completed the building of a wall in the heart of Warsaw. The wall was three meters high and topped with shards of glass marking the limits of a "zone threatened by an epidemic." A ghetto that was closed in November 1940 was where all the Jews had to go. A quarter of the million inhabitants of Warsaw had to change their places of residence: 140,000 Jews and more than 100,000 Poles.

They had no inkling of what was in store for them. Some even rushed to find the best apartments. The Przedborskis were certain that their compliance would be rewarded by a life that would perhaps be more difficult, but much safer. They wanted to be all together. All in all there were thirteen of them. In outward appearance, life continued again at its normal pace;

there were a hospital, cafés, lecture halls, even theaters and a symphony orchestra.

They all insisted that Frania join them. Her mother, Dela, Bronka. Zamutek was taken prisoner, that was enough misfortune. In such times how could you remain separate? Frania had Zbyszek; Bronka, three-year-old Maryś; Dela had Halina, more than nine years old, who would help take care of the younger children. Madzia, Frania's younger sister, had arrived from the ghetto in Ozorków with one-year-old Henryś in her arms. The family.

Frania did not move into the ghetto. She chose the Aryan side, as she had chosen more than ten years earlier when she came to Warsaw. She had a Polish husband in whom she had unbounded confidence and whose words meant more to her than the pleadings of her mother, brother, and sisters, even more than Hitlerian decrees.

I think that she lived the first few months as if the German orders did not concern her. Perhaps she didn't feel threatened, perhaps the prospect of being locked up frightened her more than the dangers of life beyond the wall. But for Oleś, Frania's moving into the ghetto was not even a possibility.

The apartment building on Okrąg Street where they had lived was now in the German sector. Therefore she proceeded to move in with Oleś's parents in the neighborhood of the Old Town. But he stayed in one of his bachelor apartments. This time he justified it as a measure of security.

A pass was necessary to visit those who were confined to the ghetto. The more resourceful arranged it with a tip to the guards watching the entrances, the German policeman, the blue Polish policeman. But you could hear the voices of your relations without authorization or any difficulty, even though isolated behind the wall. The telephone communications with the Jewish ghetto were maintained almost right up to the end.

Frania telephoned every day to the ghetto. "How are you today? What do you need?" The first months there seemed to be no need to worry. They worked, they were not hungry. They actually believed that it would not last a long time. On the telephone, Grandmother Jecia sang to little Zbyszek her song about the shoemaker's wife. Why, and for whom, will she wear paper shoes? For death.

· · ·

One winter had passed and another was coming. Frania continued working at the office on Mazowiecka Street, and Oleś's parents looked after Zbyszek. Darkness fell earlier. It was almost night when Frania opened the door to an unknown woman.

Regina Schumacher, a lawyer from Łódź, was the legal advisor to Oleś's firm before the war. When war was declared she stayed with her mother, who was increasingly frightened at the idea of living on the Aryan side. Like many Jews from Łódź she came to the Warsaw Ghetto.

Regina was resourceful. Every day she passed to the Aryan side through the courthouse to replenish provisions for the house and to learn about living beyond the wall. There were more and more people like her. They looked good, and they more or less had links with Polish culture and language. The most important was an address. Regina had chosen that of Oleś.

What made her think that he would help her? Was she one of the women with whom Director Majewski had a special relationship? He denies it. Perhaps that was what was said by his acquaintances; he knew a lot of people, and his statement of solidarity with Jews was being put to the test now, when all other possibilities had failed.

The next day, Oleś hired her as a telephone operator in the office on Mazowiecka Street.

Walls, barricades, fences, barbed wires, a typhoid zone separated from the city. A district for those people that German posters said were disgusting and fearsome. Odious, frightening effigies of Jews peered from the walls of Warsaw. Hooked noses, rapacious fingers, cupidity, infestation with lice. It was difficult to enter into the world of these people, the worst marked by the yellow star. The *wachy*—the gates to the ghetto—were under strict surveillance. Few were those who visited the closed sector. Few were those who had the need or the desire.

Frania kept her distance. She never set foot in the court-house building, never mixed in the crowd of people requesting to pass to the other side to look for their relatives. She never rode the streetcar that crossed the ghetto without stopping there. She never saw what lay behind the wall, even through a window. Sometimes by telephone she arranged with her sister or mother to meet at a place where they could see her, from their side. With her baby carriage, in a park, she sat on a bench by a fountain. She waited.

From what vantage point could you look at the Aryan side beyond walls three meters high? From the upper stories of buildings, and several other places nearer the wall, and from the wooden overpass on Chłodna Street.

No, from there you would not be able to see a baby carriage and the fountain. Frania's sisters had to go elsewhere to see greenery, a few trees, a garden to recognize her, to distinguish her from the dozens of other women strolling with children. Therefore it had to be Krasiński Park, near Franciszkańska; a fixed plan with baby carriage, fountain, and bench, over there where Frania waited for them to see her from the other side.

Oleś entered the ghetto. As an entrepreneur doing business with German firms, he possessed more valid papers than most, and he had turned over one of his shops to a high-ranking German official in exchange for facilitating commercial and financial transactions. He was, as always, energetic and bold. He had quickly succeeded in arranging for a permanent pass authorizing his visits to off-limits areas. The wall divided another of his shops in half, a big store with storage areas and warehousing on Grzybowski Square.

In the ghetto Oleś went to see the Przedborskis, first on Sienna Street, then at their other successive addresses. Thirteen people, the whole family, lived together, which gave them a feeling of security. They weren't hungry, they had enough oil for the lamps and coal for the stoves. One of the brothers-in-law was a dentist; another, an engineer, worked in a shop manufacturing for the Germans. Oleś used all his powers to persuade them to flee to the Aryan side; he offered help and papers. He admits now that he foresaw the fate awaiting the Jews. He tried to warn them, to frighten them, but none of the Przedborskis wanted to believe him. His mother-in-law reproached him for putting Frania in danger by exposing her to the daily threats beyond the wall.

How was it that Warsaw, which for many of them had been a haven before the war, seemed to them more danger-ous than the evidently cruel reality of the ghetto? Even before the final extermination of the ghetto, sometimes Jews came back, abandoning the Aryan side where they had passed, worn down by the constant tension, the need to hide, and the fear of denunciation.

Eventually they begged Oleś to stop coming to see them.

On October 15, 1941, the streets of Warsaw were plastered over with a notice from the governor general, Hans Frank, that Jews who left their quarters without authorization risked death. Also risking the death sentence were those who gave them help of any sort. The large printed letters BEKANNTMACHUNG—NOTICE—drew the attention of all passersby. Oleś and Fra-nia came upon them at every step.

They decided—he decided: it was he who, more and more often, now decided for both of them—that it would be eas-ier to hide Frania and Zbyszek if she passed for his sister. He quickly arranged for the necessary papers. But Frania, Zofia Majewska, had to remain celibate with a child out of wedlock. He arranged for the divorce in the same Russian Orthodox church where they had been married. When she said to him jokingly that he was free once again, he swore to her that he would never again marry.

Regina Schumacher was still working in Oleś's office. Her duties quickly grew beyond her work as a switchboard operator. Competent and organized, she quickly became his right hand. She changed her hairstyle and dyed her hair. She had fled the ghetto after the death of her mother. She moved in with Oleś and Frania, but I don't know which of the two proposed it. Oleś reiterates that Frania agreed without giving it a thought. They gave Regina the identity papers of Oleś's first wife. They had the same first name. Regina Schumacher, a lawyer from Łódź, became Regina Majewska, née Jakubiak, whom Oleś had married in St. Mary's Church. Their fates became more and more closely linked.

Oleś called my aunt Frania by her baptismal name, Zofia. Sometimes Frania cried. Zofia never did. She never complained, either. She took care of the baby, she went on strolls with him, ran her errands, completed her work at the office. Without a word of complaint. Sprinkled with holy water, Zofia make herself act as if the war had never thrown the shadow of her origins over her. Zofia was stronger, better, the Aryan incarnation of herself, Frania from Przedrynek in Łęczyca; Zofia did not distinguish herself from the Polish women from before the war who attended balls and worldly social gatherings. No one would have ever connected Zofia with Krochmalna or Nalewki Street.

Oleś mixes up the years. He helped Jews, he got many of them out of the ghetto, procured papers for them, and arranged hiding places. Who, when, by what means, he doesn't remember. He doesn't know if he first helped Bronka, Frania's sister, out of the ghetto, or if their acquaintances from Łódź had asked him for help earlier. He doesn't speak about it; besides, he has no proof, but then he never tried to obtain any. So he remains silent.

I know for a fact that he got Bronka out through the courthouse building. It wasn't easy; someone had spotted them, another carriage was following them. He asked the driver to take them to Szucha Avenue, to the Gestapo. It was only at the last minute, when you could see the badges on the German guards, that the blackmailers finally gave up.

I also know that it was Oleś who paid the money to ransom my grandmother Dela. I know that it was a friend of Oleś, from the Underground, a go-between in the Home Army, who took little Maryś, Bronka's son, out of the ghetto through the courthouse. Oleś also pulled him out of there.

Without Oleś, the Polish husband of Celina Franciszka Przedborska, the man she fell in love with and married against the objection of her family, without him, without you, my uncle, there would be no trace of any of us. I would never have come into this world, because my mother and her mother, Dela, would never have gotten out of the ghetto. My grandmother would not have received from fate the gift of several additional months of life.

I am the last link in this chain. Grandmother Dela, Halina, the escape through the courthouse, the blackmailers, the coach, the Gestapo. If you had hesitated then, if you had been frightened, if you had been tired or momentarily absent, Dela and Halina would never have come out of the building on Szucha Avenue. There wouldn't have been any sequel.

Dela would have perished right then. Halina would not have found her father again, would not have fallen in love, would not have made a home and given birth to a daughter. She wouldn't have had anything to remember. She would have had nothing to forget. And I . . . I would not have experienced the flavor of my heritage. I would not have known my grandfather's sisters, because Bronka and her son would have perished in Treblinka, or behind the wall; Frania and her child could not have managed on the Aryan side. I would not have discovered, years later, my cousin Adaś Herman, placed with a Polish family; he would have been gassed together with his mother. And others whose fate is not intimately linked to mine.

· · ·

Oleś speaks of these things without being dramatic, systematically and in order. How, when, where, what had to be anticipated, the addresses, the documents, the housing, the certificate of residency, the food. A concrete plan. And another in reserve in case the first one failed. Helping Jews required renewed vigilance, not only in relation to the Germans but to the Poles also. Money was important, but people were even more so.

Was he afraid? He was a member of the Resistance, and a genuine agent never speaks of fear. He had entrusted no one with his secret activities. That was the safest way. During the Occupation in Poland, they condemned and executed people for possession of a weapon, a radio, gold, or false papers, for giving help to Jews, and for the black market—you risked death for everything. He took that into account in his planning related to the war.

I have never heard any boastfulness in his voice, or pride. Maybe only when he told about how he succeeded in deceiving the Germans, or covering his trail, confounding the blackmailers, evading pursuit, escaping raids. When they arrested Frania, Oleś got her out of the police station. He made a scene with the policemen. He presented himself as a collaborator of the Reich. In this case, his unflinching confidence, his daring, his arrogance, was the only hope.

I listen as if to a war adventure series that I know; however, it holds a drama more anguishing than a Greek tragedy.

Oleś, Frania, Zbyszek, their young son. Regina. How many similar scenarios has the war created? It's not a very original situation, but I know that it was very real. I followed its path ever since childhood, at first unconsciously but now with a thirst to explore the recesses of the past. I don't know what her young employer, a fine-looking man, represented for Regina Schumacher, for whom, more than just work, he offered security and a roof over her head. Oleś had removed her death sentence, which had seemed irrevocable. Was she then in love with him?

I don't know. But Oleś claims that it was she, Regina, who said that she wanted to have a child by him.

They moved to the other side of the Vistula River. Saska Kępa, Francuska Street, with villas and gardens. There was no

ghetto on this side of the river. Or rather, the ghetto was on
the other side. The two Majewskas, the wife and the "sister"
of Oleś, lived in a small building on Szczuczyńska Street. How
were the household chores divided, and the rooms?

Frania kept quiet. She was silent for months, all during Regina's pregnancy. The third month, the fifth, the eighth month—
next to her was developing her husband's child. In another
woman's womb. It was the longest pregnancy she knew. Oleś
was good to her. However, she saw him less; he disappeared
completely for days and nights, going between Warsaw and
Łódź. In May 1942 Regina gave birth to a son, Andrzej. He was
different from Zbyszek, blond.

On July 22, 1942, the first transports to Treblinka left
Umschlagplatz.

I don't know if anyone from my family realized that they
were going to a certain death. Officially they spoke of transfers
to the east for work. First they took the youngest of the sisters,
Madzia, with the baby and her dentist husband, who earned a
good living in the ghetto. He remained ignorant of what was
happening till the end. Then they took all those whom Oleś
had not succeeded in saving.

In the autumn of 1942, after the transport to the gas chamber of 250,000 inhabitants of the ghetto, more than 20,000
Jews were hiding in Warsaw. There were three times that number of Poles to help them.

They couldn't buy too much food; it would have aroused
suspicion. They had to have a big celebration of Frania's
name day—Zofia's, his pretend sister Zofia's—as was required
by Christian custom, and invite the tenants in the building.
Bronka shouldn't have to recite any poems when she was looking for work as a cleaning woman. Dela had to know the price
of a ticket on the streetcar.

By the end of 1942, in the four extermination camps on Polish soil, more than two million Jews had been murdered.

The smell of fear, I think about it. Perhaps that was the most
important. More important than appearance and the way of

life. Bronka, my grandfather's sister, had been baptized on the Aryan side in the most rudimentary fashion, at home with a few drops of holy water. A Polish acquaintance had said to her then that she finally no longer smelled Jewish. But it wasn't true. They smelled Jewish. Before and after. And her sister, her mother, her cousins, all of them. Frania also, even if she was baptized a little sooner out of love, and it seemed that such a fear would never overtake her.

The odor was in them even before; the Occupation had simply liberated and made it stronger. Now special skills were required to get rid of it. They smelled of fear. Fear, that is to say, a Jew.

· · ·

How did they feel danger over there, on the other side of the Vistula? When I find myself in front of the house where Oleś is still living, I have the impression that the Saska Kępa neighborhood has preserved the soul of a little provincial town, where time flows differently and the people are closer to one another. Even a few years ago, Saska Kępa seemed to me from the prewar era—vegetable stands, leather workshops, manicurists. Private libraries.

All her life my aunt Frania escaped from her solitude into the world of books. She avidly read novels, historical narratives, murder mysteries. From the apartment on Szczuczyńska Street, she went to the neighboring library, she searched through their catalog-card files. During the first three years of the war she telephoned the ghetto using the pay phone on the wall.

Was someone listening to her conversation? Did she have as good an appearance as Oleś imagined? When I look at her photo from the time of her baccalaureate degree, wearing a blouse with a navy collar in fashion at the time, the photo preserved in the archives of the University of Warsaw, her attractiveness corresponds to the information written next to it: "of Mosaic faith." In a photo dating from the Occupation, she has full lips and dark, curly hair. She looks sad.

She was denounced in the autumn of 1942. She was returning from summer vacation, she and Regina. They were walking confidently, and, according to their agreed signal, the open
curtains in the dining room meant there was no danger. Just
as they got to the door, the concierge made them turn around,
warning them that the Germans were upstairs.

They had come for Zofia Majewska, the wife of Aleksander.
For Frania.

Oleś denied it. His wife was Regina and not Zofia. He
showed them the marriage license; they wanted to see it in
broad daylight. They pulled open the curtains. The signal. He
was waiting for the women to come in at any moment.

Oleś—Aleksander Majewski—and his wife had to appear
the next day at Gestapo Headquarters, Szucha Avenue, with
the required documents. They had to verify the denunciation.

"We knew only too well that Frania would not survive the
confrontation," Oleś told me. "But it was Regina herself, on
her own initiative, who proposed to accompany me to Szucha
Avenue. As my wife."

That night they made a hiding place in the big armoire
in the entrance hall. The next day, Frania slipped inside the
moment they closed the door and left the apartment. They had
to get through this, they had to, they couldn't leave her alone.
It was about the children, his sons. She did not pray. No doubt
she no longer knew how to pray. Besides, how could she have
prayed to the Jewish god when she had been at war with him
for years? She had married a Pole, she had converted, she had
renounced her heritage. And now she was hiding solely to save
her own skin.

It didn't last more than two hours. Footsteps, the sound
of the lock, the squeaking of the floorboards. They had both
returned. Frania didn't look her in the face when she told her,
"Regina, I will never forget what you did for me."

Regina had saved her life. Frania was in her debt. She was to
remain that for the rest of her life. Always.

Perhaps Regina had saved her life, but why? "Perhaps," it

has to be written, "she saved her life. But before that she had become pregnant by her husband."

They didn't laugh, they didn't weep with joy. The feeling of relief had a bitter taste.

I don't know how much time Frania spent in her hiding place. How many hours, days, months. I don't know if her sleepless nights have to be counted in years, or seasons. She went inside whenever someone visited them or knocked on the door. Zbyszek was little when he had to learn to stay away from her. Oleś's mother looked after him. He wouldn't stop crying when someone else was rocking him.

Frania was seated on a board fixed to the back of the armoire, the biggest one, with three doors and an oval mirror. Holes had been bored in the plywood, round openings, not very big—she stuck her fingers through them, tired of inactivity. Darkness. There was no question of reading, or darning or crocheting. Kill time, put aside the persistent images, tenacious as the day and night, noontime and sunset all the same, crowding together upon her. Her father repeating in a monotonous voice, "Daughter, take care of yourself, look after your mother," the sons in tears, Salomea Herman in a big bed, motionless, the cherries on the lamp in the dining room on Poznańska Street, the fruit still there, red and shining. A moment later, again everything was blurred. Her little boy, her little Zbyszek, singing the song of the shoemaker's wife with paper shoes; he didn't know how to cry, but he could speak. "Don't worry, sweetheart, everything will turn out fine," he repeated, taking her in his arms.

But she was Jewish also, the other. The other one in the lighted room. The other with her husband.

They were both on Szczuczyńska Street, two Jewish mothers. But one was more favored than the other. One was secretly in the hiding place. Why her? Did her appearance really mark her to such a degree? Was she so non-Aryan, and what if it was they who had persuaded her of it? She thought about it at times, I know she must have, seated in her hiding place in the hallway—they must have thought it up in order to have more time to themselves. Time and quiet. Perhaps she bored Oleś, he was tired of her, she bothered him. However, he continued to come to her at night. To her also. She played with Andrzej, imagining that he was Zbyszek. He was less willful.

What did she hear? How was her time spent, made up of noises, the sound of steps, shoes, boots, running, jumping? Pulse of the stairwell, noticeable noises; years later she was still capable of speaking about them. Opening of doors, echoes of greetings and goodbyes, echoes or repetitions, echoes of anger or joy, even sometimes melodies filtered through the door. Bits of Christmas carols during the holidays, songs from the summer, the one about the soldier with a heart in his knapsack.

There was clothing hanging in the armoire. Dresses, a blue dress in cretonne, that she wore in the evenings after a day on the water kayaking. He called her, affectionately, "Psiapsia" at the very beginning.

It had gathered lace purchased to replace some that had burned on her in the forest near Czorsztyn, when a gas container had exploded and they thought that she would die from her burns. Ever since, she never undressed except in the dark. And for the first time she had stopped looking at herself in the mirror. She had stopped looking in the mirror for the second time during the second year of the war.

That last summer, they had gone back to the lake, this time as husband and wife, she in a green dress, on the motorcycle. The one with the poppies all crushed in the fields near Narocz, when she finally became pregnant.

She explored with her fingers the undulations of the wood, a board, knots, pine, ash, what was this wood? Musical notes, they seem so simple, but the fingers are not used to it. The names of the violin makers, her father taught her, not the Italians but the Polish ones. She couldn't remember a single one. She traced with her finger, with all her fingers, the streets of Łęczyca, then the river and the fields, the streets, the streams, the trash, must not evoke those odors.

It turned out that the informer who denounced her was the owner of the neighborhood library. Oleś double-checked his suspicions. Then he personally oversaw that the sentence handed down by the Resistance for "actions against the Polish people" was duly carried out. The Underground had started belatedly to punish those who blackmailed the Jews. The credible figures are missing. After the summer of 1943 perhaps twenty of the four thousand informers (*szmalcownicy*) in Warsaw were executed.

Frania had taken the room looking out on the street. I don't know under what circumstances they decided to permanently close the sliding door. She installed her sofa and the kilim rug from Łęczyca. It is still there. Everything on it is from a fairy tale: the big oak tree with the owl, the witch who tries to lure the children with a red apple, the taste of evil and the promise of a happy ending. Oleś continued his conjugal visits to her at night. Perhaps the kilim was there by chance, like the mirror on her mother's armoire. From Łęczyca it was moved to Okrąg Street, and from there to Saska Kępa; the family had not wanted to bring it to the ghetto. A mirror didn't seem necessary. They didn't have the strength to look at themselves in it.

. . .

About some people they knew nothing; about others they didn't want to know anything. They had lost contact. They didn't know their fate. There was the news that Frania was incapable of accepting. About her mother, her grandmother, her sister. They came from the provinces; but the others, elegant, learned, wealthy, Polish? Uncle Janek and his Polish nose. The same oven for all?

Dr. Przedborski, Samuel Janas as listed in the wartime documents, had remained in the ghetto until the Janusz Korczak Orphanage was evacuated. He wrote down what he experienced in school notebooks. The notebooks survived; he didn't. They are in the archives of the Jewish Historical Institute in Warsaw, and in them is the narrative of his fate in the ghetto.

A narrative interrupted. No one knows where he hid after the summer of 1942, and the whole following year. In July 1943 he turned himself over to the Hotel Polski on Długa Street, where the Germans had set a trap for the Jews hiding in Warsaw by offering them the promise of immigrating to South America in exchange for a considerable sum. Nearly all perished in Auschwitz.

They had to close the door. But these rumors came to her even through closed doors. Difficult to define. Two people in darkness, trying to be as quiet as possible. Could this not be painful, to be received as if under anesthetic, as if in a numbness, a prolonged stupor? To be in a prolonged state of detachment from oneself, me and not me, without feeling anything? It lived in her and was happening again and again. How many times? Did she stop her ears with her hands? Panting breath. Theirs, hers.

What did Regina hear?

· · ·

Frania never went near the window. She spoke less and less. And then the ghetto burned. It was Easter and people were going to church. Oleś's mother came to the house with a little basket of blessed Easter eggs. She had prayed for the resurrection of Jesus Christ. Not one of the three had accompanied her.

· · ·

What was it that made their daily lives the most painful? Their mutual presence, the constant tripping over each other, fear lurking in every corner? In the kitchen and in the bathroom. Day and night. Often Oleś was not there. He left in the morning and returned after nightfall; he had had to settle problems, take part in things, organize. They never asked any questions. It was the need to take care of the children, to feed them, to play with them, to put them to bed, to decide the rhythm of their days. They both put on the appearance of good cheer at work. Feeling genuine tenderness again. Indispensable activities. That moment when Regina appeared for the first time on the threshold of their apartment seemed to go back to remote times. Her marriage to Oleś belonged to another life. Now they were both by his side; Frania was grateful to both of them for being alive.

Oleś had chosen both women and saved them. They had chosen him out of love, not knowing that he was their salvation. Frania was the first, Regina had followed her soon after. The fifth winter of the war was coming. In the courtyard, the children had built a snowman.

When Oleś joined the Uprising, for the first time in their lives together, Frania and Regina remained really alone. They knew what they had to do. Wait, survive, triumph. They sold soup in the local market and a little something of what they still had left. Their sons played under the watchful eye of their mother-in-law.

Saska Kępa came out not too badly from the bombings. Strewn with debris and broken windowpanes, their building remained standing. They had a roof over their heads. Oleś returned from his German imprisonment at the end of January 1945.

In the middle of the room there was a little smoking bandy-legged stove.

They drank boiled water. They were saved.

Ninety-eight percent of the Jews of Warsaw had perished.

A RIGHTEOUS MAN

*I*started to love Frania too late. By then she was already
fading. I had never really dared to ask her anything, not
even about the war, or about her family, her home, and
the reasons why she wanted so badly to free herself of all that
and leave Łęczyca.

She lived as if she had no past.

I didn't really believe Oleś's stories. I couldn't believe that
Frania had decided her own fate. Rebellious, proud, independent as a young girl and as a mature woman, as a wife, mother,
lover until the outbreak and all during the war. What had happened after that to transform her into a victim? What hap-

ALEKSANDER MAJEWSKI,
FRANIA'S HUSBAND, OUR FAMILY'S
HERO, AT THE AGE OF ONE
HUNDRED IN 2005

pened to her appetite for the world, for love, for knowledge? Why, of her own free will, had she shared her husband with another woman? To my eyes she was a victim. She awakened a tenderness in me with a shade of pity, never admiration.

When the war was over Frania registered herself with the Committee for Polish Jews. Bronka and Szymon did the same. I don't know whose idea it was, but nearly all the Jews who had survived had themselves registered. It was the only time that Frania officially admitted who she was. She never again declared herself Jewish. She also wrote in the documents that she was single, making official the separation her husband had arranged during the war. Under the heading "Method Used to Survive," she wrote, "The Aryan side."

She had no other address.

She must have been exhausted. I don't know if she felt the postwar euphoria, the awareness of having to restart her life from the beginning. I think that she felt herself liberated from the need to fight. Never again would she take a leading role.

Beginning in 1945 Oleś and Regina, without Frania, started to stay more often in Łódź. Regina had to reclaim her old apartment on Piotrkowska Street, the main street of the town, which had been relatively spared. There they could be together, just the two of them, without a silent, omnipresent witness. They went out as a couple, even though officially they were not married. Oleś claims that he did not want to break the promise he had made to Zofia. The papers from the war defined their roles.

After a time they lived in Łódź, where Regina Schumacher, now Regina Majewska, had reconnected with the clients of her practice. On Sundays and holidays they returned to Warsaw and the children, whom they had left with Frania.

Under the heading "Education," Aleksander Majewski, a self-styled intellectual, had written with subversive pride: "Four Years in Secondary School." He highlighted his peasant origin, which in postwar Poland was a great advantage. But his privileges stopped there. Hostile to communism, he never joined the Party. And yet he didn't do badly for himself. Enterprising and full of ideas, he held many positions and trades. He had experience in transportation and in the sale of liquid fuel. And he had also worked as an economic advisor. Often he helped Regina prepare the documentation for her cases, and even her counsel's speeches.

I think that he made all the decisions. He knew what was best for them collectively and for each separately. For Regina he reserved the public domain, the law courts, the drawing room, the role of representing them; and for Frania, it was the home and the children. At first Frania worked for a state institution. Zamutek, their brother, had hired her and Bronka for the Office for the Reconstruction of the Capital. But Oleś was an entrepreneur in his soul. In the building where they lived he had rented additional space, where he installed knitting machines abandoned by the Germans. The firm AMA—short for Aleksander Majewski—manufactured sweaters. There was always a demand for them in Warsaw, so poorly heated. He needed someone trustworthy to oversee the operation: Frania. She left the Office for the Reconstruction, she left her brother and sister as she had left twenty years earlier and during the war. "Fortunately Mother never lived to see this," sighed Bronka after Frania had paid a flying visit. Zamutek remained silent. He was almost always silent.

I also heard that Frania had become pregnant again after the war. But it was Regina who bore Oleś a third son in 1947. They called him Piotr.

And yet they knew how to be a happy family. I have seen many photos of them on vacation together, the three of them with the three boys, at the seaside, on lakes, in the mountains. Only Frania went to the parent-teacher meetings. She intervened as the mother of the three boys. I don't know what they called her when they were little, but it was to her that they reached out, and on her shoulder they would cry about a scraped knee.

She is not smiling in any photographs. She has a serious

face, especially compared to Regina, who was always smiling. Regina had gotten past the war. I understand that as a concrete action, like a bird shaking drops of water from its wings, or a person awakening from a nightmare. That's how I see Regina. I remember her as different from Frania; she smelled good and spoke easily. Yet a stranger.

In Frania the war had left a black residue. A burden she was incapable of shedding. She tried sometimes to smile. It wasn't right for her. It was as if she knew all the reasons that make joy unsuitable.

Frania had an ear for music. She knew how to play the piano well. At the house in Przedrynek, concertos, sonatas, waltzes, nocturnes. In the apartment in Saska Kępa, there was no piano. Instead, Oleś gave her an accordion. The accordion had 120 basses, and Frania had a marvelous way of using them to play anything requested, relying on her ear for all sorts of melodies. She sang with an alto voice. She knew many arias by heart, dating from the period when she played with her brother in Łęczyca. Perhaps she had had some talent. Everything she had was gone. Talent, dreams, love. During the Christmas holidays they sat near the Christmas tree and sang carols accompanied by the accordion.

Oleś oversaw the order and set the discipline at home. Those who had less sympathy called it training. He never raised his voice, and he never had to repeat anything twice. He governed the home and didn't even try to give it a semblance of being democratic. He raised his sons with a firm hand. The children listened. "Papa, can we put on some tea?" He had trained his children and later, his grandchildren. "Grandfather, can I take the bicycle?" In time, it would be to their advantage.

He decided where they would go on vacation, and the gas station where they would stop for fuel, whether they were sick enough to call the doctor, whether to drink the coffee in cups or in glasses, questions that had to be settled, how and where. Nothing escaped his control.

They had come to an agreement, all three as always, that

Frania was not keen on socializing. They didn't make her take part in all the visits and receptions. She remained at home with the children. They had decided she was not fond of dressing up. It was Regina who wore the pretty dresses sent by the American cousins. They called her "Lala" (Dolly); Frania was "Psiapsia," which is to say the one who makes hard-boiled eggs and clears the table.

She never complained. She didn't struggle against her destiny. It was safer in the shadows. She wanted to persevere, to fulfill her daily duties. Look through the window to see how life had matured everybody else.

During this time, Regina thrived in her professional and social life. She fought for the rights of women, abused, exploited, humiliated. She had organized free legal aid in the context of the Women's League; she advised on how to escape oppression, drew up legal appeals. Those who remembered her in the law courts claim that she represented the law at a higher level.

It's about a tangled skein of loyalty. During Hitler's time Oleś helped his two women, he protected them, and he was ready to do anything to save their lives. After the war, as a former Home Army soldier, he was himself exposed to danger. A number of underground soldiers had already spent some time in the prisons of the Polish People's Republic. Oleś remembers this time of threat. Perhaps because of that he provoked and irritated people with his undisguised anticommunism, his needling personality, his innate intelligence. He railed against the ideological commitment of Frania's brother, Szymon, of their sister Bronka, and his brother-in-law Danek. At the afternoon teas to which he invited them, he would purposefully choose anti-Soviet jokes and cite compromising quotes from the Party papers. He used the term "savages" to describe the ruling Party leaders whose names were written on all the posters, to whom the Przedborskis had pledged loyalty and promised to serve for the benefit of the People's Republic. He showered his guests with jeers and didn't mince his words. The brothers-in-law Szymon and Danek, Bronka's husband, weren't able to hide their dislike of Oleś.

He still doesn't believe in disinterested relationships between people. Those closest to him will testify to it. He continued to repeat that nothing was free. If someone gave something, it was because it served his interests. Every present had its price. And his sons also learned this. Only reciprocal exchanges existed. Those were the rules of the game that he imposed. Four pounds of apples were worth a package of coffee.

How does that go with his generosity during the Occupation? What he did for others, it would be impossible to calculate its value in monetary terms.

And yet Oleś was not the darling of the Przedborski family. Those whose lives he saved continued on their way. They did not celebrate his deeds among themselves, and when they met they never mentioned the Occupation. It was as if they felt no gratitude, but rather a sorrow for Frania's wasted life.

Let's draw up a ledger. The Przedborskis: Frania, her sister Bronka with little Maryś, who really looked unmistakably Jewish. Dela and Halina, my mother. And by indirect consequence, me. Adaś Herman. Dr. Stupaj, related by marriage.

They were the only Przedborskis who survived. Not counting Szymon—Zamutek—a Polish officer who survived the Oflag.

They remembered he kept Dela's dining-room furniture. Szymon reminded him about it.

They see him in the role of despot. For him they felt neither any warmth, nor admiration, nor gratitude. Perhaps that wasn't the case, but that is how I understood their gestures, their words, their behavior. Had they forgotten what he did for them? And why had they allowed themselves to forget it? Perhaps the memory had something humiliating about it. They saw him only as ruining their sister, their family, our Frania, and they secretly sympathized with her, without noticing to what extent they themselves were entangled with and had been dependent on her Polish husband. They had eliminated all feelings of gratitude for their survival. And he allowed them to do it, by not mentioning the Occupation, the ghetto, Hitler. They behaved as if that did not concern them. They didn't want to be concerned. And he, by his silence, gave them his consent. To them as well as to himself.

Oleś could not be a hero in this family. He couldn't be because the stability of this family, Jewish but Polish, rested on the denial of their identity and centuries-old history. They accepted being saved by the hands of Oleś, and after some time they considered it normal. Offered. It didn't require eternal gratitude.

Aleksander Majewski never received the medal of the Righteous Among the Nations that Israel bestows on gentiles who saved Jews. And he doesn't want it. He insists that he could not have behaved otherwise. And besides, it only concerned those closest to him.

Oleś had always been self-reliant. He carried on about the thugs and criminals who ruled the country. Thus it was easier for him to live without illusions. In time he bought a piece of land in the countryside where his family had come from and built a wooden cabin. It wasn't about having a getaway place for summer vacations but rather about having a hiding place in case of disaster, famine, or war. He took the threat seriously and did everything possible to make others aware of it also.

The events of March 1968* confirmed his political opinions about the perversity of the authorities in power as well as the long reach of anti-Semitic slogans. After the events in March, Frania lost her sister. Maryś, his wife, and their young child emigrated to Denmark. Bronka and her husband followed them.

That's when Oleś, who had never spoken of love and, according to him, had never been in love, could not accept this

---

* The authorities removed from a Warsaw theater the posters for *Dziady* (Forefathers' Eve) by Adam Mickiewicz; the resulting protest by the students in the capital brought manifestations of support in every university town in the country. The authorities suppressed them brutally and attacked intellectuals before finally blaming the Jews and launching a violent anti-Semitic campaign. (A.T.)

separation. He would not allow either one of his two women to leave. The three were intertwined, they could not imagine another life, they didn't know how to be alone each on his or her own. They settled everything by mutual consent, from running errands to the bedrooms. I can hear his voice, hear him say this, years after the death of his two women. He had spent sixty-three years with Frania; Regina shared half a century with them. They were used to one another.

Was it enough for a life? Being used to one another? Always in threes, never isolated, rarely alone. Vacations together, first in Poland, at the seaside, photos of Frania somewhere in Łeba or in Ustka, like a seal on the beach. Later, when finally people could travel, they drove all through Europe by car. They visited seventeen countries, Oleś in the driver's seat, Frania in the front passenger's seat with the map, Regina in the back. From monument to monument, by the Colosseum, the Bridge of Sighs, the Louvre, old amphitheaters, from tent to tent, from campsites by lavender fields and the Riviera, always in threes, among them nothing but consideration. "Consideration." It rings like an insult. The three of them for half a century. Magical triangle.

Frania was alone only when she visited her sister Bronka in Copenhagen. Those were the only two weeks in the year she spent apart from them. It didn't add up to more than one hundred days, the last time in 1978. Her first trip by airplane revived all her old fears. Again she was only an object; she was passed from hand to hand, customs officers, civil servants, military men, questions, documents, more and more, incomprehensible and confusing. She was impatient to be sitting together again at the kitchen table. The table in Copenhagen was smaller than at home, but the tea had the same taste. However, when Bronka proposed that she come live there, Frania refused to even speak about it.

She returned to the familiar entrance hall, found her chopping block and the oven. The time had passed when anything could be changed. She had experienced everything.

She had tried to leave once. Her grandchildren were already born. She had moved to a studio apartment the family owned for some time. After two weeks, Oleś came to take her back home.

Why do I still have my doubts about this trio? Because I have seen all three of them at the table. Because it seemed to me that Frania's eyes said something other than what I was told to believe—their common happiness, their harmony. I had the impression that someone ruled Frania's destiny. It was as if she were here with us but in reality was elsewhere. She carried herself with great pain; weariness slowed her movements. Welcoming by nature, she made an effort to serve, always bringing the platter cautiously, without smiling, almost apologetically.

I know that she was glad to see us, but I also felt her sense of relief as she stood on the threshold of the door and said goodbye to us. It was less painful when everything was quiet. The room overlooking the street, the one that was less safe, was where she kept the little tapestry with the witch from Prze-drynek whence she had fled.

I can't imagine how things were when she and Regina remained alone. Together. This was much later, when life had passed by, when Regina had been decorated for her service to the bar, and Frania was baking for the grandchildren small apple pancakes lightly sprinkled with confectioner's sugar. How could they stand one another during those empty hours under the same roof, how could they tolerate one another? How their mutual presence must have irritated them, and the memories and the absence of memory.

In bed, at the window, at the table, they knew by heart the noises they made. Through walls, behind walls. They had shared so many smells and so many kinds of sorrows. Who washed their sheets? They both washed in the same small bathroom without a sink, more and more slowly, more and more powerless.

Time and dust invaded the apartment; they had less and less room and still so many people in photographs. Both with their children, the family, everything concerning the family; so many pictures of summers and winters. The children mattered and the adults, fathers with their own children; the rest was only decoration, a stage setting. Less and less necessary.

In Frania's room, a picture of Bronka. The telephone used to call the ghetto, the telephone for calling Copenhagen. Which was farther? Bronka, all the same, survived; she had been saved. And now she had moved farther away again, beyond the ocean, because her son had settled in the United States with his family, her cherished grandson. It had to be done. Frania told him not to move so far, a new change of life at his age, a different air to breathe, problems of language.

And then there was the afternoon when Bronka did not wake up. For Frania the world ended when she passed away. She didn't have anyone left. She wept. Then she fell silent. Almost completely.

Until finally Regina started losing her memory, slowly, not all at once. At first she forgot what she had just said and she asked the same question several times, then she made slips of the tongue, and she was mistaken. She searched for the right word, she clung to shreds of the past. She begged Frania to change her day off because she hadn't finished reading to her. Already she was beginning to lose her eyesight. They still carefully put on her wig and seated her at the table for meals. Finally words began to separate from their meaning; she called the samovar a water lily, and a loan became a shampoo. She remained seated in her bed and chattered like a capricious little girl. Frania fed her with a teaspoon.

Frania died in the hospital on March 9, 1993, under the name of Zofia Majewska. Alone, when everyone had stepped outside. She was buried in the Majewski family vault in Warsaw.

I was traveling. My mother wrote in a letter that finally, after sixty years, Franuchna was going to be able to be alone.

Regina died several years later. Her body was buried under the same tombstone.

IX

Maryś

MARIAN MARZYŃSKI, MY MOTHER'S COUSIN,
IN THE MOUNTAINS AFTER THE WAR. HIS MOTHER,
BRONKA, AND MY MOTHER'S FATHER,
SZYMON, WERE SIBLINGS.

*M*aryś (diminutive of Marian) Marzyński. He was my mother's closest cousin.

They were united by many things. They had much in common. For years I never understood to what extent. Today they are, assuredly, the last witnesses of this world they had in common.

The much-beloved only son of Aunt Bronka had from the very beginning special privileges within the family. Family legend claims that he was allowed to sit on his potty in the center of the table, when the guests were gathered around drinking their tea. It was before the war.

Maryś also remained unbearable afterward, but people rarely took him to task for it. I understood that if he was forgiven more things than others, there was a reason for it. He talked a lot, and loudly; he gesticulated a lot. He was allowed to pick the raisins out of the cake, eat from the platter with his hands, and get up from the table in the middle of a meal. He caused total chaos, would throw himself on his mother and cover her with kisses, hug her without rhyme or reason, and a moment later announce to everyone that the elastic holding up her underwear had given way in the middle of the street, and only when the pink panties fell around her ankles and prevented her from walking did she understand what had happened. He told this story with glee while watching its effects.

He was into everything. He knew what took place in the garden and who read what in the bathroom. He loved to provoke. He was curious about his parents' bedroom and the intimate details of the life of the housewife. He was always in search of food; that's why he felt happiest in the kitchen, next to the refrigerator. Wetting a finger with saliva, he would pick up the crumbs from the tablecloth. Nothing intimidated him.

He would scream at his mother, "Bronuchna, you've forgotten your teeth again!"

Maryś was already a journalist during my childhood; he had a special aptitude for asking questions that were disconcerting. I don't know if I was more ashamed of that or that I was afraid of him. I didn't want to be the object of his attention. When he started with his jokes, I just couldn't bear it.

I saw him on television when he was the host of a show, *The Tournament of Cities,* a popular program in which the mayors of various towns set forth the local attractions, competed in drinking beer or in a tug of war. He often traveled abroad. He would come back with a new VW Beetle, a suede vest—their Górnośląska Street house reeked of perfume and had stashes of French cognac. He would appear again on television, telling stories, gesticulating, just as he did when he held Bronka by the shoulders and pinched Halina, my mother, spreading chaos all around him.

That's how I remembered him from when I was ten years old.

My mother loved Maryś, six years younger than she, like a brother.

She loved him even if he was obnoxious because he was insolent, he always had an excuse, he always knew better than anyone else. He used to spy on her, imitate her, and make fun of her. He made faces when she looked at herself in the mirror, made fun of her to her friends, banged on the bathroom door. She loved him because he was the son of her dearest aunt, who remembered her mother, and because they had been hidden together in a basket of dirty laundry in the ghetto.

They had spent a lot of time together in successive lodgings behind the wall. Halina was the oldest of the children. She had to take care of them. Maryś was the most difficult. He would go into fits of rage. He would call Bronka for help. He was five years old and still fell asleep holding on to her ear. During the day he was excited, he sang, he ran around. She tried to explain to him that his father had come home from work after the night shift and wanted to rest; besides, it was dangerous, the Germans could come. He only continued in the same way.

But during the raid on Leszno Street, he calmed down. As if he had suddenly understood something. At first he wouldn't squeeze himself in the basket, a wicker basket with dirty sheets, napkins, clothing. There were four of them, four children under a pile of laundry. They had been given warm milk. Where did a mother find milk? But perhaps they only dreamed it? Cries in the courtyard. Quick! You have to hurry. "We won't be afraid," Halina said for everybody; "we won't smother," she decided. The youngest, Henryś, the son of Aunt Madzia, held on to her braids; little Izio, from Aunt Cenia, huddled against her, pressing against her shoulder; Maryś climbed in last. He hadn't tried to escape. No one coughed, no one sneezed, no one moved. That time, they had still all been saved.

Halina remembers it. Maryś pretends that he wasn't in the ghetto then.

It's good to have someone who remembers your deceased mother and your father, the way Maryś remembers Dela Goldstein and Halina remembers Borys Kuszner, and their grandmother who was taken to Umschlagplatz, although no one knows if she really existed. Aunts, uncles, cousins. It's a great privilege to have witnesses to one's life. Both of them were, the one for the other, these witnesses.

They became separated in the ghetto and didn't see each other for years. It was then, on Podwale Street, that Maryś screamed from the balcony to the children in the courtyard, "I can't play with you because I am Jewish and they are hiding me here." His aunt almost paid for it with her life.

He admits that something of the sort occurred, but at another address. He screamed that he wanted to go to the ghetto. He was five years old, and he missed his parents. They tried to entrust him to several people he did not know, but they had always returned him.

He spent the rest of the war in the orphanage of a convent. For a long time he believed that his faith had protected him.

He had placed himself under the protection of God, the Polish god, different from the Jewish god that was his and ruled in heaven. But he knew that salvation was assured him by belonging to the Polish god. This started with make-believe prayers and ended with a genuine feeling of belonging. The priest in his cassock became his mother and his father. And the proximity of the cassock was the safest shelter that Maryś had known at the age of six.

He couldn't remember any of the religious aspects of his home from before the war. In the ghetto also, he was not in contact with Jewish rituals. Nobody prayed, no one went to the synagogue. They formed a closed society of about ten people, the family. They cultivated Judaism exclusively as a tradition of family values. Maryś's father, Borys Kuszner, Communist, was an active atheist. Before the war in Łęczyca, he had successfully opposed his family, he refused to allow his only son to be circumcised. Also, the Przedborskis no longer belonged to the religious majority of Łęczyca Jews. The children had escaped to Warsaw and Łódź. Progressive and assimilated, they didn't have much to do with the orthodoxy.

Bronka came to fetch Maryś in the winter of 1945. An emaciated old lady with a scarf around her head. She came on foot from Warsaw, tens of kilometers. She resembled the women from the bazaar or the peasant woman who brought the meat or the eggs. He didn't remember her. "Come back some other time, madam," he told her, "then we can discuss it. Now I can't talk." It was the hour for his prayers.

He couldn't believe that she was telling the truth, that she was his mother.

Halina let herself be convinced more quickly by her father; she was afraid of him.

Bronka came three times. The last time she had her sister accompany her; Frania was proof that the family existed. Szymon had recourse to similar arguments with Halina. It happened during the same period of time. "Do you remember your aunt Frania?" Bronka asked her son. He remembered that he

had had a pretty aunt. Pretty Aunt Frania! This woman wasn't
even a bit pretty. She stood to the side, thin, frightened, a scarf
tied around her neck.

This visit upset his peace of mind. It disturbed him, interrupted something, his contemplation, his sense of order. She
came too late. It seemed that six months earlier everything
would have still appeared differently. But now he didn't want
to go anywhere; it was here that he had his church, his faith, his
familiar place. His home.

He wanted no other.

It was this eight-year-old child whom Bronka brought back
to Górnośląska Street. She promised him a Christmas tree and
that he could serve Mass. She would have promised him anything if only to get him back.

The war had taken her mother and grandmother, her
younger sister with her whole family, aunts, uncles, cousins.
It had taken her husband; without him the whole world had
crumbled. After leaving the ghetto, she wanted to throw herself
from the window when she understood that he had perished.
She couldn't do it; something ordered her to live. For her son.
She looked at him and saw Borys. He looked so much like him,
since the beginning: spontaneous, with eyes black as coal, and
dark curly hair. Curious about everything.

Bronka never spoke about Borys in my presence, or to me.
I had lived for years without knowing that Maryś had had
another father. Later, I lent an ear to the family tales about the
great love of the eldest Przedborski sister for the son of the dentist Kuszner, a family friend. In the family it was the only couple spontaneously accepted by everybody. Bronka was so pretty
and Borys so gifted; from the moment she went to his father's
office and he had opened the door for her, they had really never
left one another after that. When they went strolling hand in
hand down the tree-lined walks, she still wearing bows in her
hair, and he with his student cap of the Polytechnic School of
Warsaw, there wasn't a more handsome couple. Ideally suited
by their good looks, their background, their feelings—not

like Zamutek with the miserable Dela, or Frania and Oleś, about whom they lowered their voices in Przedrynek. Polish and divorced: it wasn't even proper to mention it. Bronka had married Borys right after passing her baccalaureate examinations, and shortly afterward Borys had completed his studies in the department of mechanical engineering of the Polytechnic School. Both settled in the capital. They lived on Wilanowska Street, not far from Łazienki Park. They had everything going for them. When their son was born in 1937, they were not thinking about war.

They went together to the ghetto with their child. Wise Borys, Borys the engineer who knew so many things about working wood, and buzz saws, about journalism and commerce, why did he let himself be locked up with the others? He managed a carpentry shop. I don't know how it happened that after several months he found himself on a transport to Treblinka. Why, when his work guaranteed him a safe life, had they sent him so quickly to Umschlagplatz? How long during the trip did it take him and his brother to succeed in making a hole in the back of the wagon? One hour, two? They jumped out near Dęblin. They reached the forest.

At this time, Bronka still had a goal in life. A Jewish policeman helped her get out of the ghetto for a certain sum. She ransomed herself then, and later, with gold crowns that she had received from her father-in-law at the start of the war. As soon as she placed her son in a safe haven with relatives, she went looking for Borys. No one knows how she found him again. They were together in a haystack next to a railroad-crossing keeper's box. Close, so close. She couldn't help herself, she went there several times. The last time she walked away from him she couldn't know that it was for the last time, she would never have allowed herself such a thought. From the train on which she was leaving, she heard the explosions near the forest. People said that Ukrainians had been stalking them for a long time. Borys was never heard of again.

Maryś did not know it then. He doesn't remember how and

when his mother told him, a dry piece of information so that it would be less painful. His mother wept often. He knew that he mustn't ask questions about the war. Halina also knew. She never asked her father about her mother. She had overheard a bit of conversation to which she reacted with panic and tears. She never dared come back to the subject.

You had to live. You had to protect yourself. And protect them, the parents, they who succeeded in escaping for their children's sake.

A little earlier that same winter of 1945, when Bronka regained Maryś, her brother had returned from Woldenberg. He had come back with a friend from the camp, Danek Marzyński, whom they knew before the war. Danek had lost his wife and young son in the ghetto and had nowhere to go. He stayed. They lived for a few months on Górnośląska Street in a construction hut on land where they were building the wooden houses from Finland, in the neighborhood of the Ujazdowski Hospital.

Zamutek was the person Maryś remembered the best— his mother's brother, a tyrant. A tall man in uniform, wearing glasses, he spoke loudly, yelled often, and gave Maryś his orders: what he must not touch, what he had to take, what to do and when. From the start there was the scene with the milk that Maryś had taken without permission and drunk as if it were his own. When Zamutek had struck him in the face, Bronka wanted to move out on the spot.

There was also Halina with her long pigtails, whom Maryś liked to tease. She screamed and he imitated her. He with his mother. And Danek of whom he was jealous, because he quickly became affectionate with and protective of Bronka.

For Bronka, a solitary widow with a child who was difficult to manage, her brother and Danek constituted a bulwark that would sustain her. Neither one nor the other had known the fear in the ghetto, and on the Aryan side, their hardships during the Occupation had not brought them the same suffering as hers. They were wounded and felt humiliated, but no one struck them during their five years of captivity; they had lived in bearable conditions and received packages from the Red Cross. They had even cultivated little gardens. For her, these survivors in the uniform of the Polish army were like brave knights on their chargers, bringing hope. I think that the presence of the child forced her to start living again.

Szymon, her brother, began working in the Office for the Reconstruction of the Capital, where he employed Danek, who was also an engineer. Danek Marzyński supervised the construction of the wooden houses from Finland in the Jazdów district, donated to the city by the government of the Soviet Union. Soon he was able to have one allocated to himself, number 6 in section I. He moved there with Bronka and her son. He made his decision quickly; he loved her, and he wanted to build a new life the way he was constructing new edifices on the ruins of Warsaw. Szymon lived with Halina not far from there, in a building that had been saved on Koszykowa Street. Every day he visited Górnośląska Street, just like Frania, inseparable from Bronka. After the Liberation they never left one another. And they spoke of the war as little as possible.

Halina's bond with Bronka was without a doubt her most important family attachment. She loved her not only as her father's sister, but also as her mother's friend; Bronka had grown up with Dela in the same courtyard in Łęczyca. It was Bronka, younger but married earlier, who had lent her wedding dress to Dela for her marriage to Zamutek. Bronka knew Dela's parents and her sisters, old Goldstein's dovecote, and the delicacy served in the house: freshly shelled peas. Bronka remembered the birth of little Halina and the midwife who brought her into the world. She took her for strolls in her baby carriage. She had seen her grow up.

My mother had kept all these pictures in her memory, hot and sweet, like the tea in Górnośląska Street. She turned to them every time she needed comforting. She didn't want to remember anything else. Yet Bronka must have witnessed other scenes, the declining fortunes of the Hermans with the death of the father, and the forced sale of the printing plant. When Halina was still very little, a hooligan had thrown a stone at her carriage, screaming, "For the Jewish brat!" The stone fell on the blanket and missed her head. But it wasn't such memories that kept them company at the kitchen table. Next to Bronka, despite everything, Halina did not feel that she was an orphan.

Bronka had been in charge of the bread supply for the workers of the Reconstruction of the Capital enterprise. Then she worked in the accounting department of the office, in charge of the construction of the chalets from Finland, and finally in human resources for the administration. Soon her neighbors on Górnośląska Street baked their cakes and babas according to her recipes. Bronka was forty years old and found consolation in helping others, in accomplishing the ordinary tasks before her, step by step. She knew how to be open to the world, totally the opposite of her brother, who had slammed the door behind him. She knew everybody in the neighborhood, and everyone knew her. She was interested in their children, their dogs, their illnesses, their hedges, and their currant bushes. Her innate optimism had saved her, this rare light that is given only to a few. She worried about her son and wondered how she was going to bring him up without a father, but daily life offered her the solution and chased the clouds away. She had Danek with her, and he dreamed of a family.

Danek arranged the pencils according to size on his desk. He tore his tramway ticket if he didn't have time to have it punched by the conductor in the car. He saw the world in black and white. Whatever held his attention, it was difficult to surpass his enthusiasm. A solid engineer, responsible, positive—a real matrimonial find. A Jewish scout in Pabianice before the war and then a member of the Jewish communist party, the Poalej Syjon-Left, Danek could vouch for the ideological loyalty of the family. After years of fear he and Bronka had found an equilibrium in their mutual relationship.

Soon they were married, and in 1948 Danek Marzyński adopted Maryś and gave him his name. In regard to the rules and regulations they became the Marzyński family. For years I didn't know he had any other name. Maryś didn't call Danek "Papa" for a long time. I don't know if he ever called him that.

He called him "Mr. Mannerek," from the German *Mann,* since he was such a suitable man. Certainly he didn't appreciate that Danek slept with his mother, and he often spied on them in their bedroom, but he recognized Marzyński's position in the house and did not rebel against it. Mr. Mannerek tried very hard to make a man out of Maryś. He used radical methods.

Above all he wanted to extirpate the boy's Catholicism, and secondly, to instruct him about his Jewish background. To explain to him who he was. He spoke strongly, insisting on each important point. He mocked religion.

One day after his return to Warsaw, while serving Mass, by a set of circumstances Maryś dropped the cruet of wine near the altar. He took it as a sign and never again took part in a religious ceremony.

He stopped attending religion classes at school. Danek had advised him to leave the classroom as soon as the priest entered, but Maryś never admitted to any of his schoolmates that he was Jewish. He announced that his parents wouldn't permit him to follow courses in religion, and he said it in the tone of someone who doesn't know why.

Danek spent a lot of energy to make him familiar with the word "Jewish." He did it publicly and in front of witnesses. He would stop in the street, near a corner or some stores, near a café or a park, where they lived in the heart of the city, and would start haranguing his adopted son by raising his voice loudly, too loudly: "Anyway, everybody knows very well that you are an ordinary little *Jjjew.*" He dragged out the *J* in a scolding tone with a grating loudness that wounded, which conjured up the distinguishing signs, the Star of David, the armband, the ghetto.

Bronka was ignorant of this therapy.

Danek Marzyński had spent the whole war in an Oflag, where he played cards and soccer and had not seen with his own eyes either the ghetto or the assassination of the Jews. He had lost all those who were closest to him in the ghetto, but he never really understood why Bronka and Frania would suddenly burst into tears without any obvious explanation. He tried to cure them also, just like Maryś, with shock therapy.

After the war they had not wanted to leave Poland. They had come back to their home. And they had only stayed where there was a Jewish cemetery. Nine Jews out of ten in Poland had perished. But nobody can live in a cemetery, especially after such a cataclysm. The world of life was a Polish world.

That's the memory Maryś has. The Poles, that was life; the Jews, that was death. The Jews were associated with nothing other than death. The word "Jew," even when used about oneself, was cursed.

Deep down within themselves, they were Jewish. They had to remember who they were, the people whom they had lost, and what their family had been. They had to remember and meditate on it. Not about the taste of the prayers, but about the feel of the community. And also thanks to the secular seders, which gathered together the family and allowed them to remember the family history. Stripped of all religious elements, like before. They didn't evoke the Jews who came out of Egypt, but those who lived in Łęczyca. They established their own Haggadah, private, lay. They repeated for themselves what Babusia (Jecia Herman) had said, and what Babunia (Salomea Herman) had said, who played the Bolero by Ravel on the piano (Bronka), who accompanied her on the violin (Zamutek), all the stories that took place in number 9 Przedrynek Place in Łęczyca and in the printing plant, and in the warehouse for wine and spirits on Poznańska Street. They conjured up the grandfather who used to read in the office, the tasting of the Tokay and the *pejsachówka,* the Passover vodka, which they inhaled instead of tasted, and the way they pretended to celebrate the Sabbath in front of the neighbors. What was known as a *bube-majses,* a comforting "grandmother's story." That's what they ought to remember.

In this house, they thought about themselves—"we, the Jews"—and they suffered for those who had broken with the family in the name of a new life. They talked about them because they had lost them, in short, for a second time. Thus the sister of Borys Kuszner, who was hidden by a Polish family who had so imbued her with anti-Semitism that the child refused to recognize her mother. The girl believed completely that Jews smelled, and she was afraid that someone would learn who she had been. Adaś, whom Halina remembered from the ghetto—he was also lost to his family as he started going around with the Poles and renounced his own.

But when they separated and went outside, these same Jews had to be Polish, full of enthusiasm, building a new prosperity in a new nation. Monolithic without any dissent, homogeneous. They had to be like the others, like everybody. Society had to forget their Jewishness. But they did not want to forget it. They only wanted to devote themselves to it in private. Behind closed doors. Among their own. "Do you understand?" Maryś had to ask. Often he ended his sentences at home with "Do you understand?" I am trying to understand.

I didn't know the word *amchu,* I didn't know where it came from and what was its association. *Amchu* meant "ours," that is to say, Jewish, one of us. *Amchu* was a personal sign of recognition. Something that you know, and I understand. *Amchu? Amchu.* Maryś remembered. Was it a widespread phenomenon, and in what circle?

"Who is the manager? Is it *amchu,* over there, is there an *amchu* in the house?"

"Yes, I am going to telephone him."

"Listen, call the manager of the textile store, she is an *amchu.* Tell her that you are an *amchu* and she will take care of you."

I had never heard this word in the mouth of my grandfather. On anyone's lips. Then this mysterious "*amchu* network" is perhaps only a fantasy?

Danek began his day with the *Trybuna Ludu,* the Tribune of the People, the daily of the Party, edited in the language of

propaganda brochures. Those he considered ideological enemies, he called "reactionary nabobs." Oleś, the brother-in-law
of Danek's wife, the same Oleś who had ripped her from the
hands of the Germans—he said that he was a troublemaker. For
the Jewish intelligentsia, for Danek, for Szymon, the war not
only was against the Germans, but also was a war to change the
social order. They had been afraid of the anti-Semitism from
before the war, from the thirties, that gave voice to the nation-
alist elements, the fascists, those from the National-Democratic
Party. They didn't want the domination of the Church.

Salvation could come from a new ideology, a faith so strong
that it would eliminate all discrimination. We are like everybody else. That was a promise of communism. Communism
helped people forget Jewishness. It effaced it, it denied it, it
annulled it. It confirmed the necessity for assimilation and con-
ferred on it a new dimension.

The conventions of the new social order prescribed the
absence of differences between people. It had to be a Poland
of only one nationality. The Poland of harmony, the Poland of
men and women, of people who were equal.

They wanted to believe in a utopia. They did believe in it.
Even though their fates before the war were completely different, my grandfather and Danek inoculated their families with
communism.

There were many people like them. They had renewed the
stereotype of the "Judeo commune." This would be used as a
tool of anti-Semitic propaganda. Vicious circle.

In postwar Poland, assimilated Jews did not call themselves
Jews. They didn't use the term, as if it were embarrassing or
shameful. And when others defined them that way, they felt as
if they were victims of a denunciation.

They felt wounded and degraded when someone from the
outside, a stranger, a Pole, Polish people, pointed them out as
Jews.

In 1968 the sixth house on Górnośląska Street was packed up
in a few weeks. They took down everything that had until then

made up a life and they put it into crates. They bought rugs and plates before leaving. Bronka fell ill with grief. She didn't want to leave the country. But her only son was leaving with her grandson; she couldn't remain behind alone.

What they couldn't take, they gave away. Earthenware pots for buttermilk, rounded, rugged, the color of faded bricks, appeared in our house at the end of 1969. At the same time, used place settings, a skimming ladle, and a cake slicer—for cakes that my mother did not know how to make, but Bronka, in Jazdów, made superbly. They were speaking all the time about the Gdańsk train station. I didn't understand what was happening. The whole family disappeared. She and Danek, the old dachshund, Tymek, and Maryś with his wife, Grażyna, even little Bartek, who had come into the world a short time earlier.

Rumors reached us after their departure. Distant.

At the beginning of the 1970s I went to Copenhagen with my mother. I remember nothing about the trip except for pornographic shops, and the fact that Danek had stopped believing in communism and spoke of "our queen," meaning the queen of Denmark. They went to the supermarket, at a distance, for fruit-flavored yogurt, or chicken, a different place for each thing in order to save a few cents. I remember that old ladies came to visit them to play cards. I started calling Bronka "Granny," without really knowing why. There, Granny started baking crusty croissants with raisins, delicacies that I discovered again years later in the Jewish bakeries of Brooklyn.

Maryś and his family were already in America.

America seemed to me to be the end of the world. To be in America meant almost not to exist at all.

When Bronka left Jazdów, left the house from Finland, she had ceased to exist. After my visit to Copenhagen she was still present for a moment. America took her from me completely.

The telegram announcing her death shattered Szymon.

From America sometimes would arrive enormous packages distressed by a trip of several weeks on a ship, cardboard boxes filled with the strangest wardrobe that I had ever seen. Night-gowns, celadon colored with nylon lace; coats and shirts with worn collars; cotton short-sleeved shirts, generally slightly torn or else stained with a spot of oil paint; pullovers with pulled stitches; a rainbow assortment of gloves, not always in pairs, shoes of different sizes; skirts cut differently than those here. We felt, my mother and I, like Cinderellas, overwhelmed—I don't know if we were more disconcerted or pleased. We made daily use of a few pieces from this unexpected carnival of sec-ondhand clothes.

Years later Maryś came to visit in Poland with his own film crew. It must have been in 1981; Solidarity, a breath of freedom. I remember that I didn't believe until the very end that I would see him. He had seemed so unreal, then. On a beautiful sum-mer day he came knocking at the door of our apartment on Kasprzak Street, he invaded the balcony with a camera and his crew, and he started filming, asking questions about other times, questions in which underwear and philosophy were in the same line. Everything happened quickly, so fast that I didn't have time to think, to prepare, to formulate. By then he was already gone. He used surprise as a journalistic method. It helped him establish his own documentary reality in which he was the main character.

He was gone. I heaved a sigh of relief. Our world had no point of contact anymore.

I hadn't realized that he was actually shooting a documen-tary, *Return to Poland,* a film about him and his family, there-fore also about mine, about his Jewish family and mine—how and why he had left Poland.

Somewhere, somehow, I must have known. Because I am in this film, I talk, I laugh, you can see my face. And his face. But at the same time, I had instantly erased it in me, hidden it, forgotten it. I did not want to be part of his family. His family—that of Maryś or that of Bronka? Who did I not want to be, with whom did I not want to be linked, intertwined, associated? And why? My father expressed antipathy about him; he considered him an aggressive opportunist. He remembered that Maryś had forced himself to break off relations with Halina when she married him. Did that cloud his views?

In the course of the following years I was afraid that Maryś would return. Even later, when I went to America for the first time, and I understood how much closer it was than it seemed. And not only much closer geographically. It was also closer to me—perhaps closer to the places that I knew.

In New York I began to breathe differently. However, "over there" was still "over there," far from Warsaw, from Poland, where I was Polish.

The last time that I was thrown into a panic because of Maryś was in Paris. It was just a few years ago. I learned that he was there, he would participate in the same conference in the Palais du Luxembourg where I was going to speak. It was about the Jewish-Polish question. I was again frightened. Frightened is to put it mildly—it was pure hysteria.

Then a friend asked me, "What are you afraid of? What can happen, what do you think he is going to do?"

I didn't want him to reveal it. To tell everybody. My secret.

X

March

STUDENT RIOTS, WARSAW, MARCH 1968

MARCH 1968

I don't remember March 1968. I can't distinguish it from any other March. Women's Day, carnations for the schoolteacher, solemn assemblies. When you are eleven or twelve, time behaves differently, as if it were infinite, without limits.

There hasn't been any past yet, and the future is measured by time spent doing lessons, gathering outside by the carpet hanger, school trips to the mountains. What is important is the beginning of the year and the vacations. Even if it announces spring, March mattered less to me than May, the month of book fairs, the Race for Peace, and my birthday.

That spring, but perhaps the preceding spring, at home on Kasprzak Street, we suddenly started listening to a Western radio station. Mother and Maciek spent a lot of time near the sputtering radio set, trying to understand something, which from the look on their faces seemed to me very difficult to grasp. When I concentrate on it, I manage to draw the word "Zionists" from my memory.

At home we didn't speak about politics and very little about daily life in the country where I lived. I only learned later everything that was happening then. In the spring of 1968, a wave of protests and demonstrations took place across Poland: students were demanding a loosening of the muzzle of censorship that the Communist authorities were tightening more and more. The militia set upon them brutally. The dreary calm of daily life was ripped by the explosion of tear gas and the roar of water cannons.

Everything occurred in the center of Warsaw, a few streetcar stops from our apartment on Kasprzak Street. I was aware of nothing. Held on a tight leash by Communist censorship, the Warsaw press remained silent. My mother also was silent.

What would change the destiny of our family began several days later. The authorities had discovered the explanation for, and the people responsible for, instigating the problems. It was the Jews, partisans of the Zionist imperialism of Israel, who disturbed the peace and happiness of the Polish people for vile objectives only they knew. Communist practice did not permit the public usage of the word "Jew," and they had therefore replaced it with the word "Zionist."

The anti-Semitic campaign of March 1968 touched almost all the remaining Jews in Poland. In offices and universities, in editorial meetings and in factories, in scientific institutions and in film studios, in Party meetings and in specially called conferences, they called Jews out by their names and, having chastised them for their hostility to communism and their hostility to Poland, dismissed them from their work and the Communist Party.

In general they were so taken by surprise that they didn't know how to defend themselves. And how do you defend yourself against accusations of Zionism and of betraying the character of Poland to benefit pro-Israeli sympathies? How do you demonstrate what was proven by your whole life until then?

Television broadcast news flashes showed meetings or crowds carrying banners demonstrating against the criminal politics of Israel and demanding the expulsion of the Jews from Poland. Even though the borders of the Communist countries were hermetically sealed, the authorities made an exceptional effort to facilitate Jewish immigration to Israel, on condition that they renounce their Polish citizenship. My friends with no memories of World War II today tell me that the terror they experienced and the intimidation to which they were subjected could be compared to nothing else.

I don't remember that the rhythm of days, weeks, and months

was disturbed. I don't know when I was told that Bronka was leaving for Copenhagen with her family. I didn't ask why, although anyone else in my place would have. I recited poems about Warsaw, I came home from school, I did my homework. As if nothing were happening, as if that were the essential in this situation where my Jewish family, collectively and individually, were living through the most trying days of the postwar period.

It was more than twenty years since the end of the war. The Przedborski and Marzyński families had solid ground under their feet, a base of construction and reconstruction, achievements and the realization of plans. Life seemed finally to have taken the form and had the meaning that mattered to them. They had educated their children. Halina worked in journalism, Marian in television. Frania's son had completed his studies, the two youngest were pursuing theirs. No sign of trouble from anywhere.

What mattered is that my mother was again beginning to be afraid. That must have been the case, although she said nothing then and doesn't speak of it today. She behaved as if nothing were happening or as if this did not concern her. She was Polish. She wanted to protect her child. The little girl with blue eyes had nothing in common with the Jews. Could have nothing in common.

Somewhere deep within her she found confirmation of the fact that her choice was well founded. Because it is easy to be stigmatized again, to be pointed out, the circumstances only have to present themselves.

You have to be white in a reality that accepts whites and is made up of whites, no other colors. You have to forget everything inside you that has a connection with black, even if it's only with a shadow.

She was again playing for me a role that demanded strength and character. She slammed the door on the world around us. She decided that the anti-Semitic campaign did not concern her.

She was still careful to observe the time for sleeping. I had to be in bed at the agreed time when she would come to kiss me and wish me good night. Whatever might have happened later occurred after they closed the door of my room, which sometimes let the light filter through. At that time things were different. I am not in a position to know whether this lasted a few nights or longer.

Maciek and she were seated in my room in the dark, bent over my big radio set with the turntable. He was in the easy chair, she was on the little wooden chair painted with red and gold fruit that my father had brought back for me from Moscow. The green band of the radio dial trembled. From the box came a static voice through the buzzing and crackling to which were added shreds of music that drowned out everything. I couldn't distinguish the words, even though it seemed to me they were speaking of war. I felt that something important was happening, because no one paid any attention to me.

I don't have any memories, for those years, of other moments of vague worrying like that one.

I know today that they were listening to the Voice of America or Radio Free Europe, broadcasts considered hostile, therefore permanently blocked. They followed the Arab-Israeli conflict, trying to understand how it was actually happening and what would be the future of the world, and to find out what was the reaction to the war in Poland. They followed the successive stages of the anti-Semitic campaign in Poland: my mother, Szymon with Żena and Danek with Bronka, Maryś and sometimes Frania, even though usually it was Oleś who informed her what she must think. For him, there was nothing new under the sun. He expected this.

The others had not.

Then in March, for the first time, they took stock of the fact of what they were in this country. In listening to the leader of the Communist Party, with whom they identified, they felt the ground crumbling under their feet.

Of the four Przedborski siblings, the children of Justyna and

Henryk, three had survived the war, a rare case among the Jews of Poland. They had rebuilt their families, Zamutek with a new wife, Bronka with a new husband, and Frania according to the arrangement dating from the war. They had exchanged Prze-drynek Place in Łęczyca for three addresses in Warsaw.

Without the war they would have been different people.

Its echo was prolonged. In every symptom of hostility real or imagined, in every anti-Semitic incident. What do you do when they hit you? How to react? And when they don't hit you, but instead they spit in your face?

All this seemed inconceivable. Suddenly every applicable law was violated. They invalidated the foundations of social life that had been respected until then. They didn't hit you, they didn't resort to physical constraints, but words wounded just as painfully.

SZYMON, AGE 64

*M*y grandfather did what he knew best in moments like these—he went to bed. He had behind him a record as a builder of the People's Poland and a worker devoted to serving his country. Spread before him—drafts for new projects. He had been cast out of his work and the Party.

"Why?" he repeated to his wife. And to the wall, because he was lying down facing the wall. He tried to analyze it. To find a logical explanation. Who was encouraging them, why did he suddenly find papers stuck under his doormat: "Moïshe (Mosiek) to Israel." Moïshe? What Moïshe was it about? Perhaps Samuel, Szmulek, Zamutek—although he had not spread abroad his childhood first name. He was good for the rubbish heap. Like all beings born of a Jewish mother, a much-beloved mother.

He should have been like everybody else. And he was like the others. He had fled his own Jewishness in the guise of a Communist. But what sort of Communist was he? He wasn't even a proper Communist: no past history in the Underground, no Spain, no prison. A Stalinist joker. His brother-in-law was right. He had nothing to be offended about, nor anything to complain of. They had exposed him. The country for Moïshe (Mosiek) was elsewhere, here they are foreigners, here they are like an ulcer. The Party members should be Polish nationals.

In the beginning he wanted to take his case to the higher-ups, appeal to the District Committee, or even the Central Committee. Before he understood that everything came out of there.

"We condemn the aggressive and exploitive politics of the State of Israel"—he remembered these slogans launched with others about the heroic people of Vietnam struggling against American imperialism. But it was no longer about Israeli aggression or the anti-imperialist front; it was about worldwide Zionism slandering the Polish state. On New Year's Eve, watching the New Year's cabaret on television, the screen was suddenly full of puppets with hooked noses. For a long while they swarmed over a terrestrial globe. He stopped going out of the house. He only went to buy rolls in the morning and fetch the paper. It would have been better had he not read *Trybuna Ludu,* his paper. The organ of the Party was leading this campaign in the press. He returned home and lay down on the sofa. He went out even more rarely since he found traces of excrement on the doorknob. His right hand in a disgusting stinking substance. Revulsion. Fear. When others left, colleagues, comrades from the Party, for a moment he also thought of leaving. Israel? But all the same it was a bourgeois Zionism, he himself had recently signed protests. Before all this happened.

A sofa on Puławska Street. No, he really didn't want another place. This bed, they wouldn't take that away, he can stay lying down here. If you don't like it, I won't elbow my way through. In the courts, in meetings, on the carpet, and for my prerogatives. But Moïshe (Mosiek) won't go to Israel. Moïshe (Mosiek) is here.

And that's how he remained. Alone. Turned to the wall.

BRONKA, AGE 62
DANEK, AGE 64

*B*ronka was different from her brother. Warm, loved by everybody. I don't know what the two of them talked about, or how. I don't remember having paid attention to their conversations. Danek, Bronka's husband, the adoptive father of Maryś, was always pointing out everybody's errors. He knew better than anyone, and any objections made him turn red. It didn't matter much if he spoke of the path spelled out by the Polish United Workers' Party or by industry, which was eleven times more developed than in prewar Poland. He had been dismissed from his position as director in charge of "establishing the resistance of materials in the technical institute for construction," and he had been expelled from the Party for lack of consideration for the employees under his direction. They knew that he had belonged to Poalej Syjon-Left before the war. They didn't want to hear that it was a Communist Jewish organization. Zionist. There was no place for him in our ranks.

He could not imagine that over there—somewhere, far away, in another language, and in different times—that over there, whatever it was still awaited him. He didn't want another place. On these sofas, low and uncomfortable, that his architect daughter-in-law had installed in every room and from which it was difficult to get up, he was at home. Every morning he went to fetch the paper with his dachshund, Tymek, near the Parliament building; the kiosk saleswoman set aside his weeklies; he met his neighbors. He was signed into this routine.

In the little house on Górnósląska Street, it was Maryś who became the most important. It was he who convinced, who incited, who explained. He had suddenly begun to understand more than his parents. Without him, those two would never have crossed their threshold. Apple and cherry trees bloomed in the garden for pies and dumplings and compotes. The guests were waiting for canasta and tea. The umbrella had to be repaired, the chairs moved to the shade. Weed the flowers and water them. After the May Day parade the season began in the garden. At the end of 1967 their grandson was born; let him sleep peacefully in the open air. Here everything belonged to them.

Give it up? In the name of what? Why? At what cost?

Bronka never made this decision. Never of her own free will would she have been separated from her brother and sister, and their children, and everything they had in common. The memory of their parents, and the proximity of Łęczyca. It didn't matter that they never went there, Łęczyca was nearby, the distance of memory. She had already packed up once in her life, for the ghetto, and she had begun again from nothing after the war. She had already been forced to become someone else. Zamutek wasn't well, he needed care. And she wasn't in the best of shape. And then she didn't know any other language, and she would learn nothing. What could she learn at her age? They would get by, they had often come through. Nobody was going to evict them from their home. They didn't invade homes, there was no deadline for delivering the furs. There's nothing that's obligatory.

Maryś decided. He would leave with his wife and child. No question of leaving his parents behind. Denmark would welcome them. The Danes had proposed financial help to give them a start. They were ready to take in the Jews driven out of Poland.

Bronka couldn't live without Poland and didn't want to. But she wouldn't have survived the separation from her son and grandson. They left.

FRANIA, AGE 61

She was looking out the window, just like when the ghetto was on the other side of the Vistula. This same crystal-clear air of the beginning of spring. She felt old and tired. She didn't know where to take herself. To her family, with her own people, behind the wall? Her husband had forbidden it to her, thanks to which she and her son had survived. Abroad into the unknown, for a new exile? Too late. Then, as thirty years earlier, she knew that she would remain on the Polish side.

She hadn't left Oleś, although Regina had stayed with them, supplanting or replacing her; they had lived as a threesome under one roof, with three sons. Why should she flee now? Ever since then she had resolved not to start a new life for herself after the war, because the children needed a father and protection, because someone had to run the errands and do the cooking, which no one could do as well as she; because of washing, darning, ironing; because of the children's homework, the sandwiches, the ribbons, the scarlet fever; because of the bicycles, the slippers, the gymnastics, the skis, the dictations, and all that on her shoulders. If she had not fled at that time, why would she become afraid now, because of the political storm that was brewing? She had already forgotten how bitter shame was.

Besides, no one knew who she was. Who they were, the one and the other. She lived in hiding. Regina also, the lawyer from law firm number 20. Zofia Majewska and Regina Majewska. None of the children knew that both of their mothers were

Jewish. A question of instinct for self-preservation, as Oleś explained it. He pointed out that they were only half Jewish, he turned them toward the world of clarity, the Polish side. But Frania constantly remembered the words of her mother about children born of Jewish mothers. They are ours. Thus constantly menaced. That's why she could not leave him, Oleś, a Pole, their protector, the father of three uncircumcised sons. He guaranteed their safety. So what if the war had ended, you have to always be on guard. Nothing was happening that he hadn't foreseen, that Oleś had not announced. In the anti-Semitism campaign of spring 1968 he found the confirmation of his political theory.

The Bolsheviks, the "savages," as he called them, had occupied Poland after the war and used the Jews to raise the new order. "Your brother was so stupid that he was incapable of understanding this, or he didn't want to. In the name of an ideal of equality and justice, in which the persecuted Jews believed with even greater fervor than the Poles, they even gave them work and positions. High positions. That's why I didn't want our children boasting in school that their mothers were Jewish. I knew very well the state of their mind." Frania sometimes had the impression that he treated her like a goose that came right out of the Old Testament; he sometimes used the expression when he was joking, as if she were a child. "Psiapsiunia, all the same you have to grasp the absurdity of this situation! Jewish directors, chairmen, with cars, telephones, business travels, and now my children have to be exposed?"

She accepted without any objections. Just as she peeled his apple, without a word, and put each piece in his mouth, one after the other; just as she gnawed on the bones she had taken from his plate. She didn't need any other proof for herself, to justify his reasons.

She didn't want to flee. For the rest, where could she have fled? She didn't know the world where you could be yourself.

HALINA, AGE 37

She worked as an editor in the cultural section of *Dzien-nik Ludowy*, the People's Daily, the organ of the ZSL, the Peasant Party. She lived in the same two-room apartment at Kasprzak Street where she had moved on leaving her father's house. She was careful to maintain good relations with her neighbors, the seamstress and the locksmith on the fourth floor, the engineer on the third floor, and the school-teacher on the ground floor. For them she remained the wife of the sports commentator of the Race for Peace, the broadcaster Tuszyński, even though they had not been together for years.

Other than Halina there were no Jews on the staff. Perhaps that's the reason she now claims that nothing, during this period, directly affected her. At *Dziennik Ludowy* they didn't organize meetings during which people would have been denounced according to a prepared list, and they didn't sign petitions condemning the Zionists. Perhaps that's why.

She remembered several events at the paper that March. An older colleague was noisily rejoicing that the Jews were finally having their noses rubbed in it. Zofia Satanowska, her supervisor in the cultural section, loyal Communist, had been in the Underground in the forests during the war, in a detachment of the Resistance. She had saved the life of her Jewish husband. In March 1968 she turned in her membership card to the Party, a courageous act that very few dared then.

Halina had the impression that all this did not concern her. What Israel? What desert, what battlefront, what Arabs? What did she have in common with the Palestinians and their land, their sand, their palm trees? She would have trouble finding it on the map. What Zionism? A palm tree instead of willows and birch trees?

This was beyond her. The demonstrations and the student strikes, the repression by censorship, the signs "Zionists back to Israel" in the May Day parades. In the hallways colleagues whispered behind her back and turned away when she passed. The author of certain articles on these people of foreign origins who should clear out of Poland would tap her on the shoulder with a wink. As if to let her know that he had to act this way, but they knew very well, the one and the other, what was the real score.

She didn't play the game, didn't discuss it, expressed no opinion. As if it didn't concern her. Her colleagues remember her seeming at a complete loss. She did not appear afraid, but rather absent, and isolated from the others.

Did she ever think: we, the Jews? I don't think so. She could think: we, the family, the Przedborskis, the father, the mother, then we, the colleagues of this group—journalists, literary critics. She never thought that such-and-such a professor had a father who was a rabbi, or that he was originally from a small Jewish town. And because of that, he would favor her, or her colleague Joanna, or Wera. None of her girlfriends was Jewish. None of them spoke badly of the Jews.

She had never thought of emigrating. She was afraid of change, she was afraid of going toward the unknown. She never lost her job. They had not deprived her of her source of income. Her troubles were at the level of the cafeteria staff, and a loudmouthed accountant, the guarded look of mailroom staff, and a certain discomfort when in the midst of people. The question in their eyes, do they know, do they recognize, what will be their reaction? Who will call her *żydówo* (kike), and in what circumstances? In the street, in the printing shop, at the kiosk, at the vegetable stand, at the movies? I don't know to what extent she was fearful of that.

MARYŚ, AGE 31

*H*e seemed to be at the height of his career. He had an excellent position on Polish television as a journalist and the host of a weekly entertainment program. He traveled abroad and brought back Western manners and clothes, as well as a breath of fresh air. He loved his Polish wife, a talented architect who had just given birth to a son, Bartek. His parents were in good health. He was full of ideas. The whole world lay before him.

March 1968 made him aware of how tenuous was the foundation of his future. It seemed suddenly as if anyone could say to him, "You, the Jew!"—it was an insult. They could confront him with impunity, treat him as a vulgar Jew boy trying to hide who he was. He felt very vulnerable.

At the television station someone told someone and someone repeated it to him that if they could, they would crush him like a fly on the wall. He didn't believe it. He didn't even believe that he had heard it incorrectly, he knew what was happening, he read the newspapers. He refused to absorb it. He continued working. They told him that they liked him, and that's why they didn't fire him on the spot, as with others. His wife, Grażyna, considered that this was sufficient reason to leave immediately.

She had wanted to leave for a long time. She was among those Poles who dream of emigrating. For her it was the solution, a chance to free herself from this cage to reach the much-desired West. The chance to break free of a system she couldn't stand, which held her captive and troubled her in all its manifestations. She didn't like those people, or their way of life, or their relationships, or their compromises, or the sick way they related to one another. The absence of smiles, the waste, the lies.

Maryś felt she was right. He didn't want live a lie any longer, and his own success seemed ridiculous to him. His wife insisted, pushed more than he by wounded pride. Even more self-assured than he, also, that their real future and more opportunities were abroad. But it was Maryś who had to convince his parents, overcome their doubts, their resistance, and their despair. His son, Bartek—did he also have to live out his life in lies and fears? That's how he explained it to Bronka, turning back her own argument—the child was most important.

Were the three of them ever alone, Szymon, Bronka, and Frania, to sort out what had to be done? When and how did Bronka inform her brother and sister that they had made the decision to leave Poland? Szymon no longer took part in family get-togethers. They said out of compassion that he suffered from melancholia. He didn't say a word about Bronka's departure, and all the rest of what occurred after March 1968. Maryś heard Szymon say to Danek that in the West they would come under the influence of American intelligence. He said the same thing to Halina. He demanded that she break off all communication with her aunt who was leaving Poland, with the rest of the family from Łęczyca who managed to escape the extermination. Bronka preferred just not talking about it with her brother. She didn't like contradicting anyone, but her brother in particular.

Maryś and Grażyna made their final decision in the summer of 1969. The Polish authorities made it known that the special emigration privileges for Jews wanting to leave Poland would soon be canceled. Even though the turbulent anti-Semitic campaign in the media had already been reduced to a minimum by the end of 1968, the news that they were going to stop emigration provoked a new wave, even greater, of requests for authorization to leave. Maryś left first, in the autumn of 1969, with his

Volkswagen Beetle, his baggage, and his frightened old dachshund. Bronka and Danek took the train from Gdańsk Station, where the Polish friends of Jewish emigrants were gathered for a final, unforgettable, and symbolic gesture of farewell.

Halina did not go to the station.

Today she claims that Szymon forbade her. He had also forbidden her to take in Maryś's wife, Grażyna, who was staying another week in Warsaw with little Bartek. Their apartment had already been vacated, their belongings either packed up or sold off. Several days before departure. The plane ticket in her pocket. Several days, Monday, Tuesday, Wednesday, and so on until the end, seven days and nights in all, seven times twenty-four, not quite one hundred and seventy hours, half of which would be spent asleep. A humid windy November that seemed endless, when you can't get out of the house. What was Mother afraid of then? What danger could possibly be menacing her? What was still there and always would be in the Polish air, in the autumnal atmosphere of Warsaw in 1969, well after March 1968 with its great wave of hatred and panic, what was there that wouldn't allow her to offer hospitality to Grażyna and Bartek?

What did she not want to be confronted by? The secret service spying efficiently on the Jews? Or the Jews emigrating from Poland? She certainly feared that someone would make the association between her and them, put her in the same category as they. She didn't want this, either for herself or for me.

Am I permitted to judge? Mother wanted to be Polish. Completely, as soon as the war ended. She avoided situations that put her in need of defining herself. If she had to, she always selected Polishness. The Communion wafer included. She said she did it for me. I am not sure. Also for herself. That way she constructed her self-portrait. Not only in the eyes of others, but in her own eyes equally.

Szymon never saw his sister Bronka again. He would not maintain any contact with her. He did not correspond. For having betrayed her country, she was excised from the Przedborski family by my grandfather.

As a result of the events that are today defined as "March 1968," the majority of Jews who were still here left Poland. A third of them had received superior educations; they were university professors, scientists, intellectuals, students. Polish citizenship was taken away from the emigrants. At the passport office they had received a travel document authorizing travel in one direction only, without the right to return. They were given a month to leave the territory. It was generally considered that the events of March 1968 had put an end to the thousand-year presence of Jews on Polish soil. Yet a number of Polish Jews had remained.

After March 1968, several thousand Jews left Poland from Gdańsk Station in Warsaw, for Vienna and Copenhagen and from there for Israel and America. Through the train windows taking them west they saw for the last time what was most familiar to them. Today the special trains leaving Gdańsk Station are going to Rostov and Woroneż.

Thirty years later, in 1998, in Gdańsk Station they unveiled a commemorative plaque bearing an inscription from the pen of the author Henryk Grynberg: "Here, they have left more of themselves than they had." It happens that the plaque is splattered with paint and there are anti-Semitic graffiti. The word "Zionist" doesn't figure. Today they again can write "Jew."

BOGDAN TUSZYŃSKI, MY FATHER,
AT WORK AT A SPORT EVENT

BOGDAN, AGE 36

*I*n the middle of the 1960s my father caught the wind in
his sails. He married for the second time and became
father of a second daughter, and he applied himself to
his work with renewed vigor. He traveled a great deal. Not like
others, to Romania or to Bulgaria, but to the West, the real
West outside the Iron Curtain. He didn't have to wait for the
visit by the Rolling Stones to Warsaw to feel like a citizen of
the world himself. He wasn't bothered by the successive crises
of the shortage of meat, inflation, and the struggles in queuing
up at shops. More than ever, the radio was his home.

In spring 1968, in the hallway of the radio station, someone
overheard my father say, "It's a good thing that they are leaving." Someone heard him say "finally." And that there was no
way of getting rid of them, and that it was high time. They
had done enough harm. They had created disasters. They had
governed long enough, playing the petty master.

Irena, who heard this, who had always been on his side
because they had spent more than ten years at neighboring
desks in the sports section, shut herself in a room with him
and gave him a lecture. "What's the matter with you?" She
brought up his Jewish wife, his ex-wife but a great love, the life
he wanted to share with her and the child who united them.
She didn't know how he could talk that way and even less how
he thought those things. "Shut up!" she said. "Don't yell like
that in the hallways, because half the radio station is going to
vilify you."

In March 1967 he had joined the Party. The organization

condemned the aggressive and expansionist politics of the state of Israel. He had himself heard his colleagues at the radio station express loudly and clearly their joy at the Israeli army's victories during the Six-Day War. He had heard one of them speak of the victory of "our army." He was in a rage. "How the fuck is that, 'our' troops?" What sort of Poles were they when they identified with the military successes of the Jews?

Kazik Zybert was a colleague very close to my parents, ever since they were students together. On the radio he was responsible for a daily program broadcasting popular news items and commentaries.

It was undoubtedly toward the end of spring 1968. The director of the department summoned him and asked him if it was true that during the Arab-Israeli conflict a year earlier, he went to the Israeli embassy to deliver personally to the wife of the ambassador a note expressing his gratitude to the Israeli army. Kazik at first thought that it was a joke by his colleagues. He denied it, but the director said that he could no longer be in charge of the broadcast. Kazik protested; he considered the accusation a provocation. "Can you seriously believe it?" he had asked his boss. "That has no bearing on the case," answered the director.

In the Warsaw studios of Polish Radio, where numerous Jews were working, the persecution lasted a long time.

When, years later, Kazik told the story of those days, what he remembered most clearly were his friends. Those same friends who slapped him on the back before the meeting and assured him that everything would go well. Those same friends with whom he played volleyball on the grounds behind the radio building and whom he met on Saturdays for birthday parties.

There were about a hundred people in the room. They each rose in turn. To make brief statements without proof, lies, using several formats. They showed him as a reactionary and retrograde, a foreign tumor on Polish soil. Words that struck him like stones.

They didn't all accuse him. As he said years later, there were a few courageous people. But my father was not among them.

My father had been a friend of Kazik's since student days; together they had taken part in the harvests, and in collecting potato bugs in the fields, and they had taken their exams in Marxism together, and later walked along the river hugging their sweethearts. Kazik remembered my father in particular. He wasn't the only one in this business, many others also intervened, but he especially struck Kazik most violently—he declared that Kazik had lost his Polish heart.

Kazik remembered the meeting of spring 1968 just as well as my father remembered another meeting sixteen years earlier, at the University of Warsaw. There they had branded him an enemy of the people; here they set the dogs loose on a Jew.

Now as then they had recourse to the same methods, they used calumnies and lies. Then they eliminated the foreign elements on the ideological level, whether real or assumed. Here the foreign element was on the national level—that is to say, of an improper origin. My father told me that his most virulent accusers in the past were the Jews. Had an opportunity for revenge presented itself to him in 1968?

No, that would be too simple.

He was still young then, impulsive, impetuous. He spoke faster than he could think. His friends try to understand, in the name of an old friendship. They are even certain that there is no hate in him, he just gets carried away, by the force of his heightened language. This has grown more pronounced over the years.

Mother assures me that he wasn't that way when they were married.

As far back as I can remember he has gone off into tirades of this sort. Never directed toward me, as if it did not concern me. As if my heart were made of sand from the banks of the Vistula. How old was I when he began? Twelve years old? Ten? Even younger? My mother left him when I was six years old. I must say that he also never told me that she was Jewish.

How to pull it all together? Because he had a Jewish wife whom he, his family, had all embraced as one of their own. He continues to reassure me that in their household, the Jewish question didn't exist. They never spoke of it. He loved her and never asked himself who she was. Was it later, when she turned toward another, that it all came together as a sort of whole?

Couldn't my father see with whom he was falling into line at that time? He came out of a working-class tradition of the PPS, the Polish Socialist Party; there was no trace of anti-Semitic deviation in the family. He was an atheist, and he doesn't speak any better of the Church. He has no link with the heirs of Father Trzeciak* nor with the church on Zagórna Street spreading anti-Semitic publications. Then how is it possible that it is specifically Bogdan, the first boy in the family to have had an education, the youngest child of the People's Poland, who has been contaminated by something that neither his illiterate grandmother, nor his railroad-worker grandfather, nor his parents, nor his uncles and his aunts had ever suffered from? How would he have behaved as a student if they had made Halina sit separately with the other Jewish students, on the left side of the room?

I believe, I believe absolutely, that he would have seated himself next to her. Then where does all this come from? Where does he stand today with his feeling of being rejected by the young, and his complaints about his experience being undervalued, and yet having so rich a life? His bitterness is directed against the elite in power, among whom—as always—Poles of Jewish origin play their role.

When, some years ago, on a television program, *The Hour of Sincerity,* they asked my father about his favorite melody, he mentioned "If I Were a Rich Man," from the Jewish musical comedy *Fiddler on the Roof.*

---

* By his speeches and his publications, Stanisław Trzeciak was one of the leaders of anti-Semitism in Warsaw during the prewar period. Marek Edelman, one of the main figures responsible for the Warsaw Ghetto Uprising, states that most of the pogroms in the capital originated at his church on Theater Square. (A.T.)

XI

Addresses

*T*he book has not ended, since the story continues. It also has no end because I do not want to choose only one heritage. Both of them—the Polish and the Jewish—are alive in me. Both make me what I am. Even if they oppose one another and accuse each other—I belong to both. And let it remain that way.

I have a dream. I don't know whether I should call it a dream or a wish. I would like to gather them all for a moment in the same room. I want to see them all present. All of those whom I never had, whom I have not known, who were taken from me before I could get to know them, or who were silenced so that I wouldn't know. Let them come to me now. Grandmother Jecia with Henryk; her mother, Salomea Herman, with her husband the typographer who died young; her children; their children. The brothers of their father, the sisters, the grandmothers, all of them, all together for a great meeting. Let them come out of the silence, of nothingness, of nonexistence. From the smoke, from the grave, from forgetfulness. I invite you. To my home. Into my childhood room where you never came. Where you were missing. In this empty space, in this silence. There where I missed you so much although I didn't know of your existence.

I am here and I wait.

XII

My Family

MY FATHER'S FAMILY

ROZALIA KARLIŃSKA
née Krześniak, 1890–1983

JAN KARLIŃSKI, "WANIA"
1886–1962

ROMUALD TUSZYŃSKI
1913–1981

MARIANNA TUSZYŃSKA
1909–1969

STEFANIA KARLIŃSKA-BARTOSIK
1923–2001

BOGDAN TUSZYŃSKI
Born in 1932

Jan Karliński, "Wania"
1886–1962
My great-grandfather. He worked on
the railroad as a brakesman and ticket
taker on the Warsaw–Vienna Line.
Husband of Rozalia Krześniak, my
great-grandmother. He died in Łódź.

Rozalia Karlińska, née Krześniak
1890–1983
My great-grandmother. Daughter of
Agnieszka and Józef Krześniak. She
gave birth to twelve children, five of
whom reached adulthood. She died
in Łódź.

Marianna Tuszyńska
1909–1969
My grandma Mania, eldest daughter
of Jan and Rozalia Karliński. Mother
of my father and my uncle Włodek.
She died in Warsaw.

Stefania Karlińska-Bartosik
1923–2001
My great-aunt. She was the sister of
Grandma Mania, daughter of Jan and
Rozalia Karliński. She died in Łódź.

Romuald Tuszyński
1913–1981
My grandfather. Son of Walerian
Tuszyński and Maria Paulina, née
Hausman. Employed on the railroad.
He died in Łódź.

Bogdan Tuszyński
Born in 1932
My father, son of Marianna and
Romuald Tuszyński. Sports journalist
and historian.

MY MOTHER'S FAMILY

JAKUB SZLAMA GOLDSTEIN	CHANA GOLDSTEIN	HENOCH (HENRYK) PRZEDBORSKI	JACHET GITEL (JUSTYNA) HERMAN
1881–1942	1878–1942	1871–1938	1885–1942

UDEL SURA (ADELA) GOLDSTEIN-PRZEDBORSKA	SAMUEL (SZYMON) PRZEDBORSKI	EUGENIA GADZIŃSKA-PRZEDBORSKA
1902–1944	1903-1989	1916–2005

BRONISŁAWA PRZEDBORSKA (BRONKA)	CELINA FRANCISZKA PRZEDBORSKA	ALEKSANDER MAJEWSKI	HALINA SCHUMACHER	HALINA PRZEDBORSKA-TUSZYŃSKA
1905–1987	1907–1993	1905–2006	1907–1995	Born in 1931

MARIAN MARZYŃSKI
Born in 1937

Henoch (Henryk) Przedborski,
"Handsome Henio"
1871–1938
My great-grandfather. Municipal
counselor of Łęczyca. Husband of
Jachet Gitel (Justyna) Herman. Father
of four children. He died in Łódź.

Jachet Gitel (Justyna) Herman,
"Grandma Jecia"
1885–1942
My great-grandmother. Daughter of
Samuel and Sura Ruchli (Salomea)
Herman. She perished with her
mother at Treblinka.

Samuel (Szymon) Przedborski,
"Zamutek"
1903–1989
My grandfather. Son of Henryk
Przedborski and Justyna Herman.
Engineer, graduate of the Polytechnic
School of Warsaw. Officer in the
Polish army, fought in the September
Campaign, prisoner of war in
Woldenberg. He died in Warsaw.

Eugenia Gadzińska-Przedborska,
"Żena"
1916–2005
Second wife of Szymon Przedborski,
my grandfather. Worked for the
government. She died in Warsaw.

Bronisława Przedborska, "Bronka"
1905–1987
My aunt. Daughter of Henryk and
Justyna, wife of Borys ("Bolek")
Kuszner and Daniel Marzyński.
Mother of Marian (Maryś). She died
in the United States.

Marian Marzyński, "Maryś"
Born in 1937
My cousin. Son of Bronisława, née
Przedborska, and Borys Kuszner.
He is a journalist, filmmaker,
documentarian. He lives in the
United States.

Celina Franciszka Przedborska,
"Franuchna"
1907–1993
My aunt Frania, daughter of Henryk
and Justyna, wife of Aleksander
Majewski, "Oleś." Mother of
Zbyszek. She died in Warsaw.

Aleksander Majewski, "Oleś"
1905–2006
Husband of Franuchna and father of
her son, Zbyszek, and two sons by
Halina Schumacher. An entrepreneur
before the war. He saved a good part
of the Przedborski family. He died in
Warsaw.

Halina Schumacher
1907–1995
Second wife of Oleś, mother of two
sons. Lawyer. She died in Warsaw.

Jakub Szlama Goldstein
1878–1942
My great-grandfather. Proprietor
of a warehouse for coal and heating
materials. Father of six children. All,
with the exception of Dela, perished
in the ghetto of Łęczyca or in Chełmo
nad Nerem.

Chana Goldstein
1881–1942
My great-grandmother. Wife of
Jakub, mother of six children. She
died in the ghetto in Łęczyca or in
Chełmo nad Nerem.

*Udel Sura (Adela) Goldstein-
Przedborska,* "Dela"
1902–1944
My grandmother. First wife of
Zamutek, mother of little Halina, my
mother. Schoolteacher. She died in
Otwock.

Halina Przedborska-Tuszyńska
Born in 1931
My mother, daughter of Samuel
Przedborski and Dela Goldstein.
Journalist.

Acknowledgments

I worked on this book for four years. By devoting myself to those who were closest to me, for the first time I was venturing into unknown territory, which was different from writing the biographies of other people.

The subjects of my preceding books belonged to the past. This authorized me to examine them sheltered by the barrier of time. Their biographies were closed, and my intrusions into their lives did not directly affect any living persons. I never met anyone who could remember Maria Wisnowska, the turn-of-the-century actress; and the Jewish Nobel Prize winner Isaac Bashevis Singer had died a few months before my arrival in America. I knew Irena Krzywicka, the Warsaw writer, but I began working on her biography only after her death.

This book about my family represented another challenge. I had read family biographies by Americans, but there were few examples of this genre in Polish letters. Measuring myself against a family secret required as a consequence that I make my own decisions without reference to the experiences of others. Writing about those close to me who were sealed behind the wall, those in photographs, those in cemeteries, forced me to answer for myself the fundamental questions of boundaries that must not be crossed. What becomes a betrayal, and when? By what right do I have to cause others to suffer?

The answers to these questions were generally contradictory, and sometimes it was painful for me to resign myself to them.

My parents were the most important. They knew from the beginning that it would be a work touching upon a secret about which they had remained silent to their only child for many years. In countless conversations I forced my mother and father into the difficult task of discovering the extent to which they had dissimulated their memories. And yet they never refused to answer any of my questions. Their openness helped me to write what had also been difficult to narrate for me.

The picture of my family was completed by what had been told to me by my last living relatives whom I knew in my childhood—Stefa Karlińska-Bartosik, the late Aleksander Majewski, Marian Marzyński, and the late Eugenia Przedborska. In addition to family narratives, they brought to this book innumerable details and images preserved in their rich and generous memories.

I am indebted to friends and relations of my family for their precious recollections: Roma Bojmart, Irena Kiepuszewska, Hanna Lewandowska, Barbara and Daniel Lulinski, Ewa Ostrowska, Cezary Papiernik, Witold Stankowski, Marianna Zybert. Mirka Chwat of Tel Aviv is the only person who still remembers my great-grandmother. The New York journalist Michael Kaufman, my recently rediscovered cousin, shared with me what he knew of the branch of the Przedborski family in Łódź.

I worked on this book in many places, where I gathered fragments of conversations without end with friends scattered around the world. I want to thank all of them. In New York: Fela and Joasia Dobroszycki, Phillis Levin, David Margolick, Monika and Wiktor Markowicz, Shana and David Roskies, Susan Stone. In Israel: Aviva Blum and Romek Waks, Linka and Władek Kornblum, Wila and the late Michal Orbach, Gina and Kazik Rotem, Marysia and the late Bronek Thau. In Paris: Maria Brandys, Jean-Yves Erhel, Małgosia and Marc Goldberg, Irena Milewska, Antoine Perraud. In Toronto: Paula Draper, Judit Szapor, and Ewa Stachniak, the kindly disposed reader of the first draft of this book.

Undoubtedly the last link with the world of my ancestors was the late Master Ludwik Seidenman of New York, a man of great wisdom and nobility of character, my mentor and friend. I am profoundly sad that he was able to read only fragments of the text—he had passed away before I had time to complete the whole.

Carol Mann, my American agent, Victoria Wilson, my editor at Knopf, and the writers Paul Auster and Richard Lourie very early believed in the universal significance of this story of the entanglement of these Polish-Jewish lives. They helped me with their advice, their knowledge, and their experience in the New York literary world.

I would also like to thank my translators, Jean-Yves Erhel and Charles Ruas, as well as Anna Wrobel for reviewing the translation with me.

The Rockefeller Foundation, Ledig-Rowohlt, as well as the Mac-Dowell Colony, made my writing possible in their creative centers. I am equally grateful for the friendships formed with writers I met there and who cast an external glance upon my project about the closed circle of Polish Jews: Chris Hirte, Patricia Duncker, Fenton Johnson, and Guillermo Martinez.

In Poland, in the grip of my own dilemmas, made inevitable by the discovery of my family secrets, I needed special support. Stanisław Bereś, Barbara Engelking-Boni, Konstanty Gebert, Jerzy Jarzebski, Stanisław Krajewski, Tomasz Pietrasiewicz, and Janina Sacharewicz offered me their friendship and their assistance. The perspicacious comments by Irena Majchrzak have helped me to see farther into things which I had not seen until then. The memories of my childhood friend Agnieszka Lulińska have enriched and complemented mine.

For the time that they devoted to our conversations, I want to thank equally the Sadomski family of Relin, where my grandmother was hidden during the war, as well as the Joźwiak family, of Kuchary, the former estate of my great-grandfather. However, I would never have reconstituted the history of my Jewish ancestors without the immense and disinterested help of Mirosław Pisarkiewicz, whom I met during my first visit to Łęczyca, the place where my mother was born. It's to him that I am indebted for the essential archives documenting the Przedborski and Herman families.

The form of this book was gradually revealed in the course of daily conversations with my friend Ewa Junczyk-Ziomecka, the driving force behind the project for a Museum of the History of Polish Jews in Warsaw. More than most, she understood the complexity of the questions that I forced myself to unravel.

Dearest to me was the late Henryk Dasko, my life companion. He never doubted for a moment, since the beginning, that I was going to write an important and necessary book.

AGATA TUSZYŃSKA

Translator's Acknowledgments

This translation is for my brother, Alex Nelson, and my friend Mark Axelowitz, who loves literature and is a constant reader. As well, I'd like to remember my friend and advisor the late Mrs. Lewin for her generosity of spirit and unbounded optimism. I undertook this project about Polish history in memory of Constance Gloria Iwaniska Ruas, the Polish ballerina caught in the turmoil of revolutions and wars who fled eastward to China, where she met my father in Tientsin and became his first wife long before his marriage to my mother.

I am grateful to my agent, Irene Skolnick, for her advice and support. Victoria Wilson believed in this project and was its guiding spirit, and I thank her for bringing me on board. I owe special thanks to the Writers Room in New York City for providing a place for me to accomplish my work, and especially to Donna Brodie and Elizabeth Sherman and the staff, who were always generous with their time and resources. Above all, it was the invaluable assistance and painstaking vigilance of Joellyn Ausanka that made this work possible. And, as in everything else, the unfailing encouragement of Rob Wynne has been a mainstay in my life and has sustained me in this work.

CHARLES RUAS

A NOTE ON THE TYPE

This book was set in Adobe Garamond. Designed for the Adobe
Corporation by Robert Slimbach, the fonts are based on types first cut
by Claude Garamond (c. 1480–1561). Garamond was a pupil of Geoffroy
Tory and is believed to have followed the Venetian models, although he
introduced a number of important differences, and it is to him that we
owe the letter we now know as "old style." He gave to his letters a certain
elegance and feeling of movement that won their creator an immediate
reputation and the patronage of Francis I of France.

COMPOSED BY
North Market Street Graphics, Lancaster, Pennsylvania

PRINTED AND BOUND BY
Berryville Graphics, Berryville, Virginia

DESIGNED BY
Iris Weinstein